Archive, Bibliotheken und Enzyklopädien haben das Wissen in Ordnung gebracht. Abgeheftet, klassifiziert und katalogisiert liegt es bereit in analogen oder digitalen Speichern. Es gehört zu den Erwartungen von Wissensgesellschaften, dass es tagein, tagaus zu massenhaften Zugriffen auf diese Speicher kommt. Denn nur wenn das sorgsam gespeicherte Wissen aus der Sterilität der Aufbewahrungsorte befreit wird, nur wenn das Wissen zirkuliert, nur wenn es abgerufen und angewandt wird, kann sich die Menge des verfügbaren Wissens weiterhin vergrößern.

Dies gilt selbstverständlich auch im Bereich der Architektur. Doch wie die vorangegangen, so zeigt auch diese dritte Ausgabe von *Candide*, dass die Architektur eigene Wissenskulturen hervorbringt. Denn das Wissen der Architektur liegt nicht sorgsam abgeheftet in Archiven zum Abruf bereit, sondern steckt in Entwurfswerkzeugen, Arbeitsabläufen, Wohnräumen oder Fensterdetails. Als forschende Architekten und Wissensarchäologen ihrer eigenen Disziplin entdecken die Autorinnen und Autoren nicht nur Fundorte des Wissens, sondern beschreiben jeweils die für architektonische Belange unauflösliche Verbindung von Wissen und Erfindung, von Erkenntnisgewinn und Projekt.

Die Architekturhistorikerin Elâ Kaçel dokumentiert am Beispiel des Hilton Hotels von Istanbul, einem vielbeachteten Bau der Nachkriegs- moderne, die Verwerfungen, welcher der Import von Wissen und Arbeits- weisen im beruflichen Selbstverständnis türkischer Architekten ausgelöst hat. Andrew Witt, Forschungsdirektor von Gehry Technologies in Paris, reaktiviert für uns die hochentwickelten Ellipsografen, Helikografen und Spirografen des 19. Jahrhundert. Witts historischer Exkurs zur Geschichte der Entwurfswerkzeuge erinnert in höchst eindringlicher Weise an den überaus fruchtbaren Zusammenhang von Geometrie, Instrument und Entwurf, der als Synthese die Produktion von Architekturwissen vorantreibt. In der Rubrik Fiktion präsentiert uns der in Chicago ansässige Jimenez Lai eine Parabel in Form eines Bilderromans. Sie geleitet uns in eine phantastische Welt, wo eine kanonische Sammlung geometrischer Figuren zur Trieb- abfuhr bereitsteht. Doch Lais fiktionales Reich ist nicht frei von kulturellem Unbehagen. Dies entsteht, wenn die Libido nicht zu den verfügbaren und kollektiv abgesegneten Formen passt. Oliver Schetter, der als Architekt in der Entwicklungszusammenarbeit in Mozambik arbeitet, untersucht die Wohnbauten des Landes. Anhand architektonischer Details zeigt Schetter wie Wissensfragmente der Kolonialzeit mit lokalen Praktiken fusionieren. Architekturtheoretikerin Amy Kulpers Beitrag beschließt das Heft und führt uns zurück zur unserer anfänglichen Frage nach dem Wissensspeicher und seiner möglichen Öffnungen. Kulper examiniert hierzu das literarische Œuvre von Georges Perec und entdeckt dabei jene akribische Methoden und minutiösen Beschreibungen, mit denen Perec der notorischen Langeweile von Listen, Archiven und Taxonomien ein ungeahntes kreatives Potenzial entlockt.

Die Herausgeber
Axel Sowa, Susanne Schindler

Recommendations for the submission of manuscripts

Candide. Journal for Architectural Knowledge is a scholarly journal published in English and German. Its peer review process corresponds to internationally accepted scholarly criteria.

Candide is dedicated to exploring the culture of knowledge specific to architecture. How is architectural knowledge generated, collected, presented, and passed on? Which forms of architectural knowledge can be observed? How can knowledge generated in reference to a specific task be applied to other contexts? Which experts, designers and users, which institutions and organizations are involved? Which techniques, tools and methods are instrumental? What do graduates of architecture schools know? What did architects of different periods know? Through which media is architectural knowledge disseminated? These are some of the central questions that *Candide* invites authors to address.

Each issue of *Candide. Journal for Architectural Knowledge* is made up of five distinct sections. This framework responds to the diversity of architectural knowledge being produced, while challenging authors of all disciplines to test a variety of genres to write about and represent architecture.

Essay

provides a forum for discourse on architectural knowledge. The editors are interested in publishing both fundamental research into and speculative arguments on the nature of knowledge, coming from philosophical, historic, or anthropological perspectives.

Analysis

allows for in-depth examinations of built architecture. The editors are interested in demonstrations of how knowledge that was invested and is embodied in buildings can be extracted retrospectively. How can the detailed reading of existing structures promote the creative re-use of existing knowledge?

Project

is directed primarily at architects who both practice and theoretically reflect on their work. Moving beyond the constraints of context, clients, and the task at hand: How can a specific design project become a model of thought, an example to be emulated? How can a project reorganize available knowledge or expand on it?

Encounters

gives access to the personal knowledge of renowned, unjustly forgotten, or entirely unknown protagonists of architecture. Accordingly, the section provides ample space for interviews, dialogues, and testimonies.

Fiction

reflects the editors' conviction that fictional stories often tell us more about architecture than scientific explanations. The editors are interested in fables, aphorisms, utopias, comic strips, or photographic novels that expand the formal spectrum used to generate and present architectural knowledge. Reflections on the relationship of fiction and architecture will also be considered.

Candide. Journal for Architectural Knowledge accepts previously unpublished, original articles which are not being considered for publication elsewhere. Articles may be submitted at any time, in either English or German. On receipt of a submission, the editors make a first decision on its suitability for publication. Manuscripts submitted to any of the five sections —*Essay, Analysis, Project, Encounters, or Fiction*— are then subject to a double-blind peer review by at least two referees. After initial submission, authors will hear back within two weeks as to whether their manuscript has been accepted to be reviewed or not. If it is, the peer review process is expected to take eight weeks. The authors will receive the peers' reviews. If "accepted for publication with revisions", the authors will receive enough time to revise their papers. Prospective authors are welcome to discuss their proposals with the editors in advance of making a formal submission.

Before submitting papers, authors are invited to read the detailed guidelines online: **www.candidejournal.net**

Contents   Inhalt

Archives, libraries, and encyclopedias have brought order to knowledge. Filed away, classified, and cataloged it awaits use in analog or digital storage. It is part of the expectations of our knowledge-based societies that day in and day out this stored information is accessed on a massive scale. For only if the carefully stored knowledge is liberated from the sterility of its holding areas, only if knowledge circulates, only if it is retrieved and put to use, does it make sense to continue increasing the knowledge made available.

Clearly, this also concerns the discipline of architecture. However, as the preceding two issues of *Candide* have shown, the present one too demonstrates that architecture has developed its own, specific cultures of knowledge. For architectural knowledge is not carefully stored in archives awaiting retrieval, but it resides in tools of design, in processes of work, in spaces of dwelling, in details of windows. As researching architects and archeologists of architectural knowledge, the authors discover not only sites of knowledge, but describe the intrinsic and fundamental connection of knowledge and invention, insight and project.

Architectural historian Elâ Kaçel, using the example of the Hilton Hotel in Istanbul, a central building in Turkish postwar modernism, analyzes the dislocations caused by the import of knowledge and organizational methods in the professional self-image of Turkish architects. Andrew Witt, director of design innovation at Gehry Technologies in Paris, brings to life the sophisticated ellipsographs, helicographs, and spirographs of the nineteenth century. Witt's foray into the history of design tools forcefully reminds us of the productive relationship of geometry, machine, and design, that, as a synthesis, significantly furthers the production of architectural knowledge. In Fiction, Chicago-based architect Jimenez Lai offers a parable in form of a comic strip. The narrative takes us to a fantastic world in which a canonical collection of geometric figures is available to satisfy inhabitants' physical desires. However, Lai's fictional empire is not free of cultural anxiety, resulting from the fact that libido does not always match collectively authorized figures. Oliver Schetter, currently working in development cooperation in Mozambique, explores the country's dwellings. Looking at the details of their architecture, Schetter shows how fragments of knowledge dating back to colonial times have amalgamated with local practices. Architectural theorist Amy Kulper's essay concludes the issue and brings us back to our opening question regarding the storage of knowledge and its potential opening. Kulper analyzes Georges Perec's literary œuvre and unravels his meticulous methods and scrupulous descriptions, methods that elicit an unsuspected, creative potential from the notorious tedium of lists, archives, and taxonomies.

The editors
Axel Sowa, Susanne Schindler

Hinweise für Einsendungen von Manuskripten

Als deutsch-englisch sprachiges Medium, dessen Peer-Review-Verfahren international geltenden, wissenschaftlichen Kriterien entspricht, fördert *Candide. Journal for Architectural Knowledge* die Erforschung einer spezifisch architektonischen Wissenskultur.

Wie wird das Wissen der Architektur generiert, gesammelt, aufbereitet und weitergegeben? Welche Formen des Wissens lassen sich beobachten? In wie weit ist kontextgebundenes Wissen auf andere Lagen übertragbar? Welche Personen, Institutionen und Verbände sind an der Wissensproduktion beteiligt? Welche Techniken, Instrumente, Verfahren und Methoden spielen dabei welche Rolle? Was wissen Absolventen von Architekturfakultäten? Was wussten Architekten verschiedener Epochen? Durch welche Medien erfährt das Wissen der Architektur seine Verbreitung? Dies sind einige der zentralen Fragen, zu deren Beantwortung *Candide* einladen möchte.

Der Aufbau von *Candide* trägt der Vielfalt möglicher Forschungsansätze Rechnung und befördert die Genres mittels der Architektur untersucht und dargestellt werden kann. Jede Ausgabe von Candide ist daher in maximal fünf Rubriken unterteilt:

Essay

bietet ein Forum für Diskurse zur Wissenskultur der Architektur. Beiträge, die zur Veröffentlichung in dieser Rubrik in Frage kommen, sollten sich forschend oder spekulativ mit der spezifischen Natur des architektonischen Wissens in philosophischer, historischer und anthropologischer Perspektive auseinandersetzten.

Analyse

ermöglicht die eingehende Untersuchung gebauter Architektur. Die Herausgeber möchten Autorinnen und Autoren einladen, der Frage nachzugehen, wie Wissen in Gebäude investiert und inkorporiert wurde, bzw. wie Wissen aus bestehender Architektur gewonnen werden kann. Kann ein aufmerksames Lesen von Architektur, die schöpferische Wiederverwertung von existierendem Wissen befördern?

Projekt

Diese Rubrik richtet sich in erster Linie an praktizierende Architekten, die ihr Handeln einer theoretischen Reflektion unterziehen. Hier sollen modell- und beispielhafte Entwürfe zur Sprache kommen, welche über die Einmaligkeit von Bindungen durch den Kontext oder die Bauaufgabe hinausreichen. Wie können Projekte verfügbares Wissen neu organisieren oder erweitern?

Begegnung

bietet einen Zugang zum Wissensschatz von berühmten, ungerechtfertigter Weise vergessenen oder ganz unbekannten Persönlichkeiten der Architektur. Dieser Rubrik bietet Raum für Dialoge, Interviews sowie das lebendige Gedächtnis von Zeitzeugen.

Fiktion

Mit dieser Rubrik bekunden die Herausgeber ihre Überzeugung, dass zuweilen fiktionale Geschichten mehr über Architektur auszusagen vermögen, als Erörterungen im wissenschaftlichen Stil. Daher soll in dieser Rubrik in Form von Fabeln, Aphorismen, Utopien, Comics oder Photoromane das Spektrum der Arten über Architektur nachzudenken bereichert werden.

Candide. Journal for Architectural Knowledge nimmt unveröffentlichte Artikel an, deren Veröffentlichung nicht bereits in einem anderen Medium geplant ist. Aufsätze können jederzeit in deutscher oder englischer Sprache eingereicht werden. Nach Erhalt der Einsendung entscheiden die Herausgeber, ob eine Veröffentlichung grundsätzlich in Frage kommt. Ist dies der Fall, werden die, für eine der fünf Rubriken Essay, Analyse, Projekt, Begegnung oder Fiktion eingereichten Manuskripte in einem anonymisierten Verfahren durch mindestens zwei Gutachter bewertet. Innerhalb von zwei Wochen nach Einsendung ihres Manuskripts werden die Autorinnen und Autoren über die Zulassung ihres Manuskripts zum Gutachterverfahren benachrichtigt. Das Verfahren selbst wird dann in der Regel acht Wochen in Anspruch nehmen. Den Autorinnen und Autoren werden die Gutachten zugestellt. Sollten sich die Gutachter für eine Veröffentlichung mit Auflagen aussprechen, so wird den Autorinnen und Autoren Zeit zur Bearbeitung der Auflagen einberaumt. Die Herausgeber sind gerne bereit, im Vorfeld der Einsendungen deren mögliche Inhalte mit den jeweiligen Autorinnen und Autoren zu diskutieren.

Vor jeder Einsendung sollten die weiteren Hinweise unter **www.candidejournal.net** beachtet werden.

Candide —
Journal for Architectural Knowledge

Candide is a scholarly journal published twice a year at the Department for Theory of Architecture, Faculty of Architecture, RWTH Aachen University.

The editors would like to thank the Faculty of Architecture as well as the Rectorate of RWTH Aachen University for supporting Candide.

Candide is funded in part by the German Research Foundation's program "Scientific Journals."

Candide ist eine wissenschaftliche Zeitschrift, die zweimal jährlich am Lehr- und Forschungsgebiet Architekturtheorie, Fakultät für Architektur, RWTH Aachen herausgegeben wird.

Die Herausgeber bedanken sich bei der Fakultät für Architektur sowie bei der Hochschulleitung der RWTH Aachen, die das Projekt unterstützen.

Candide wird im Rahmen des DFG-Programms „Wissenschaftliche Zeitschriften" gefördert.

Editors / Herausgeber
Axel Sowa
Susanne Schindler

Editorial Contributor /
Redaktionelle Mitarbeit
Ariane Wilson

Administration / Sekretariat
Doris Mangartz

Board of Advisors /
Wissenschaftlicher Beirat
Mario Carpo,
Professor, College of Architecture, Georgia Institute of Technology, Atlanta
Michael Guggenheim,
European anthropologist and sociologist, London
Susanne Hauser,
Professorin für Kunst- und Kulturgeschichte, Universität der Künste, Berlin
Eva Kraus,
Director, Galerie Steinle Contemporary, München
Wilfried Kuehn,
Architekt und Professor für Ausstellungs-design und kuratorische Praxis, Hochschule für Gestaltung, Karlsruhe
Sébastien Marot,
Professeur, École d'Architecture de la Ville et des Territoires, Marne-la-Vallée
Ingeborg Rocker,
Architect and Assistant Professor, Harvard Graduate School of Design, Cambridge (MA)
Irénée Scalbert,
Architecture critic, London
Angelika Schnell,
Universitätsprofessorin für Geschichte und Theorie der Architektur, Akademie der Bildenden Künste, Wien

Gestaltung / Design
Katja Gretzinger, Graphic Design Studio, Berlin, mit Fides Sigeneger
www.katjagretzinger.com

Proof Reading / Lektorat
Joachim Geil
Amanda Fernandez

Printed and bound by / Druck und Bindung
DZA, Druckerei zu Altenburg

Publisher / Verlag
transcript
Verlag für Kommunikation, Kultur und soziale Praxis
Mühlenstraße 47
D-33607 Bielefeld
T +49 (0)521 393 797 -0
F +49 (0)521 393 797 -34
www.transcript-verlag.de

Price individual Issue /
Preis Einzelausgabe
17 € / $ 24.95

Subscriptions and distribution for Germany, Austria, and Switzerland /
Abonnements und Bestellungen für Deutschland, Österreich und Schweiz
transcript Verlag, Bielefeld
bestellung@transcript-verlag.de
T +49 (0)521 393 797 -0
F +49 (0)521 393 797 -34

Global distribution outside Germany, Austria, and Switzerland /
Abonnements und Bestellungen außerhalb Deutschlands, Österreichs und der Schweiz
Transaction Publishers
Rutgers University
35 Berrue Circle
Piscataway, NJ 08854, USA
www.transactionpub.com
T +1 (732) 445-2280
F +1 (732) 445-3138
For orders (U.S. only): toll free
888-999-6778

The articles in this issue are papers presented at the conference "Constructing Knowledge" in Aachen in November 2009 that have since been revised for publication. The abstracts to these papers were selected on the basis of a double-blind peer review in the summer of 2009.

Die Beiträge dieser Ausgabe sind Vorträge, die auf der Tagung „Constructing Know-ledge" in Aachen im November 2009 gehalten und zum Zweck der Veröffentlichung überarbeitet wurden. Die Abstracts dieser Vorträge wurden im Sommer 2009 auf der Grundlage eines anonymisierten Gutachter-verfahrens ausgewählt.

Submissions / Einsendungen
Submissions to the sections Essay, Analysis, Project, Encounters, and Fiction are possible at all times. Please see the more detailed information on submissions guidelines and the peer review process at www.candidejournal.net.

Einsendungen zu den Rubriken Essay, Analyse, Projekt, Begegnung und Fiktion sind jederzeit möglich. Bitte lesen Sie die näheren Erläuterungen zu der Form der Einsendungen sowie zu dem Gutachterverfah-ren unter www.candidejournal.net.

Candide. Journal for Architectural Knowledge
Faculty of Architecture
Department for Theory of Architecture
RWTH Aachen University
Templergraben 92
D-52056 Aachen
T +49 (0)241 80 935 -71/-72
F +49 (0)241 80 925 72
candide@theorie.arch.rwth-aachen.de
www.candidejournal.net
theorie.arch.rwth-aachen.de

Elâ Kaçel

Hiltonculuk and Beyond
The Dialectics of Intellectualism
in Postwar Turkey

The spread of the International Style in 1950s
Turkey is often interpreted as an inevitable outcome of the so-called Americanization of
modernism. A closer look at the conditions of
practice and knowledge production in architecture, however, shows that the appropriation
of modernism was problematic. Referring to the
repeated imitation of Istanbul's Hilton Hotel,
the critic Şevki Vanlı at the time coined the term
"Hiltonculuk" (Hiltonism) to mock an uncritically and widely accepted architectural ideology.
Kaçel, in contrast, speaks of "common-sense
modernism" to denote in the affirmative the values
shared by Turkish architects. With reference to
Antonio Gramsci's critique of intellectuals
and Karl Mannheim's sociology of knowledge,
Kaçel depicts architects not as creative,
autonomous figures but as intellectuals whose
practices need to be analyzed in relation to the
social relations in which they are embedded.

Elâ Kaçel

Hiltonculuk und die Folgen
Die Dialektik des Intellektualismus in der Türkei
nach dem Zweiten Weltkrieg

Die Verbreitung des Internationalen Stils in der
Türkei der 1950er Jahre wird oft als unumgängliche
Folge der sogenannten Amerikanisierung der
Moderne interpretiert. Ein näherer Blick auf die
Bedingungen von Berufspraxis und Wissensproduktion in der Architektur zeigt dagegen, dass
die Aneignung der Moderne nicht unproblematisch
war. Mit Bezug auf die wiederholte Imitation von
Istanbuls Hilton Hotel mokierte sich der Kritiker
Şevki Vanlı damals mit dem Begriff „Hiltonculuk"
(Hiltonismus) über eine architektonische Ideologie,
die unkritisch von der Mehrheit der Architekten
übernommen wurde. Die Autorin spricht dagegen
von einem „Alltagsverstand des Modernismus",
um im Affirmativen die gemeinsamen Werte türkischer Architekten zu beschreiben. Bezugnehmend
auf Antonio Gramscis Intellektuellen-Kritik und
Karl Mannheims Wissenssoziologie, stellt Kaçel
Architekten nicht als kreative, autonome Personen
dar, sondern als Intellektuelle, deren Praktiken
in Bezug zu den sozialen Beziehungen, in die sie
eingebettet sind, analysiert werden müssen.

The Istanbul Hilton Hotel is considered an icon of the so-called International Style era in 1950s Turkey. Yet before heralding the International Style, the hotel primarily manifested the Cold War politics and ideologies of modernization advanced under the auspices of the United States. From the project launch in New York in 1951 to the building's opening in 1955, the officials of the partnered contracting organizations in Turkey and the United States undertook a publicity campaign that popularized the political ideologies and cultural policies embodied by the hotel; the designers—a collaborative effort between Gordon Bunshaft of the New York–based Skidmore, Owings & Merrill (SOM) and the Turkish architect Sedad Hakkı Eldem—are rarely mentioned in the governmental publicity materials. For the readers of Turkish popular media, just one or two images would have sufficed to visualize the country's prospect of becoming a "little America," as realized in this new building [→ fig. 1].

Featured in several trade magazines abroad, the pure prismatic, reinforced-concrete volume of the hotel perforated by a crate of balconies would have been a rather familiar structure to an international audience, considering its forerunners, from Le Corbusier's Unité d'Habitation (1947–52) in Marseilles to the Caribe Hilton (1946–49) by Toro Ferrer y Torregrosa in Puerto Rico. In the contemporaneous scene in Turkey, however, the architecture of the Istanbul Hilton was familiar neither to architects nor to the public. From the outset, therefore, every effort was undertaken to make the hotel an exceptional showcase. Located on a hill overlooking the Bosphorus, the hotel was the largest and even highest structure in the city at the time. With its imposing scale, it easily prevailed over nearby public buildings, including those of a university—the former military barracks from the nineteenth century—and the Istanbul Radio building belonging to the Turkish Radio Television, built in the style of the nationalist revivalism of the

1 For a detailed account of the hotel's design, see Wharton 2001. For studies that discuss the significance of the Istanbul Hilton as an icon of postwar Turkish architecture, see Bozdoğan 2008, Wharton 2001, and Akcan 2001.
2 The suffixes -cu and -luk in the term "Hiltonculuk," which Vanlı coined, imply two meanings. First, the word connotes a professional practice and its ideology of designing Hilton-like buildings. "Hiltonism" would be the closest translation with regard to this meaning. At the same time, the word also alludes to a game in which participants (architects, in this case) pretend to be "experts of Hiltonculuk." Thus, in a single word, Vanlı was able to indicate both the realities and the make-believe character of the practice of Hiltonculuk. Vanlı 1958: 21f.
3 Vanlı 1958: 20.

1940s [→ fig. 2]. Various novelties that the hotel deployed—such as its exceptional site at the edge of a public park, high standards for construction techniques, new recreational urban spaces, and interiors that blended American modernism with stylized Turkish decorative arts—underscored its design as a monumental achievement.[1]

Yet the appropriation of the hotel as a prototype of a new, International Style architecture among Turkish architects proved to be problematic. Several versions of the Hilton Hotel were soon designed—as hotels or as office buildings—without the associated discourse being questioned. Starting as early as 1953 with Istanbul City Hall by Nevzat Erol, the pattern of the perforated prismatic box was repeated in the designs of the Porsuk Hotel in Eskişehir by Vedat Dalokay (1956), the Grand Efes Hotel in Izmir by Paul Bonatz and Fatin Uran (1957), the Tarabya Hotel by Kadri Erdoğan (1957), and the Çınar Hotel in Istanbul by Rana Zıpçı, Ahmet Akın, and Emin Ertan (1959) [→ fig. 3].

In 1958, only three years after the opening of the Hilton, Şevki Vanlı, a practicing architect, was the only critic who pointed out the absurdity of an architectural practice that he called "Hiltonculuk."[2] He mocked local architects who took the Hilton as a design scheme and produced replicate buildings all around the country as experts of Hiltonculuk. What concerned Vanlı most was a professional practice and discourse that gave credit to the Hilton and then reused similar schemes without reservation. Vanlı's criticism was two-sided. With the term "perfect mediocrity,"[3] Vanlı criticized the commercialized aspects of bureaucratic architecture in 1950s

Das Istanbul Hilton gilt als ein Symbol der sogenannten Ära des Internationalen Stils in der Türkei der 1950er Jahre. Doch bevor es den Internationalen Stil einläutete, stand das Hotel in erster Linie für die Politik des Kalten Krieges und die Ideologien der Modernisierung, die unter der Federführung der Vereinigten Staaten betrieben wurden. Vom Projektstart in New York im Jahr 1951 bis zur Einweihung des Gebäudes im Jahre 1955 veranstalteten die Vertragspartner-organisationen in der Türkei und den Vereinigten Staaten eine Werbekampagne, die die von dem Hotel verkörperten politischen Ideologien und kulturpolitischen Grundsätze popularisierte. Die Architekten – Gordon Bunshaft, Partner in der New Yorker Niederlassung von Skidmore, Owings & Merrill (SOM), und der türkische Architekt Sedad Hakkı Eldem – werden in dem behördlichen Werbematerial selten erwähnt. Den Lesern der türkischen Massenmedien dürften jedenfalls wenige Abbildungen genügt haben, um sich ihr Land als ein zukünftiges „Klein-Amerika" in der durch dieses neue Gebäude angedeuteten Prägung vorstellen zu können [→ Abb. 1].

Der internationalen Öffentlichkeit muss der von einem Balkonraster perforierte, geometrisch ungebrochene Stahlbetonbaukörper des Hotels, der in mehreren ausländischen Fachzeitschriften besprochen wurde, ein ziemlich vertrauter Anblick gewesen sein, angesichts seiner Vorläufer, von Le Corbusiers Unité d'Habitation (1947–52) in Marseille bis zum Caribe Hilton (1946–49) von Toro Ferrer y Torregrosa in Puerto Rico. In den damaligen türkischen Kreisen war die Architektur des Istanbul Hilton jedoch weder Architekten noch der Öffentlichkeit geläufig. So wurden von Anfang an große Anstrengungen unternommen, das Hotel zu einem außergewöhnlichen Vorzeigeprojekt zu machen. Auf einem Hügel mit Blick über den Bosporus gelegen, war das Hotel damals das größte und auch das höchste Gebäude der Stadt. Mit seinen imposanten

Ausmaßen behauptete es sich mühelos gegen die umliegenden öffentlichen Gebäude, einschließlich einer Universität in den Gebäuden einer ehemaligen Kaserne aus dem 19. Jahrhundert und dem Istanbuler Rundfunkgebäude der Türkischen Rundfunk- und Fernsehanstalt, erbaut im Stil der Zweiten Nationalen Architekturströmung der 1940er Jahre [→ Abb. 2]. Nicht zuletzt dank der zahlreichen Neuheiten, mit denen das Gebäude aufwartete – etwa seine außergewöhnliche Lage am Rande eines öffentlichen Parks, hohe bautechnische Standards, neue städtische Freizeiträume und Interieurs, in denen sich amerikanische Moderne mit stilisierter türkischer dekorativer Kunst vermischte – galt der Hotelentwurf als eine enorme Leistung.[1]

Doch erwies sich die Aneignung des Hotels als Prototyp einer neuen Architektur, des Internationalen Stils, unter türkischen Architekten als problematisch. In schneller Folge wurden mehrere, dem Hotel nachempfundene Gebäude entworfen – als Hotels oder Bürogebäude – ohne dass der damit verbundene Diskurs kritisch hinterfragt wurde. Bereits 1953, mit dem Rathaus von Istanbul von Nevzat Erol, wurde das Muster des perforierten Kastens wiederholt, und anschließend bei der Gestaltung des Porsuk Hotel in Eskişehir von Vedat Dalokay (1956), des Grand Efes Hotel in Izmir von Paul Bonatz und Fatin Uran (1957), des Tarabya Hotels von Kadri Erdoğan (1957), und des Çınar Hotel in Istanbul von Rana Zıpçı, Ahmet Akın, und Emin Ertan (1959) [→ Abb. 3].

Im Jahr 1958, nur drei Jahre nach der Eröffnung des Hilton, kritisierte Şevki Vanlı, ein praktizierender Architekt, die Absurdität einer Architekturpraxis, die er in einem Kommentar auf der Kommentarseite der illustrierten Wochenzeitschrift *Kim* als „Hiltonculuk"[2] bezeichnete. Er verspottete jene Architekten, die das Hilton als Entwurfsvorlage nahmen

---

1 Für eine ausführliche Darstellung des Hotelentwurfs siehe Wharton 2001. Für Studien, die sich mit der Bedeutung des Istanbul Hilton als Ikone türkischer Nachkriegsarchitektur befassen, siehe Bozdoğan 2008, Wharton 2001 und Akcan 2001.

Abb. 1
Das Cover der Wochenzeitschrift *Hayat* präsentiert das Istanbul Hilton als Hintergrund modernen Lebens. *Hayat*, 11. September 1959.

Fig. 1
The cover of the weekly magazine *Hayat* presents the Istanbul Hilton as the backdrop for modern living. *Hayat*, September 11, 1959.

und dann als „Hiltonculuk-Experten" im ganzen Land Replikate produzierten. Was Vanlı am meisten Sorgen bereitete, war eine Berufspraxis und ein Diskurs, die das Hilton und die vorbehaltlose Wiederverwendung ähnlicher Vorlagen befürworteten. Vanlıs Kritik war zweifacher Art. Mit dem Begriff „perfekte Mittelmäßigkeit"[3] kritisierte Vanlı die kommerzialisierten Aspekte bürokratischer Architektur im Amerika der 1950er Jahre, wie sie von Architekturbüros wie SOM praktiziert wurde. Vanlı übernahm den Terminus der bürokratischen Architektur (*bureaucratic architecture*) von dem Architekturhistoriker Henry-Russell Hitchcock, der die Architekturproduktion in zwei Gruppen einteilte, in eine bürokratische und gewöhnliche sowie eine von Genialität (*genius*) geprägte, ikonische.[4] Gleichzeitig richtete sich seine Kritik gegen die unkritische Aneignung amerikanischer Architektur à la Internationaler Stil in der Türkei, in deren Verlauf eine bürokratische Architektur in ein hehres Vorbild für die Praxis verwandelt wurde.

Indem er die negativen Auswirkungen von Hiltonculuk auf die Architekturszene in der Türkei betont, stellt Vanlı Hiltonculuk lediglich als Ideologie dar und kritisiert die Ideologie der Architekturpraxis nach dem Krieg. Doch mit dieser Kritik impliziert Vanlıs Definition von Hiltonculuk auch eine Form der Wissensproduktion, die Hand in Hand geht mit einer Ideologie der Architekturpraxis, die von der Mehrheit der Nachkriegsarchitekten in der Türkei geteilt wurde, einschließlich Eldem, dem türkischen Partner des Teams, das das Istanbul Hilton entwarf. Und in der Tat lieferte Eldem kurz nach Erscheinen von Vanlıs Kritik höchstpersönlich einen Beitrag zu Hiltonculuk. Um die Kapazität des Hotels um weitere hundertfünfzig Zimmer zu erhöhen, manipulierte er den ursprünglichen Entwurf und erweiterte einfach den Block in der Länge, indem er weitere sieben identische Schotten hinzufügte. Während Bunshaft eine derartige Erweiterung des Gebäudes missbilligte und damit den Gefahren von Hiltonculuk aus dem Weg ging, trug Eldems Beteiligung dazu bei, die Praxis

unter türkischen Architekten weiter zu legitimieren [→ Abb. 4 und 5].

In seinem Kommentar beschreibt Vanlı die Arbeitsbedingungen von Architekten, die in der Türkei der 1950er Jahre Wettbewerbsbeiträge entwarfen. Diese Architekten, schreibt Vanlı, bezogen die Anregung für ihre Praxis von Hiltonculuk in erster Linie aus ausländischen Zeitschriften, in denen ähnliche Projekte wie das Hilton-Gebäude abgebildet waren:

„Inzwischen ist allgemein bekannt, dass überall in diesen Büros Vorlagen zu finden sind, die aus ausländischen Publikationen ausgewählt wurden – an den Wänden, wo die Vorbereitung für die Wettbewerbsbeiträge im Gange ist, und auf den Schreibtischen, wo die Zeichnungen für den Beitrag erstellt werden. Es liegt in der Tat auf der Hand, dass für kreatives Arbeiten keine Zeit mehr ist, wenn für mehrere Wettbewerbe gleichzeitig entworfen wird. Jedenfalls ist zweifelhaft, ob die Projekte irgendein überzeugendes Ergebnis erzielen können, wenn sie auf diese Art und Weise vorbereitet werden. Und alle Ergebnisse haben die Gestalt von ‚Hiltonculuk', wie wir es nennen. Die Bewerber wählen aus griffbereiten

2 Die Suffixe -cu und -luk in dem Begriff „Hiltonculuk", den Vanlı prägte, implizieren zweierlei Bedeutungen. Erstens konnotiert das Wort eine Berufspraxis und ihre Ideologie, Hilton-ähnliche Gebäude zu entwerfen. „Hiltonismus" würde dem bedeutungsmäßig am nächsten kommen. Gleichzeitig ist das Wort auch ein versteckter Hinweis auf ein Kinderspiel, bei dem der Teilnehmer (in diesem Fall Architekten) vorgeben, „Experten für Hiltonculuk" zu sein. Somit gelang es Vanlı, mit einem einzigen Wort sowohl die Wirklichkeit wie auch den Scheinwelt-Charakter der Praxis von „Hiltonculuk" auszudrücken. Vanlı 1958: 21f.
3 Vanlı 1958: 20.
4 1947, als er Architekten und ihre Produktion in zwei Gruppen einteilte – der bürokratischen und der genialen – war Hitchcock auf der Suche nach einer „intellektuellen" und wissenschaftlichen Erklärung für das Geschäftsmäßige der Architekurpraxis in den Vereinigten Staaten. In seiner Analyse unterscheidet er zwischen besonderen Gebäuden und gewöhnlichen Gebäuden – zwischen dem Kunstwerk eines genialen Architekten und dem normalen Gebäude eines Architekten aus einem Architektenkollektiv von eher bürokratischer Prägung. SOM gehörte zu den Beispielen, die er für das bürokratische Praxismodell anführte. Hitchcock 1947.

America as it was practiced by corporate architectural offices such as SOM. Vanlı borrowed the notion of a bureaucratic architecture from the architectural historian Henry-Russell Hitchcock, who divided architectural production into two groups, bureaucratic and ordinary on the one side, genius and iconic on the other.[4] At the same time, his criticism was directed at the uncritical appropriation of American architecture à la International Style in Turkey, in the process of which bureaucratic architecture was turned into a sublime model of practice.

By emphasizing the negative impacts of Hiltonculuk on the architectural scene in Turkey, Vanlı depicts Hiltonculuk merely as an ideology, and critiques the ideology of postwar architectural practice. However, beneath this criticism, Vanlı's definition of Hiltonculuk also implies a mode of knowledge production that goes hand in hand with an ideology of architectural practice that was shared by the majority of postwar architects in Turkey, including Eldem, the Turkish partner of the team designing the Istanbul Hilton. In fact, shortly after Vanlı's critique, it was Eldem himself who made a contribution to Hiltonculuk. In order to accommodate another one hundred and fifty rooms in the hotel, he manipulated the original design, simply extending the length of the block by adding another seven identical bays. While Bunshaft disapproved of the expansion of the building in this way and, thus, saved himself the stigma of practicing Hiltonculuk, Eldem's involvement in it reinforced the legitimacy of the practice of among Turkish architects [→ figs. 4 and 5].

In his op-ed piece, Vanlı describes the working conditions of architects designing competition entries in 1950s Turkey. For these architects, Vanlı writes, images of Hilton-like projects from foreign journals were the main sources for practicing Hiltonculuk:

> By now, it is common knowledge that there are documents selected from foreign publications everywhere in these offices—on the walls where the preparation for competition entries is

going on and on top of the desks where the entry drawings are being drafted. As a matter of fact, it is obvious that there won't be enough time for any original work when drafting for several competitions at once. Anyway, it is doubtful that the projects can reach a fair result when prepared in this manner; and all the results are in the form of what we call "Hiltonculuk." The reason is that the contestants select "neutral" examples rather than strong ones, from documents ready in hand, in order to avoid the risk of distinctive architecture to be easily recognized.[5]

In Vanlı's view, this way of working was "oversimplified."[6] Yet the practice of Hiltonculuk generated some consensus among architects who believed that they had found in it the rationale of their intellectual practice as architects. In the absence of any constructive criticism in postwar Turkey, the ideology of Hiltonculuk was completely internalized and widely shared by architects, becoming the major paradigm of postwar architectural practice. For this reason, Vanlı's critique of Hiltonculuk led to absolutely no self-critical reflection among professionals at the time, and thus remained only a marginal, almost irrelevant, personal remark.[7]

In his criticism of Hiltonculuk, Vanlı attempted to unmask the collective unconscious of contemporary architects. In so doing, he undermined the intrinsic qualities of Hiltonculuk because he treated it merely as an ideology and ignored the aftereffects

4 In 1947, when dividing architects and their production into two groups—the bureaucratic and the genius—Hitchcock was in search of an "intellectual" and scholarly explanation for the business-like nature of architectural practice in the United States. In his analysis, he differentiates between special buildings and regular buildings—the former being a work of art by a genius architect and the latter being an ordinary building by an architect of a multi-partnered office with a more bureaucratic character. SOM was one of his examples of the bureaucratic model of practice. Hitchcock 1947.
5 Vanlı 1958: 22 [Engl. trans.: Elâ Kaçel].
6 Vanlı 1958: 22.
7 I use the term *common sense* with reference to Antonio Gramsci. Common sense, for Gramsci, is the uncritical, passive, and unconscious way of being in the world that becomes commonly accepted. Gramsci 2003 [1971].

Abb. 2
Das Istanbul Hilton an seiner außergewöhnlichen Lage vor
bestehenden Bauten entlang der Hauptstraße. Das Istanbuler
Rundfunkgebäude befindet sich ganz rechts, hinter dem Hotel.

Fig. 2
The Istanbul Hilton shown on its exceptional site in front of
existing buildings lining the main street. The Istanbul Radio
building is to the far right, behind the hotel.

Rasyonalizmin kalıpları ile Türkiye'ye gelişi...1950'ler

Bu kalıbın kapsamında en ilginç denemeler, Le Corbusier ile Terragni'nin ürettikleri ve geliştirdikleri kartezyen petek ızgaradır... İstanbul'da Büyükada Anadolu Kulübü, Hilton, Çınar, İzmir'de Efes, Eskişehir'de Porsuk gibi beş otelle başlanılan, döşemelerin ve bölme duvarlarının kapalı, oda sınırlarından taşarak balkon oluşturmasıyla sağlanan bir düzenlemedir. Sonunda uzun yıllar, vasat yerli yapı tipolojisi olmuş, binlerce kez yinelenmiştir.

Daha önce geleneksel heveslerle mimarlığı yaşamış kişiler, yeni bir yaklaşımı hedef edinmekte güçlük çekmişlerdir... Herkes bulunduğu yerden bu modern, akılcı sürece girmiştir. Akılcılık, daha çok mimarın paylaşabileceği bir yaklaşım olarak yayılmış, gelişmiş, çoğalmıştır.

Tarabya Oteli'nde ise, bu ızgarayı farklılaştırma girişimi vardır.

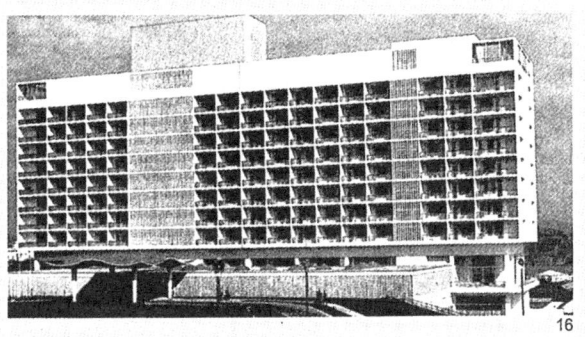

16

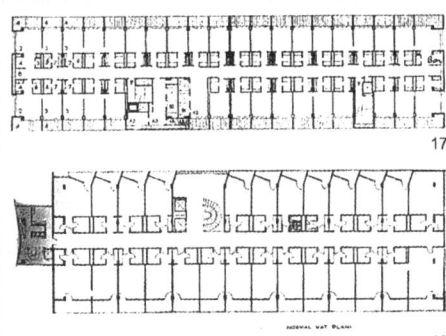

17

19

18

21

20

16, 17. SOM, Sedad Hakkı Eldem, İstanbul Hilton Oteli, 1952.
18, 19. Rana Zıpçı, Ahmet Akın, Emin Ertan, Çınar Oteli, İstanbul, 1950'ler.
20. Vedat Dalokay, Orduevi (Porsuk Oteli), Eskişehir, 1956.
21. Kadri Eroğan, Tarabya Oteli, İstanbul, 1957.
22. Paul Bonatz, Fatin Uran, Büyük Efes Oteli, İzmir, 1957

22

Abb. 3
Eine Seite voller Beispiele von Hiltonculuk aus Şevki Vanlıs letztem Buch. Vanlı 2006: 211.

Fig. 3
A full-page layout of examples of Hiltonculuk, featured in Şevki Vanlı's last book. Vanlı 2006: 211.

Vorlagen eher ‚neutrale' Bespiele aus als originelle, um sich im Vergleich zu anderen nicht mit einem unverwechselbaren Entwurf zu exponieren."[5]

Nach Vanlıs Meinung war diese Arbeitsweise „übersimplifiziert".[6] Doch bewirkte die Praxis von Hiltonculuk auch einigen Konsens unter Architekten, die meinten, darin die Maxime ihrer intellektuellen Praxis als Architekten gefunden zu haben. Mangels jedweder konstruktiver Kritik in der Türkei der Nachkriegszeit wurde die Ideologie von Hiltonculuk vollständig verinnerlicht und von vielen Architekten angenommen, wodurch sie zum hauptsächlichen Paradigma der Architekturpraxis nach dem Krieg avancierte. Aus diesem Grund führte Vanlıs Kritik an Hiltonculuk zu keinerlei selbstkritischer Reflexion in der damaligen Fachwelt und blieb somit nur eine marginale, beinahe irrelevante persönliche Meinung.

In seiner Kritik an Hiltonculuk versuchte Vanlı das kollektive Unbewusste zeitgenössischer Architekten zu entlarven. Damit unterminierte er die inhärenten Vorzüge von Hiltonculuk, weil er es lediglich als Ideologie betrachtete und die Nachwirkungen dieser Ideologie ignorierte, unter anderem den aufkommenden Alltagsverstand[7] und die Wissensproduktion, die in der Moderne der Nachkriegszeit in Erscheinung traten. Wie ich im Folgenden ausführen werde, verhilft uns Hiltonculuk sogar zu einem neuen Verständnis des Intellektualismus und der unterschiedlichen Arten, wie Architekten in ihrer Berufspraxis die Beziehung zwischen Ideologie und Wissensproduktion gestalten.

Ideologie, Wissensproduktion, Intellektuelle

Folgt man Karl Mannheim, so besteht das Studium der Architekurideologie hauptsächlich darin aufzuzeigen, wie sich die verschiedenen intellektuellen (oder ideologischen) Standpunkte, die Architekten einnehmen, zu ihrer Berufspraxis verhalten und wie Ideologie und Praxis im Verlauf von gesellschaftlichem und intellektuellem Wandel interagieren. Antonio Gramsci hingegen berücksichtigt auch die gesellschaf-

lichen Bedingungen intellektueller Mediation und ihre Folgen – sei es Entfremdung, Hegemonie, Scheinautonomie oder die Schaffung von „Alltagsverstand".

Es steht außer Zweifel, dass Architekten ihre berufliche Legitimation vor allem über ihr Fachwissen beziehen und dieses Wissen innerhalb und zwischen mehreren spezifischen beruflichen Bereichen wie dem Büro, der Baustelle oder der Bauindustrie weitergeben. Im öffentlichen Sektor sind es dann Fachschulen, Verbände und Zeitschriften, die dieses Wissen über verschiedenene Medien in Umlauf bringen und Fachkollegen sowie der allgemeinen Öffentlichkeit zugänglich machen. Mit Rückverweis auf Mannheim könnte man das spezialisierte Wissen der Architektur als „relationales Wissen" bezeichnen, aufgrund seines nicht-autonomen und objektiven Wesens, seiner wechselseitigen Funktionsweise und seiner Dynamik.[8]

Es ist die Beziehung zwischen Geistesleben und gesellschaftspolitischen Kräften, die, so Mannheim, als Gegenstand einer „Wissenssoziologie" oder eines „wertfreien Ideologiebegriffs" untersucht werden muss. Dabei unterlässt es Mannheim, die Grenzen der Bereiche des Geisteslebens genau zu definieren, wie Gramsci es versucht. Derselbe Mangel zeigt sich in Vanlıs Kritik an Hiltonculuk, die keinerlei Trennung zwischen kritischen und unkritischen Ansätzen gegenüber dem Hiltonculuk vornimmt. Sämtliche Praktiken des Intellektualismus werden in die Schublade von Hiltonculuk gesteckt. Aus der Sicht praktizierender Architekten stellt sich die Beziehung zwischen Ideologie und relationalem Wissen jedoch komplizierter dar. An dieser Stelle kommt nun der Frage nach den Bewusstseinsarten eine zentrale Bedeutung zu, um die Struktur des Intellektualismus zu verstehen.

---

5 Vanlı 1958: 22 [Dt. Übers.: Matthias Müller].
6 Vanlı 1958: 22.
7 Ich verwende den Begriff Alltagsverstand (senso commune) im Sinne Antonio Gramscis. Unter Alltagsverstand versteht Gramsci die unkritische, passive, unbewusste Art des menschlichen Existierens, die in einer Gesellschaft allgemeine Zustimmung gefunden hat. Gramsci 2003 [1971].
8 Mannheim 1978 [1929].

of this ideology, including the emerging common sense and the knowledge production that came with it in postwar modernism. In fact, as I will now show, Hiltonculuk provides us with a new understanding of intellectualism and of the ways in which architects relate ideology to knowledge production in their profession.

Ideology, Knowledge Production, Intellectuals

With reference to Karl Mannheim, the study of architectural ideology would mainly involve showing how intellectual (or ideological) standpoints of architects are connected with their professional experience in practice, and how ideology and practice interact in the course of social and intellectual change. Antonio Gramsci, in contrast, accounts for the social conditions of intellectual mediation and its consequences—whether it is alienation, hegemony, quasi-autonomy, or the creation of a "common sense."

There is no doubt that architects legitimize their profession through their specialized knowledge of architecture, and transmit that knowledge within and between several specific professional domains such as the office, the building site, and the building industry. Public domains, such as professional schools, organizations, and journals, then circulate and disseminate this knowledge through various media to professionals and the general public. Referring back to Mannheim, one could call the specialized knowledge of architecture "relational knowledge" because of its nonautonomous and objective nature, its reciprocal operation, and its dynamism.[8]

It is the relationship between intellectual life and socio-political forces that needs to be studied, Mannheim argues, as a theme of a "sociology of knowledge" or a "non-evaluative study of ideology." Mannheim does not precisely define the limits of the domains of intellectual life as Gramsci tries to do. Ironically, the same shortcoming is apparent in Vanlı's criticism of Hiltonculuk in that he does not differentiate between critical and uncritical approaches to Hiltonculuk. All practices of intellectualism are swept under

8 Mannheim 1936 [1929].

9 The curators of an exhibition on Turgut Cansever depicted the architect's two identities as two sequential themes of the exhibition—Cansever as an "architect" and as a "man of thought." My critique of this approach is that Cansever was turned into a genius by the exhibition's curatorial framing in that it sublimated his individualism and isolated him from the social context of the architectural discourse. See the exhibition catalogue, which includes interviews with the architect. Tanyeli/Yücel 2007.

10 In particular, sociologists who work in the field of social network analysis provide us with an eye-opening approach to reciprocity: " [I]f we ignore social relations and adopt 'separate' actors as the basic assumption, we are left with an 'undersocializing' theory of the individual." Degenne/Forsé 1999: 8.

11 Eldem and Arkan are two prominent Turkish architects who led the introduction of modern architecture into Turkey as educators and practitioners after being educated in Germany. For 1930s modernism in Turkey, see Bozdoğan 2001. Taut and Holzmeister are the most significant figures of those who were officially invited to Turkey in the 1930s and employed by the government to teach and practice architecture. For a detailed study of architects in exile in Turkey, see Nicolai 1998.

the rubric of Hiltonculuk. Seen from the perspective of professional architects, however, the relationship between ideology and relational knowledge seems to be more complicated. It is at this point that modes of consciousness become central in order to understand the structure of intellectualism.

What makes an architect predominantly an intellectual? Consciousness, "intellectual restlessness" (to use Mannheim's term) that simply comes with one's intellectual practice as an architect, or rather embellishments, judgments of historians and critics projected onto the architect's intellectualism, sometimes even arbitrarily? And can any architect be identified as a "man of thought,"[9] regardless of whether the architect is a state or private employee, an academic, or a business owner?

Architecture is certainly not exempt from the criticism of social scientists who attack theories that "undersocialize" the individual.[10] It is precisely the focus and priority given to "undersocialized" individuals that has recently surfaced as a conundrum in the historiography of Turkish modernism. One can easily argue that, in Turkey, singular figures such as Sedad Hakkı Eldem, Seyfi Arkan, Bruno Taut, and Clemens Holzmeister, among others, and, by consequence, singular discourses, dominate the trajectory of modern architecture.[11] Yet the professional

Was macht einen Architekten in erster Linie zum Intellektuellen? Bewusstsein und intellektuelle Ruhelosigkeit, die mit der eigenen intellektuellen Praxis als Architekt einhergeht, oder eher Ausschmückungen, Urteile von Historikern und Kritikern, die auf den Intellektualismus des Architekten projiziert werden, manchmal sogar willkürlich? Und kann jeder Architekt als ein „Denker"[9] bezeichnet werden, ungeachtet dessen, ob der Architekt sich in öffentlicher oder privatwirtschaftlicher Anstellung befindet, ob er Akademiker ist oder Unternehmer?

Die Architektur ist von der Kritik durch Sozialwissenschaftler sicherlich nicht ausgenommen, wenn sie Theorien angreifen, die das Individuum „untersozialisieren".[10] Und just der Nachdruck auf „untersozialisierte" Individuen hat sich in jüngerer Zeit als Dilemma in der Geschichtsschreibung der türkischen Moderne herausgestellt. Nun kann man durchaus vorbringen, dass in der Türkei ja auch singuläre Persönlichkeiten wie Sedad Hakkı Eldem, Seyfi Arkan, Bruno Taut, Clemens Holzmeister und entsprechend singuläre Diskurse den Verlauf der modernen Architektur bestimmen.[11] Doch die berufliche Autonomie dieser Persönlichkeiten war eine relative, denn sie waren in den 1930er und 1940er Jahren ohne Ausnahme unter staatlichem Patronat tätig. Wie Gramsci deutlich macht, ist jede Autonomie, die Intellektuellen aufgrund ihrer Funktion in einer staatlichen oder zivilgesellschaftlichen Organisation gewährt wird, in Wirklichkeit nur eine Scheinautonomie. Ungeachtet der Illusion, über „totale" Autonomie zu verfügen, nahmen diese Architekten der 1930er und 1940er Jahre, die sich im Fach etablierten, vielfältige privilegierte Identitäten an – als praktizierende Architekten, als Lehrende und als Angehörige der nationalen Elite, und zwar aufgrund ihres intellektuellen Funktionierens in der Gesellschaft. Das band sie natürlich in diese Gesellschaft ein. In seiner Intellektuellenanalyse unterstreicht Gramsci auch die Tatsache, dass kein Intellektueller hinsichtlich der Funktion, die er in einer gegebenen Gesellschaft einnimmt, dem anderen gleicht. Gramsci zufolge ist

somit eine Unterscheidung zwischen „traditionellen" und „organischen" Intellektuellen unvermeidlich, da sich jeder Architekt in seiner Ortung im sozialen Netzwerk von dem anderen unterscheidet. „Traditionelle Intellektuelle", so Gramsci, handeln unabhängiger und verfügen vermeintlich über mehr Macht im Vergleich zu „organischen Intellektuellen", die von den Organisationen abhängig sind, die sie geschaffen haben.

In Eldems Fall war es seine Vorrangstellung in Hochschule, Staat und Diskurs, die ihn als traditionellen Intellektuellen etab-lierte. Die gesellschaftliche Macht und Autorität des traditionellen Intellektuellen – wie Gramsci sie definiert – ist eher auf Autonomie gebaut denn auf Einbettung in ein soziales Netzwerk. Gerade diese relative Autonomie hatte Eldem ausgeübt, um seine Vorrangstellung zu erhalten und sich von seinen Zeitgenossen abzuheben – seien es traditionelle oder organische Intellektuelle, „Experten" oder Kritiker in Sachen Hiltonculuk. Sein hohes Ansehen als traditioneller Intellektueller bewahrte ihn auch davor, von seinen Zeitgenossen als „Experte für Hiltonculuk" kritisiert zu werden, als er das ursprüngliche Hilton erweiterte.

9 Die Kuratoren einer Ausstellung über Turgut Cansever stellten die beiden Identitäten des Architekten als zwei aneinandergereihte Themen der Ausstellung dar – Cansever als „Architekt" und als „Denker". Meine Kritik ist, dass diese kuratorische Rahmung Cansever in ein Genie verwandelte, indem sie seinen Individualismus sublimierte und ihn vom gesellschaftlichen Kontext des Architekturdiskurses ausnahm. Siehe den Austellungskatalog, der ein Interview mit dem Architekten enthält. Tanyeli / Yücel 2007.

10 Vor allem Soziologen, die auf dem Gebiet der sozialen Netzwerkanalyse arbeiten, bieten uns einen überzeugenden und sinnfälligen Ansatz zum Verständnis von Gegenseitigkeit: „...wenn wir gesellschaftliche Beziehungen ignorieren und von der Grundannahme ausgehen, dass wir es mit ‚einzelnen' Akteuren zu tun haben, ergibt das eine ‚untersozialisierende' Theorie des Individuums." Degenne / Forsé 1999: 8.

11 Eldem und Arkan sind zwei prominente türkische Architekten, die, nach ihrer Ausbildung in Deutschland, als Hochschullehrer und Praktiker maßgeblich an der Einführung der modernen Architektur in der Türkei beteiligt waren. Zur Moderne der 1930er Jahre in der Türkei siehe Bozdoğan 2001. Unter den Architekten, die in den 1930er Jahren offiziell vom Staat in die Türkei eingeladen und angestellt wurden, um Architektur zu unterrichten und zu praktizieren, zählen Taut und Holzmeister wohl zu den bedeutendsten. Für eine detaillierte Studie über Architekten im Exil in der Türkei siehe Nicolai 1998.

autonomy of each of these figures was relative, as in the 1930s and 1940s they all practiced under the patronage of the state. As Gramsci clearly shows, any autonomy that is awarded to intellectuals because of their function in the organization of either the state or civil society is, in reality, only quasi-autonomy. Despite the illusion of holding "total" autonomy, architects of the 1930s and 1940s who established themselves in professional practice in fact assumed multiple privileged identities—as intellectuals, educators, and members of the country's elite—because of their intellectual functioning in society; this, of course, implicated them in that society. In his analysis of intellectuals, Gramsci also underlines the fact that no intellectual has the same function in a given society. According to Gramsci, a differentiation between "traditional" and "organic" intellectuals is inevitable, considering that each architect's position is distinct from another's in how one is situated in a social network. "Traditional intellectuals," Gramsci argues, act more independently and supposedly have more power in comparison to "organic intellectuals," who are dependent on the organizations that create them.

In the case of Eldem, the privileged positions he held in academia, the state, and the discourse established him as a traditional intellectual. The social power and authority of the traditional intellectual—as Gramsci defines it—is primarily constructed on autonomy rather than on connectedness in a social network. It is precisely this relative autonomy that Eldem had been exercising in order to retain his hegemonic position and to differentiate himself from his contemporaries—whether traditional or organic intellectuals, experts or critics of Hiltonculuk. His highly respected position as a traditional intellectual also saved him from being criticized by his contemporaries as an expert of Hiltonculuk when he extended the original Hilton.

From the early 1950s on, however, young architects experienced an inevitable split among the formerly conjoined intellectual identities as professionals, educators, and as elite members of society. Eldem was the only

12 Historians, too, were susceptible to Eldem's dominance. The first English monograph on a modern Turkish architect was in fact written about Eldem. See Bozdoğan/Özkan/Yenal 1987.
13 Mannheim 1936 [1929]: 3.

architect who could preserve all three identities for himself well into the 1970s. His quasi-independent position in architecture, in contrast to that of young architects who struggled to survive in the professional market by serving both public agencies and private entrepreneurs, armed him with representational power in education, practice, and discourse. As a matter of fact, for three consecutive decades, it was always his buildings that heralded and established a new discourse: as a reaction to 1930s international modernism, the Turkish Pavilion at the 1939 New York World's Fair, co-designed with Sedat Zincirkıran, initiated a nationalist revivalism in the country, which prevailed until it became dated by Eldem and SOM's Istanbul Hilton (1952–55). The International Style introduced by the Hilton in turn lasted for about a decade until Eldem, with the design of the Social Security Agency Complex (1963–70) in Istanbul, shifted his—and the discourse's—attention to vernacularism.[12] Being a traditional intellectual in the Gramscian sense, Eldem established absolutes rather than generate debates on the themes he helped to frame, including historicism, vernacularism, traditionalism, and even Hiltonculuk. It was, therefore, absolute knowledge, not relational knowledge, that Eldem established as a norm in architectural discourse. This mode of knowledge production, however, was soon to be challenged by the first multipartnered architectural offices and groups in the country.

Code 17171: Challenging Ideology through Collective Practice

Two features characterize Mannheim's methodology of the sociology of knowledge. First, the unit of analysis is not individuals and their thoughts, but rather relational interactions. As a member of a group, individuals not only find themselves in "a ready-made situation" but also "in an inherited situation with patterns of thought."[13]

Abb. 4 und 5
Das Istanbul Hilton vor und nach der Erweiterung
des ursprünglichen Blocks.

Figs. 4 and 5
The Istanbul Hilton before and after the expansion of
the original block.

Doch ab Anfang der 1950er Jahre erlebten junge Architekten eine unvermeidliche Spaltung zwischen den ehemals verbundenen intellektuellen Identitäten als Berufsausübende, Lehrer und Angehörige der Elite. Eldem war der einzige Architekt, der alle drei Identitäten für sich erhalten konnte, bis weit in die 1970er Jahre hinein. Seine quasiunabhängige Position in der Architektur – im Gegensatz zu jener junger Architekten, die sich abmühten, auf dem Markt zu überleben, indem sie sowohl öffentlichen Stellen wie auch privatwirtschaftlichen Unternehmern dienten –, stattete ihn mit repräsentativer Macht aus. Tatsächlich waren es für drei aufeinanderfolgende Jahrzehnte stets seine Gebäude, die einen neuen Diskurs ankündigten und etablierten: Als Reaktion auf die internationale Moderne der 1930er Jahre leitete der türkische Pavillon auf der Weltausstellung von 1939 in New York, an dessen Entwurf Sedat Zincirkıran mitwirkte, die Zweite Nationale Architekturströmung im Lande ein, die anhielt, bis sie durch das Istanbul Hilton von Eldem und SOM (1951–55) überholt wurde. Der Internationale Stil, vom Hilton initiiert, hielt seinerseits etwa ein Jahrzehnt an, bis Eldem, mit dem Entwurf des Komplexes der Sozialversicherungs-Agentur (1963–70) in Istanbul seine Aufmerksamkeit – und die des Diskurses – zum ortsüblichen, traditionellen Baustil[12] verlagerte. Eldem begründete als traditioneller Intellektueller im Sinne Gramscis eher absolute Setzungen, anstatt Debatten zu den Themen auszulösen, die er umriss, einschließlich Historismus, Vernakularismus, Traditionalismus und sogar Hiltonculuk. Es war daher absolutes Wissen und nicht relationales Wissen, das Eldem als Norm im Architekturdiskurs etablierte. Diese Art der Wissensproduktion sollte jedoch bald von den ersten Architekturbüros und -gruppen im Land infrage gestellt werden.

Code 17171: Infragestellung der Ideologie durch kollektive Praxis

Zwei Merkmale kennzeichnen Mannheims Methodik der Soziologie des Wissens. Erstens, die Einheit der Analyse sind nicht Individuen und ihre Gedanken, sondern relationale Interaktionen. Als Angehörige einer Gruppe befinden sich Individuen nicht nur in einer „fertigen Situation" sondern auch in einer „ererbten Situation mit Denkmodellen".[13] Zweitens, kollektives Denken ermöglicht „kollektives Handeln", durch das eine gegebene Gruppe aneinander gebundener Individuen daran arbeitet, sich den bestehenden Bedingungen um sie herum zu widersetzen oder aber sie zu erhalten.[14] Mit diesem relationalen Ansatz macht sich Mannheim an die Untersuchung von Ideologie, und durch das Konzept des „kollektiven Handelns" deckt sich seine Kritik der Ideologie mit der Gramscis. Beide interessieren sich für die Frage, welche Konsequenzen für die Ideologie entstehen, wenn Individuen in Gruppen eingebunden sind. Nur aus der Perspektive des Kollektivs und der Ideologie der Gruppe, so lautet ihr Argument, kann die Kritik einer Individualideologie entwickelt werden.

In der Türkei bedeutete das Aufkommen der ersten Architekturbüros Anfang der 1950er Jahre einen Wendepunkt in der Art und Weise, wie der Berufsstand in der Wissensproduktion tätig war. Es war nämlich in der Praxis einiger dieser Büros – tatsächlich war Eldems Zusammenarbeit mit SOM ein Vorläufer –, und nicht in der von Einzelpraktikern, in der sich „kollektives Handeln" zum ersten Mal ansatzweise zeigte, und damit auch die Möglichkeit, eine Kritik der Ideologie in der Architektur in Gang zu setzen. Historiker und Wissenschaftler haben jedoch die geschichtliche und theoretische Bedeutung dieser ersten Partnerschaften – zu ihnen gehören İMA, Baysal-Birsel, Birol-Gürel-Defne, und Tekeli-Sisa-Hepgüler – wegen ihres bürokratischen Charakters unterbewertet. Die ersten Architektenpartnerschaften in der Türkei machen allerdings deutlich, dass eine solche scharfe Trennung, wie sie Hitchcocks Einteilung zwischen dem Bürokraten und dem Genie vornimmt, den

---

12 Auch Historiker konnten sich Eldems Dominanz nicht entziehen: Die erste englischsprachige Monografie über einen modernen türkischen Architekten wurde tatsächlich über Eldem verfasst. Siehe Bozogan/Özkan/Yenal 1987.
13 Mannheim 1978 [1929]: 5.
14 Mannheim 1978 [1929]: 3.

14 Mannheim 1936 [1929]: 4.

Second, collective thinking enables "collective activity," through which a given group of individuals bound together works to resist or preserve the existing conditions surrounding them.[14] With this relational approach, Mannheim proceeds to study ideology, and the concept of "collective activity" brings his critique of ideology in line with that of Gramsci. Both are interested in the implications for ideology when individuals are bound together in groups. Only from the perspective of the collective and the group's ideology, they argue, can a critique of individual ideology be developed.

In Turkey, the emergence of the first multipartnered architectural offices in the early 1950s constitutes a pivotal moment in how the profession was engaged in knowledge production. It is the practice of some of these offices (Eldem's collaboration with SOM in fact being a forerunner), not that of single practitioners, where the first glimpses of "collective activity" appeared, and with it, the potential to generate a critique of ideology in architecture. Historians and scholars, however, have underrated the historical and theoretical significance of these first partnerships—they include İMA, Baysal-Birsel, Birol-Gürel-Defne, and Tekeli-Sisa-Hepgüler—because of their bureaucratic character. What the first architectural partnerships in Turkey prove, though, is that such a clear-cut schism as is laid out by Hitchcock's division between the bureaucratic and the genius cannot do justice to the architects' identities. Looking closely at the organizational structure of each of these partnerships, one finds that none of the founding architects either consented to becoming a bureaucrat architect or aspired to be a genius architect.

Rather, by 1950, at a time when eighty percent of architects were hired by the public and governmental agencies in Turkey, the newly founded offices of the young partnerships were seeking independence from public employment. Their independence, however, was relative because they continued to bid for state-issued and -funded designs and planning commissions. Especially architectural competitions, which governmental agen-

cies started to launch as a mode of commissioning architects in the mid-1950s, provided a new field in the profession. As Ilhan Tekeli points out, competitions became a platform on which young architects could declare "the manifesto of the new," that is, of the International Style. Through competitions, these architects viewed modern architecture to be practiced as on a tabula rasa, beyond what was regarded as everyday, businesslike, ordinary practice. At the same time, these competitions created the new common sense, one that perpetuated the practice of Hiltonculuk, as Şevki Vanlı would show in 1958.

It is in one such collaborative working model, formed by architects from İMA, Baysal-Birsel, and Birol-Gürel, where discussions of Hiltonculuk and the paradoxical relationship between knowledge and ideology emerged. Aside from their everyday practices in separate offices, up to ten architects from these three partnerships formed a think tank. Its members included Maruf Önal, Abdurrahman Hancı, Turgut Cansever, Süha Toner, Şahap Aran, Haluk Baysal, Melih Birsel, Radi Birol, Sedat Gürel, and Faruk Sırmalı, and single practitioners such as Faruk Sırmalı would occasionally join. The formation of such a team was the first of its kind in Turkey. The architects' intentions in joining together were to generate collective thinking, incisive criticism, and open discussion, and to make these instrumental in their collaborative work, which primarily involved entering architectural design and urban planning competitions as one large team.

The think tank received several first and second prizes in about twenty major competitions in the 1950s. The only signifier of the anonymous think tank was a five-digit code, 17171, which they used to identify their entrances to blindly reviewed design competitions. The think tank's identity became public to the architectural community for the first time in 1955 when their winning design for the State Highways General Directorate's new building in Ankara was

Identitäten der Architekten nicht gerecht wird. Unterzieht man die organisatorische Struktur jeder dieser Partnerschaften einer eingehenden Prüfung, so stellt man fest, dass die Gründungsmitglieder tatsächlich andere Ziele hatten.

Im Gegenteil, schon um 1950, zu einer Zeit als achtzig Prozent der Architekten in der Türkei ihre Aufträge von öffentlichen und staatlichen Stellen erhielten, strebten die neugegründeten Büros der jungen Partnerschaften gerade die Unabhängigkeit von öffentlicher Anstellung an. Ihre Unabhängigkeit war jedoch relativ, denn sie bewarben sich weiterhin für staatlich vergebene und finanzierte Entwürfe und Planungsaufträge. Vor allem Architekturwettbewerbe, die ab Mitte der 1950er Jahre von staatlichen Stellen als Instrument der Auftragsvergabe eingesetzt wurden, eröffneten neue Möglichkeiten in der Branche. Wie Ilhan Tekeli betont, wurden Wettbewerbe zu einer Plattform, auf der junge Architekten das „Manifest des Neuen", d.h. des Internationalen Stils verkünden konnten. Diese Architekten betrachteten Wettbewerbe als Projektionsfläche für die moderne Architektur, für alles, was über die normale, geschäftsmäßige Alltagspraxis hinausging. Gleichzeit schufen diese Wettbewerbe den neuen Alltagsverstand, der die Praxis von Hiltonculuk verewigte, wie Şevki Vanlı bereits 1958 gezeigt hatte.

In einem solchen kollaborativen Arbeitsmodell, das von Architekten der Büros İMA, Baysal-Birsel und Birol-Gürel gebildet wurde, entstanden Diskussionen über Hiltonculuk und die paradoxe Beziehung zwischen Wissen und Ideologie. Neben dem Tagesgeschäft ihrer jeweiligen Büros bildeten bis zu zehn Architekten dieser drei Partnerschaften eine Denkfabrik. Zu den Mitgliedern gehörten Maruf Önal, Abdurrahman Hancı, Turgut Cansever, Süha Toner, Şahap Aran, Haluk Baysal, Melih Birsel, Radi Birol, Sedat Gürel und Faruk Sırmalı, aber auch selbständige Architekten wie Faruk Sırmalı nahmen hin und wieder teil. Das so gebildete Team war das erste seiner Art in der Türkei. Die Architekten sahen das Ziel ihres Zusammenschlusses darin, kollektives Denken, einschneidende Kritik und eine offene Diskussion zu fördern und für ihre kollaborative Arbeit nutzbar zu machen, die hauptsächlich darin bestand, sich als ein großes Team bei Architektur- und städtebaulichen Wettbewerben zu bewerben.

Die Denkfabrik erhielt mehrere erste und zweite Preise in etwa zwanzig wichtigen Wettbewerben der 1950er Jahre. Die einzige Referenz der anonymen Denkfabrik war ein fünfstelliger Code, 17171, den sie verwendete, um ihre Entwürfe für anonyme Wettbewerbe zu kennzeichnen. Die Identität der Denkfabrik wurde zum ersten Mal 1955 der Architektengemeinde bekannt, als ihr Siegerentwurf für das neue Gebäude der staatlichen türkischen Generaldirektion für das Fernstraßenwesen (KGM) in Ankara in *Arkitekt* veröffentlicht wurde.[15] Es ist erwähnenswert, dass dieser preisgekrönter Entwurf, ein auf Pilotis erhöhter Kasten, auf den ersten Blick dem Istanbul Hilton in Baukörper und Proportionen ähnelt [→ Abb. 6]. Selbst wenn die Fassade anders als im formelhaften Ansatz von Hiltonculuk gestaltet ist, wäre der Entwurf insgesamt von Vanlı als Hiltonculuk kritisiert worden. Vanlı erwähnt den Entwurf in seinem Kommentar auf der Kommentarseite von 1958 nicht, sondern erst beinahe fünfzig Jahre später in seiner letzten Buchveröffentlichung, in der er den Entwurf als eines der damaligen neuen aber „monotonen" öffentlichen Gebäude bezeichnet, das aus dem in der Architektur vorherrschenden rationalistischen Ansatz hervorgegangen sei[16] [→ Abb. 7].

Dieser Kommentar ist aus zweierlei Gründen von Bedeutung. Erstens verrät er Vanlıs Geringschätzung für die „perfekte Mittelmäßigkeit", die der universellen, rationalen, doch gewöhnlichen Architekturpraxis in der Türkei zugrunde liegt. Zweitens veranschaulicht er, wie Vanlı, vielleicht wegen seiner Geringschätzung, die Tatsache einfach

15 Zu den preisgekrönten Projekten siehe „Karayolları Umum Müdürlüğü Binası Proje Müsabakası", *Arkitekt* 1955.
16 In dem dreibändigen Opus, dessen Titel man mit „Reden über Architektur" übersetzen kann, bringt Vanlı Dutzende von „no-name" Architekten ans Licht, deren Arbeiten bis vor Kurzem noch in der Mainstream-Geschichte der türkischen Architektur des 20. Jahrhunderts vernachlässigt worden waren. Vanlı 2006: 334.

published in *Arkitekt*.[15] It is noteworthy that at first sight this winning design, a prismatic box raised on pilotis, resembles the Istanbul Hilton in its volume and proportions [→ fig. 6]. Even though the façade is handled differently from the formulaic approach of Hiltonculuk, the overall design would have been criticized by Vanlı as such. Although not included in his op-ed piece of 1958, the design was featured in Vanlı's last book, published almost fifty years later, as one of the new but "monotonous" public buildings of its time that came out of the rationalist approach prevalent in architecture[16] [→ fig. 7].

This comment is crucial for two reasons. First, it reveals Vanlı's resentment of the "perfect mediocrity" that underlies the universal, rational, yet ordinary architectural practice in Turkey. And second, it illustrates how Vanlı, perhaps because of his resentment, had simply overlooked the fact that, in 1950s Turkey, the profession and the discourse were constructed at the same time. In other words, the iconization of bureaucratic architecture in the discourse went hand in hand with the bureaucratization of the profession through the establishment of large, multipartnered firms, on the one hand, and the establishment of the Chamber of Architects as a new professional body, on the other. Indeed, the debates relating to the role of intellectualism—as exemplified by the discussion around Hiltonculuk—all related to this simultaneous, unsettled construction of profession and discourse. For this reason, the think tank's winning design for the State Highways General Directorate's new building in Ankara needs to be considered in light of the subtleties that the think tank's "collective activity" and "cultural contact" (Gramsci) to common sense entailed. A close analysis of the think tank's organizational structure and methods of collective practice shows that it presented new models for intellectual activity as well as for doing business. Both models were constructed not on the vision of a single, leading individual but on that of a team of professionals. Rather than claiming an absolute knowledge (as Eldem did), the think tank used relational knowledge as a design motivation and as a

15 For the prize-winning projects, see "Karayolları Umum Müdürlüğü Binası Proje Müsabakası," *Arkitekt* 1955.
16 In the three-volume opus, the title of which translates as "Talking architecture," Vanlı brings dozens of "no-name" architects into light whose work had been written out of mainstream history of twentieth-century Turkish architecture until very recently. Vanlı 2006: 334.

group ideology. Vanlı's criticism of Hiltonculuk vigorously implied that alienation was the fundamental deficiency of the followers of Hiltonculuk and of the "experts" who drafted Hilton-like buildings in their offices. Vanlı even hinted at some modes of consciousness as being concomitants of practicing Hiltonculuk, including isolation, disconnectedness, lack of enthusiasm, and even loss of ethics. It is precisely these concomitants of the widespread practice of Hiltonculuk that the think tank tried to avoid. Via collective activity and relational knowledge, the team sought a way to raise their work above the limits of Hiltonculuk and, hence, to propose a remedy to the alienation of architectural practice. At the same time, however, the collaborative did not risk stepping beyond the architectural common sense that had been established after the universal and rational values of International Style modernism and appropriated among Turkish architects as such—a point that Vanlı observed in his remarks on why architects prefer to come up with neutral rather than provocative designs.

For this reason, the think tank's winning design became vulnerable to criticism of Hiltonculuk. Yet, being conscious of the fact that they had to operate within the existing common sense, the think tank actively engaged with and took on the International Style. Rather than resorting to the established models of bureaucratic architecture in Turkey, they tried to initiate a discourse on International Style modernism by introducing a steel structure and curtain wall construction in their design, which were novelties in Turkey at that time. In this way, the cultural contact that they established to common sense differentiated them from the "experts of Hiltonculuk" on the one side and from dominant, singular figures like Eldem on the other.

After being awarded first prize for the State Highways office building, the think tank

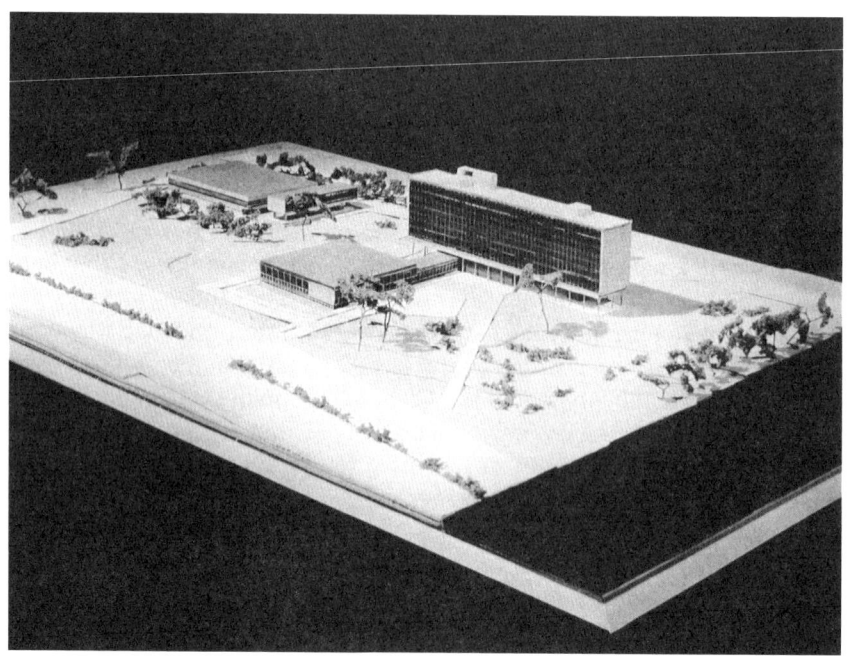

Abb. 6
Modell des preisgekrönten Wettbewerbsentwurfs der
Denkfabrik für die staatliche Generaldirektion für das
Fernstraßenwesen in Ankara.

Fig. 6
Model of the think tank's winning competition entry for the
State Highways General Directorate, Ankara.

Türk mimarları rasyonel / akılcı olmanın ilk yaklaşımı prizmalara alışıyor... 1950'ler

İlginç olan, bu önerilerin günümüze çok da ters düşmediği... B. Taut'un "Türkçe Mimarlık Bilgisi" kitabında dediği gibi, aynı prizmayı yatay veya dik koyabilirsiniz... Ben de ekliyorum, dikine koyarsanız 1950'ler 2000'ler oluyor. Bugünkü pek çok yaklaşımı rasyonel saymakta haksız olmadığımı görüyorum...

Modernizm, akılcı, ekonomik, aydınlık yüzüyle, öncesinin aynı öğelerini evirip çevirip kullanan, pahalı, kolay kirlenen, karanlık ve yeni işlevlere yabancı neoklasik veya zoraki Milli Mimarinin yerine geçti.

İşlevden sonraki en önemli niteliği, önceki insana meydan okuyan görkemin yerini alan, insana yakın, işleve uygun iç ölçü, sadelik, proje ve üretim kolaylığı idi. Buradaki örneklerden oluşacak bir çevre, çağdaş ve geleceğin toplumlarının yüzü gibi aydınlık olacaktır.

Fakat cephelerdeki doku düzeninde çok kez cam cephelerin tekdüzeliği de, özel bir istek iletmediği gibi sanki insanlara bir beklenti hakkı da tanımıyor... Bunu, yapıyla insan arasındaki iletişimi en aza indirmek isteği gibi de yorumlayabiliriz. 1956'da yarışma kazanarak uygulanan, rasyonel modernizmin yaklaşım ve anlatımına sahip başarılı, öncü bir kamu yapısı, Kortan, Yaubyan, Vapurciyan ve Andonyadis'in Sakarya Hükümet Konağı olmalıdır.

Bu yapılar tekdüze olsalar da, yeni bir dünya, yeni bir çevre ve yaşamın aydınlık temsilcileridirler...

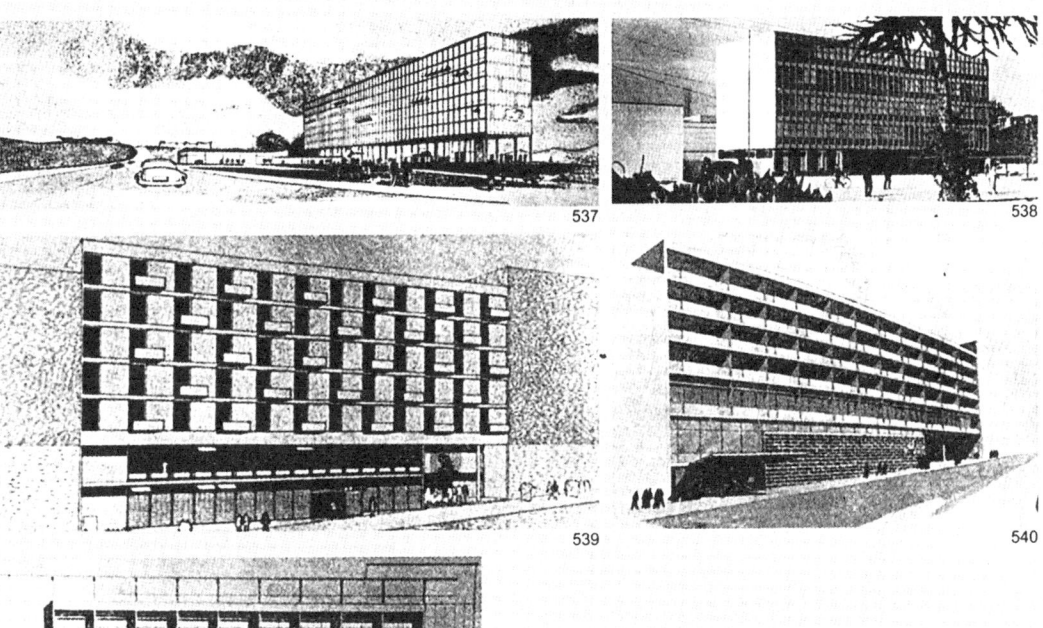

537

538

539

540

29

541

1950 sonrası egemen yaklaşımdan örnekler
537. H. Baysal, M. Birsel, R. Birol, S. Gürel, A. Hancı, Karayolları Genel Müdürlüğü Mimari Proje Yarışması, 1950'ler. 1. ödül.
538. E. Kortan, N. Yaubyan, H. Vapurciyan, A. Andonyadis, Sakarya Hükümet Konağı, Adapazarı, 1956. 1. ödül.

Türkiye İş Bankası'nın Banka, Otel ve Sinema Binası Mimari Proje Yarışması, Ankara, 1955.
539. K. Bayur, T. Aka, N. Durunay, 1. ödül.
540. E. Bahtoğlu, F. Kaskal, 2. ödül.
541. Kadri Eroğan, 3. ödül.

334

Abb. 7
Eine Seite mit „rationalistischen" Entwürfen der 1950er Jahre aus Şevki Vanlıs letztem Buch. Oben links ist eine Darstellung des preisgekrönten Entwurfs der Denkfabrik für die staatliche Generaldirektion für das Fernstraßenwesen in Ankara. Vanlı 2006: 334.

Fig. 7
A full-page layout of „rationalist" designs of the 1950s, featured in Şevki Vanlı's last book. On the top left is a rendering of the think tank's winning entry for the State Highways Gerneral Directorate, Ankara. Vanlı 2006: 334.

übersehen hatte, dass in der Türkei der 1950er Jahre sowohl der Berufsstand als auch der Diskurs parallel aufgebaut wurden. Mit anderen Worten, die Ikonisierung der bürokratischen Architektur im Diskurs fand gleichzeitig mit der Bürokratisierung der Architekturpraxis und des Berufsstands statt – die Gründung großer Architekturfirmen einerseits und die Schaffung der Architektenkammer als ein neuer Berufsverband andererseits. Tatsächlich bezogen sich sämtliche Debatten, die um die Rolle des Intellektualismus kreisten, auf diese simultane, noch unabgeschlossene Konstruktion von Berufsstand und Diskurs – wie an der Diskussion um Hiltonculuk veranschaulicht wird. Aus diesem Grund muss der preisgekrönte Entwurf der Denkfabrik für das neue Gebäude der staatlichen Generaldirektion für das Fernstraßenwesen in Ankara im Licht der Feinheiten betrachtet werden, die ihr „kollektives Handeln" und „kultureller Kontakt" (Gramsci) mit dem Alltagsverstand verband.

Eine eingehende Analyse der Organisationsstruktur der Denkfabrik und ihrer Methoden kollektiver Praxis zeigt, das sie neue Modelle sowohl für intellektuelles Handeln als auch für die Geschäftspraxis anbot. Die Modelle wurden nicht aufgrund der Vision einer tonangebenden Einzelperson entwickelt, sondern von einem Team von Fachkollegen. Anstatt ein absolutes Wissen zu beanspruchen (wie Eldem es tat), benutzte die Denkfabrik relationales Wissen als Entwurfsmotivation und als Gruppenideologie.

Vanlıs Kritik an Hiltonculuk implizierte nachdrücklich, dass die Befürworter von Hiltonculuk und die „Experten", die in ihren Büros Gebäude im Hilton-Stil entwarfen, an einer prinzipiellen Schwäche litten, nämlich an Entfremdung. Vanlı deutete sogar einige Bewusstseinsformen an, die Begleiterscheinungen der Praxis von Hiltonculuk seien, u.a. Isolation, Zusammenhanglosigkeit, mangelnde Begeisterung und sogar Verlust von Ethik. Es waren genau diese Begleiterscheinungen der weitverbreiteten Praxis von Hiltonculuk, welche die Denkfabrik zu vermeiden versuchte. Doch zugleich wagte die Arbeitsgemeinschaft nicht den Schritt über den Alltagsverstand der Architektur hinaus.

Dieser war auf der Grundlage der universellen und rationalen Werten der Moderne des Internationalen Stils etabliert worden und türkische Architekten hatten ihn als solchen angenommen. Dies war ein Punkt, den Vanlı unterstrich, als er sich dazu äußerte, warum Architekten es vorziehen, eher neutrale denn provokative Entwürfe vorzulegen.

Dies machte den preisgekrönten Entwurf der Denkfabrik anfällig für Vorwürfe von Hiltonculuk. Doch da den beteiligten Architekten wohl klar war, dass sie innerhalb des herrschenden Alltagsverstandes operieren mussten, ließen sie sich aktiv auf den Internationalen Stil ein. Anstatt auf die etablierten Modelle bürokratischer Architektur in der Türkei zurückzugreifen, versuchten sie einen Diskurs über die Moderne des Internationalen Stils in Gang zu setzen, indem sie für ihren Entwurf eine Stahlkonstruktion mit Vorhangfassade vorsahen, damals beides ein Novum in der Türkei. Dadurch dass sie den kulturellen Kontakt zum Alltagsverstand herstellten, unterschieden sie sich einerseits von den „Experten von Hiltonculuk" und andererseits von dominanten, singulären Persönlichkeiten wie Eldem.

Nachdem ihnen der erste Preis für das Bürogebäude der Generaldirektion für das Fernstraßenwesen zuerkannt worden war, richtete die Denkfabrik ein neues Büro für die Ausführungsplanung ein.[17] Doch der Vorschlag der Architekten für eine Stahlkonstruktion wurde von den staatlichen Funktionären verworfen, trotz der entschlossenen Unterstützung des türkischen Staates für den Internationalen Stil als Architektur eines neuen Staates, die vom Istanbul Hilton eingeläutet worden war. Weitere Konflikte zwischen Architekten, Bürokraten und staatlichen Funktionären resultierten in der Einstellung des Projektes.[18]

17 Der Architekt Erdem Talu wurde für diesen Zweck gewonnen und leitete das neue Büro.
18 Der Vertrag, der zwischen den Architekten und dem Minsterium für öffentliche Bauten unterschrieben worden war, wurde einseitig von Minister Tevfik Ikeri gekündigt. Für weitere Einzelheiten über die Konflikte siehe Kaçel 2007, Önal 2006: 34ff und Hasol 2003.

established a new office for the preparation of construction drawings.[17] However, the architects' proposal for a steel construction was rejected by government officials despite the Turkish state's fearless support of the International Style, following the construction of the Istanbul Hilton, as the architecture of a new state. Further conflicts among the architects, bureaucrats, and state officials ended in the cancellation of the project.[18]

Conclusion: Modernism as Common Sense

From the end of the Second World War on, when modernization in Turkey was modeled after the United States, the ideological aspects of the process had several cultural implications, including those in the architectural discourse and the profession.[19] For recent historians of postwar modernism, the Istanbul Hilton—the popular and political icon of modern Turkey—fully affirms the Americanization of modernism in Turkey on the one hand and the export-import rhetoric on the other.[20] Yet even before architectural historians assigned any historical value to the hotel, the architect Şevki Vanlı reminds us that, in 1958, the Hilton had already turned into an architectural cliché. Modeled after the Hilton, the practice of Hiltonculuk had become the common practice among Turkish architects. This came with a series of problems, as Vanlı fearlessly pointed out, and which the "experts of Hiltonculuk" blandly ignored.

Since the major characteristic of the International Style as practiced in Turkey was that it had been appropriated uncritically and passively, I interpret the practices of postwar modernism as common sense and coin the term "common-sense modernism" to denote the affirmative shared by postwar Turkish architects. I consider common sense to constitute a more fundamental aspect of postwar modernism than its "Americanization" for understanding and explaining both the affirmations and challenges to modernism from within the architectural context of Turkey. Even though Bunshaft had been cautious about Hiltonculuk, it was ultimately the temporary partnership between Bunshaft and

17 The architect Erdem Talu was hired for this immediate purpose and headed the new office.
18 The contract signed between the architects and the Ministry of Public Works was one-sidedly annulled by the minister, Tevfik İleri. For further details on the conflicts, see Kaçel 2007, Önal 2006: 34ff, and Hasol 2003.
19 The sociologist Daniel Lerner had been the advocate of modernization theory in developing countries in the Middle East, among which Turkey is illustrated as the model for the region. Accordingly, Lerner also imagined the prevalent International Style as an enduring, exclusive architecture culture for Turkey. Lerner/Riesman 1955. For a detailed analysis of Lerner's study (1958) and of the implications of modernization theory in Turkey, see Kaçel 2009.
20 For various depictions of "Americanization of modernism," see Ockman 1993: 16-19; Bozdoğan 2008. For narratives based on export-import rhetoric, see Wharton 2001; Cody 2003.
21 For the practical implications of common-sense modernism in Turkey, see Kaçel 2010.
22 In an analysis of the Baysal-Birsel partnership, for example, the architectural historian Uğur argues that the partnership legitimized itself as nothing but a new "business model," when established in 1952. Such a perspective, however, closes off any discussion of intellectualism from the outset. See Tanyeli 1998.

Eldem that set the standards for common-sense modernism in Turkey in the same way as the standards for practice were set by SOM in the United States. By the time Eldem agreed to expand the building in the late 1950s, International Style modernism promoted in its Americanized form had already created a new common sense. It was precisely this common-sense modernism and the underlying anti-intellectualism that frustrated Vanlı at the time.[21]

The first multipartnered firms in the country were able to avoid Hiltonculuk by making use of relational knowledge and social networks in their practices. However, because of their bureaucratic structuring, the design work of these firms has been conceived by historians as less intellectual in comparison to sole practitioners (such as Eldem), who could operate with a relatively high degree of autonomy and control over their intellectual production.[22]

In summary, rather than depicting architects as autonomous, creative figures, I consider them as both practitioners and intellectuals—that is to say, not only as executors of architectural practice and designers of buildings, but also as producers of ideas, conceptions, and consciousness with regard to their profession and its social impact. In architecture, for that reason, the practices

Fazit: Modernismus als Alltagsverstand

Ab dem Ende des Zweiten Weltkriegs, als die Modernisierung in der Türkei nach amerikanischem Vorbild gestaltet wurde, hatten die ideologischen Aspekte des Vorganges mehrere kulturelle Implikationen, die auch den Architekturdiskurs und den Berufsstand betrafen.[19] Für jüngere Historiker der Nachkriegsmoderne ist das Istanbul Hilton – die populäre und politische Ikone der modernen Türkei – eine unzweifelhafte Bestätigung für die Amerikanisierung des Modernismus in der Türkei.[20] Doch selbst bevor Architekturhistoriker dem Hotel irgendeinen historischen Wert beimaßen, erinnerte uns der Architekt Şevki Vanlı daran, dass im Jahr 1958 das Hilton bereits ein architektonisches Klischee geworden war. Die Praxis von Hiltonculuk, die aus dem Hilton hervorgegangen war, hatte sich zur gängigen Praxis unter türkischen Architekten entwickelt.

Man kann sagen, dass das Hauptmerkmal des Internationalen Stils, wie er in der Türkei praktiziert wurde, darin bestand, dass er unkritisch und passiv rezipiert wurde. Somit lassen sich die Praktiken der Nachkriegsmoderne als die Bildung eines gemeinsamen Nenners innerhalb des Alltagsverstands deuten, zwei Begriffe, die ich hier zu Modernismus des Alltagsverstands (*common-sense modernism*) verbinden möchte, um das Affirmative zu bezeichnen, das türkische Architekten der Nachkriegszeit miteinander verband. Meiner Meinung nach stellt der Alltagsverstand einen wesentlicheren Aspekt der Nachkriegsmoderne dar als ihre sogenannte Amerikanisierung, um sowohl die Annahme der Moderne als auch ihre Ablehnung innerhalb des Architekurkontextes der Türkei begreifen zu können. Wenn auch Gordon Bunshaft sich in Sachen Hiltonculuk eher zurückhaltend gezeigt hatte, war es letzten Endes die zeitweilige Partnerschaft zwischen Bunshaft und Eldem, welche die Standards für die Moderne des Alltagsverstands in der Türkei setzte, in der gleichen Weise wie die Praxisstandards in den Vereinigten Staaten von SOM gesetzt wurden. Als Eldem sich bereit erklärte, das Gebäude Ende der 1950er Jahre zu erweitern,

hatte der Internationale Stil, der in seiner amerikanisierten Form gefördert wurde, bereits einen neuen Alltagsverstand geschaffen. Es war genau diese Moderne des Alltagsverstands und der Anti-Intellektualismus, der ihr zugrunde lag, was Vanlı damals so entmutigte.[21]

Die ersten Architektenbüros der Türkei, die von mehreren Partnern gleichzeitig geführt wurden, konnten Hiltonculuk vermeiden, indem sie in ihrer Praxis von relationalem Wissen und sozialen Netzwerken Gebrauch machten. Doch aufgrund ihrer bürokratischen Struktur wurden die Entwürfe dieser Firmen von Historikern als weniger intellektuell eingeschätzt im Vergleich zu jenen von Einzelpraktikern (wie Eldem), die mit einem relativ hohen Grad an Autonomie und Kontrolle über ihre intellektuelle Produktion agieren konnten.[22]

Zusammenfassend ist zu sagen, dass meines Erachtens Architekten weniger als autonome, kreative Persönlichkeiten zu sehen sind, sondern eher als Praktiker *und* Intellektuelle, d.h. nicht nur als Ausführende einer Architekturpraxis und Entwerfer von Gebäuden, sondern auch als Produzenten von Ideen, Konzepten und Bewusstsein in Bezug auf ihren Berufsstand und dessen gesellschaftlichen Auswirkungen. Aus diesem Grund sind in der Architektur die Praktiken des Intellektualismus ebenso entscheidend wie die Endprodukte, d.h. die Gebäude selbst.

---

19 Der Soziologe Daniel Lerner war der Befürworter der Modernisierungstheorie in den Entwicklungsländern des Nahen Ostens gewesen, unter denen die Türkei als Modell für die Region angeführt wird. Entsprechend stellte sich Lerner auch den vorherrschenden Internationalen Stil als eine dauerhafte, exklusive Architekturkultur für die Türkei vor. Lerner/Riesman 1955. Für eine ausführliche Analyse von Lerners Untersuchung (1958) und die Implikationen der Modernisierungstheorie in der Türkei siehe Kaçel 2009.

20 Für verschiedene Darstellungen der „Amerikanisierung der Moderne" siehe Ockman 1993: 16–19 und Bozdoğan 2008. Siehe auch Wharton 2001, Cody 2003.

21 Für die praktischen Implikationen der Moderne des Alltagsverstands in der Türkei siehe Kaçel 2010.

22 In einer Analyse der Baysal-Birsel-Partnerschaft zum Beispiel argumentiert der Architekturhistoriker Uğur Tanyeli, die Partnerschaft habe sich lediglich als ein neues „Geschäftsmodell" legitimiert, als sie im Jahr 1952 gegründet wurde. Doch solch eine Perspektive macht von vornherein jegliche Diskussion über Intellektualismus unmöglich. Siehe Tanyeli 1998.

of intellectualism are as crucial as the end products—buildings—themselves. By drawing on the practices of intellectualism within common-sense modernism, we may start to differentiate among architects—whether they be traditional intellectuals, experts of Hiltonculuk, partners in multipartnered offices, or members of unique collaborations—and various ways in which they produce knowledge in relation to ideology.

As Vanlı first pointed out in 1958, the clear-cut dichotomies of postwar modernism—bureaucratic versus genius, ordinary versus iconic—neither apply to the Istanbul Hilton nor legitimize the so-called Americanization of modernism in Turkey. Instead, turning to the ways in which intellectualism is practiced, and extrapolating from modes of knowledge production and modes of consciousness, certainly provides more explanation and insight into the intricacies of modernism.

Indem wir die Praktiken des Intellektualis- die sogenannte Amerikanisierung der Mo-
mus innerhalb der Moderne des Alltagsver- derne in der Türkei. Stattdessen dürfte es
stands heranziehen, ist es uns vielleicht entschieden mehr Aufschlüsse über die
ansatzweise möglich, zwischen Architekten Fein-heiten der Moderne liefern, wenn man
– seien es nun traditionelle Intellektuelle, sich der Frage widmet, wie Intellektualismus
Experten von Hiltonculuk, Partner von großen praktiziert wird, und von den Formen
Architekturbüros oder Mitglieder einmaliger der Wissensproduktion und den Bewusst-
Kollaborationen – und den unterschied- seinsarten entsprechende Rückschlüsse zieht.
lichen Formen zu differenzieren, in denen
sie Wissen im Verhältnis zu Ideologie produzieren.

Wie Vanlı erstmals 1958 betonte, treffen
die eindeutigen Dichotomien der Nachkriegsmoderne – bürokratisch versus genial,
gewöhnlich versus ikonisch – weder auf
das Istanbul Hilton zu noch bestätigen sie

Danksagung
Ich möchte den Herausgebern von
Candide, Axel Sowa und Susanne
Schindler, sowie Angelika Schnell
und Robert Gassner für Ihre wertvollen
Anmerkungen danken. Ich bin auch
Dominic Boyer und Geoff Waite
für ihre Einblicke in die theoretischen
Diskussionen, die in diesem Beitrag
dargestellt werden, zu Dank ver-
pflichtet.

Acknowledgements
I would like to thank the editors of
Candide, Axel Sowa and Susanne
Schindler, and also Angelika Schnell
and Robert Gassner for their valu-
able comments. I am also grateful to
Dominic Boyer and Geoff Waite for
their insights into the theoretical discussions presented in this article.

Elâ Kaçel ist Assistenzprofessorin an
der Bahçeşehir Universität, Istanbul.
Sie promovierte 2009 an der Cornell
University im Fach Architekturgeschich-
te. Ausgehend von Fallstudien aus der
türkischen Nachkriegsmoderne untersucht sie in ihrer Forschungsarbeit die
Rolle des Intellektuellen im Kontext
des sozialen Wandels, wobei auch Faktoren wie Kulturpolitik, Konsumismus
und Wissensproduktion im Berufsleben
berücksichtigt werden. Zu ihren Ver-
öffentlichungen zählen Buchkapitel in
den Publikationen *Haluk Baysal – Melih
Birsel* (Müge Cengizkan, Hrsg., Ankara:
Mimarlar Odası Yayınları 2007) und
Third World Modernism (Duanfang Lu,
Hrsg., London: Routledge, 2010) sowie
divese Artikel in *Cogito*, *Arredamento
Mimarlık* und *Domus m*.

Elâ Kaçel is an assistant professor
at Bahçeşehir University, Istanbul.
She received her PhD in the History of
Architecture from Cornell University
in 2009. Drawing on case studies from
postwar Turkish modernism, her research
considers the role of intellectuals in
the context of social change, taking
into regard the role of cultural politics,
consumerism, and knowledge production
in professional life. Her publications
include book chapters in Müge Cengizkan
(ed.), *Haluk Baysal—Melih Birsel* (Ankara: Mimarlar Odası Yayınları, 2007),
Duanfang Lu (ed.), *Third World Modernism* (London: Routledge, 2010), and
several articles published in *Cogito*,
Arredamento Mimarlık, and *Domus m*.

Deutsche Übersetzung:
Matthias Müller.

References

Akcan, Esra. 2001. "Americanization and Anxiety: Istanbul Hilton Hotel by SOM and Eldem." In: Michelle A. Rinehart, ed. *Oriental-Occidental Geography, Identity, Space: Proceedings, 2001 ACSA International Conference, Istanbul, Turkey*. Washington, DC: ACSA Press.

Bozdoğan, Sibel. 2001. *Modernism and Nation Building: Turkish Architectural Culture in the Early Republic*. Seattle: University of Washington Press.

———. 2008. "Democracy, Development, and the Americanization of Turkish Architectural Culture in the 1950s." In: Sandy Isenstadt and Kishwar Rizvi, eds. *Modernism and the Middle East: Architecture and Politics in the Twentieth Century*. Seattle: University of Washington Press. 116–138.

Bozdoğan, Sibel/Suha Özkan/Engin Yenal. 1987. *Sedad Eldem: Architect in Turkey*. Singapore: Concept Media.

Bunshaft, Gordon. *Gordon Bunshaft Architectural Drawings and Papers, 1909–1990*. Department of Drawings and Archives, Avery Architectural and Fine Arts Library, Columbia University.

Cody, Jeffrey W. 2003. *Exporting American Architecture, 1870–2000*. London: Routledge.

Degenne, Alain/Michel Forsé. 1999. *Introducing Social Networks*. London: Sage Publications.

Gramsci, Antonio. 2003 [1971]. *Selections from the Prison Notebooks*. [*Quaderni del carcere*, 1929–35] Quentin Hoare and Geoffrey Nowell Smith, eds and trans. New York: International Publishers. DEUTSCH: 1991. *Gefängnishefte. Kritische Gesamtausgabe*. Hans Bochmann, Hrsg. Hamburg: Argument.

Hasol, Doğan. 2003, June. "Bizden Mimarlık Öyküleri: Mimarların Çilesi," *Yapı*: 49–50.

Hitchcock, Henry-Russell. 1947, January. "The Architecture of Bureaucracy and the Architecture of Genius." *Architectural Review*: 3–6.

Kaçel, Elâ. 2007. "Fidüsyer: Bir Kolektif Düşünme Pratiği." In: Müge Cengizkan, ed. *Haluk Baysal-Melih Birsel*. Ankara: TMMOB Mimarlar Odası. 7–31.

———. 2009. *Intellectualism and Consumerism: Ideologies, Practices and Criticisms of Common-Sense Modernism in Postwar Turkey*. Unpublished dissertation, Cornell University.

———. 2010. "This is not an American House: Good Sense Modernism in 1950s Turkey." In: Duanfang Lu, ed. *Third World Modernism: Architecture, Development and Identity*. London: Routledge. 165–186.

"Karayolları Umum Müdürlüğü Binası Proje Müsabakası." 1955. *Arkitekt* 25 (282): 167–177.

Lerner, Daniel. 1958. *The Passing of Traditional Society: Modernizing the Middle East*. New York: Free Press of Glencoe.

Lerner, Daniel/David Riesman. 1955. "Self and Society: Reflections on Some Turks in Transition." *Explorations* 5: 67–80.

Mannheim, Karl. 1978 [1929]. *Ideologie und Utopie*. Frankfurt/Main: Schulte-Bulmke. ENGLISH: 1936. *Ideology and Utopia: An Introduction to the Sociology of Knowledge*. Louis Wirth and Edward Shils, trans. London: K. Paul, Trench, Trubner.

Nicolai, Bernd. 1998. *Moderne und Exil: deutschsprachige Architekten in der Türkei 1925–1955*. Berlin: Verlag für Bauwesen.

Ockman, Joan. 1993. *Architecture Culture 1943–1968: A Documentary Anthology*. New York: Rizzoli.

Önal, Maruf. 2006. *Maruf Önal. Oda Tarihinden Portreler 2*. Interview by Mücella Yapıcı. Istanbul: TMMOB Mimarlar Odası Istanbul Büyükkent Şubesi.

Tanyeli, Uğur/Atilla Yücel. 2007. *Turgut Cansever: Düşünce Adamı ve Mimar*. Istanbul: Osmanlı Bankası Arşiv ve Araştırma Merkezi.

Tanyeli, Uğur. 1998, April. "Haluk Baysal-Melih Birsel." *Arredamento Mimarlık*: 72–79.

Vanlı, Şevki. 2006. *Mimariden Konuşmak: Bilinmek Istenmeyen 20. Yüzyıl Türk Mimarlığı Eleştirel Bakış*, 3. vols. Ankara: Şevki Vanlı Mimarlık Vakfı.

———. 1958, 28 November. "Hiltonculuk." *Kim*: 21–22.

Wharton, Annabel Jane. 2001. *Building the Cold War: Hilton International Hotels and Modern Architecture*. Chicago: University of Chicago Press.

Picture Credits

Fig. 1 Photo: Suavi Sonar.

Fig. 2 Courtesy of the Office of the Prime Minister, Directorate General of Press and Information (DGPI).

Fig. 3 Used with the permission of the Sevki Vanlı Architecture Foundation.

Figs. 4 and 5 Courtesy of the Office of the Prime Minister, Directorate General of Press and Information (DGPI).

Fig. 6 Courtesy of the Şener Özler Archive and Documentation Center at the Istanbul Metropolitan Branch of the Chamber of Architects of Turkey, UTCEA.

Fig. 7 Used with the permission of the Şevki Vanlı Architecture Foundation.

Andrew J. Witt

A Machine Epistemology in Architecture
Encapsulated Knowledge and the
Instrumentation of Design

Contemporary architecture is preoccupied with
radical formal experimentation, enabled in
particular by the computer and computer-controlled machines. Such ambitious architectural
form- making requires a virtuosic mastery of spatial
geometry, a specific kind of design knowledge
that is often specialized and difficult to deploy.
Machines, including computers, provide a way of
encapsulating this knowledge in a more usable
and repeatable way. Such machines raise certain
epistemic challenges: they abstract systems
and detach the user from operative logic, requiring
more instrumental and less design knowledge
from the user. While contemporary architects are
increasingly testing the relationship of design
knowledge to instrumental knowledge, we may
draw lessons from the broad use of mechanical
drawing instruments for design and design-based
computation in the nineteenth century. In this
historical context we can see key relationships
between instrumental knowledge and design
knowledge that are fundamental to understanding
our own increasingly mechanized approach to
contemporary design.

Andrew J. Witt

Epistemologie der Maschine in der Architektur
Maschinengespeichertes Wissen und die
Instrumentalisierung des Entwurfs

Die zeitgenössische Architektur ist geprägt von radikalen, formalen Experimenten, die vor allem durch Computerprogramme und computergesteuerte Maschinen möglich geworden sind. Diese anspruchsvolle Art der architektonischen Formgebung erfordert die Meisterung der Berechnung räumlicher Geometrien – das heißt ein Entwurfswissen, das vielfach hoch spezialisiert ist und besondere Schwierigkeiten bei der Umsetzung bereitet. Maschinen, einschließlich Computer, bieten die Möglichkeit, dieses Wissen auf anwenderfreundliche, wiederholt abrufbare Art und Weise zu speichern. Derartige Maschinen stellen den Benutzer vor bestimmte erkenntnistheoretische Herausforderungen, indem sie die der Maschine zugrunde liegenden Systeme abstrahieren und den Benutzer von ihrer operativen Logik trennen. Sie erfordern folglich mehr Instrumenten- und weniger Entwurfswissen. Während Architekten heute zunehmend die Beziehung zwischen Entwurfswissen und Instrumentenwissen ausloten, lassen sich aus den im 19. Jahrhundert üblichen, als Entwurfs- und Berechnungshilfen genutzten mechanischen Zeichenmaschinen etliche Lehren ziehen. Im historischen Kontext können wir zentrale Bezüge zwischen Instrumentenwissen einerseits und Entwurfswissen andererseits erkennen, welche die Grundlagen für ein Verständnis unseres heutigen, zunehmend mechanisierten Entwerfens bilden.

1   Aranda/Lasch 2006: 9.
2   Mallgrave 2010: 216.
3   Wood 2002: 49.
4   Wood 2002: 50.
5   Kalay/Swerdloff/Maikowski: 50.
6   Kalay/Swerdloff/Maikowski: 51.

A Contemporary Polemic,
A Historic Analog

For the last several years we have found ourselves in a design context deeply preoccupied by the formal possibilities of design technology, particularly the computer. Once the purview of experimentalists, design computation has become one of the most vital strains within contemporary practice. By allowing the automation of complex processes and the rule-based means to resolve challenging problems of geometry, economy, representation, and construction, the computer acts as an instrument that extends the capacity and ability of the architect to manage problems and forms that would not be possible otherwise. By scripting and programming software, architects can even have the computer carry out complex custom calculations of their own invention, essentially encapsulating the knowledge and formal volition of the architect within the software itself.[1]

Yet architects maintain an ambivalent if not conflicted view of technology in general and the computer in particular. The heroic view of architecture as an autonomous and unmediated manifestation of the will of the architect still holds public and private fascination. Even technical innovators may duly defer to this self-characterization of architecture, and are often at pains to characterize their work as design as opposed to engineering, which has become a pejorative term. The advent of a technology that is so powerful, fast, automatic, even intelligent, presents a subversive confrontation to the architect's sufficient and autonomous will or knowledge. The perceived association of the computer with striking formalism and tentative material resolution makes it only more suspicious to the traditional understanding of design.[2]

The appearance of technologies so disruptive to the practice and self-understanding of architecture has implications for the postmodern project of textual, theoretical, and historical autonomy of design. Autonomy implies an independence of the syntactic and rational systems of architecture from extrinsic technical or ideological constraints.[3] It also affirms the role of the architect's will, whose syntactic choices in turn sustain the autonomy project.[4] This truly autonomous act of will implies a sort of epistemic self-sufficiency: the designer has a specific knowledge to create form, and any instruments that could imply that the designer's knowledge or capacity are incomplete call into doubt this heroic view of architecture and authorship. Thus the disciplinary implications of the computer hinge on questions of knowledge: does the computer, as an intelligent tool, enhance or diminish the knowledge of the architect? Can the computer or software encapsulate knowledge? If yes, can a user be said to know a process that is abstracted, encapsulated, and automated in a machine? Do machines in and of themselves represent a sort of latent knowledge?

At the core of the polemic is an implicit distinction between two types of knowledge: design knowledge and instrumental knowledge. *Design knowledge* is an intrinsic understanding by the architect of formal organization principles such as the relationship of parts to whole, and interrelationships of program constraints, spatial organization, ranges of material effects, and use of geometric methods. It may include disparate and heterogeneous organizational schemes and diagrams.[5] These general principles may be redeployed in various contexts, and need not be tied to particular working methods or automatic tools. In this sense, *geometric knowledge* is a particular kind of design knowledge: although it may be deductive and procedural, it is not automatic and its application requires a synthetic understanding of design constraints.[6] Design knowledge is the most enduring epistemic content of architecture as a discipline, sometimes even hastily equated with architectural knowledge itself.

Andrew J. Witt
A Machine Epistemology

Candide No. 3, 12/2010
Essay

Zeitgenössischer Disput und historische Analogie

Seit etlichen Jahren sind Architekturdiskurs und -praxis zutiefst von den formalen Möglichkeiten der Entwurfstechnologien, insbesondere des Computers, bestimmt und geprägt. Einst die Domäne experimentell orientierter Architekten und Randfiguren der Disziplin, ist das computergestützte Entwerfen (design computation) inzwischen zu einer der vitalsten Bewegungen der zeitgenössischen Architektur avanciert. Indem wir die Automatisierung komplexer Entwurfsprozesse und regelbasierter Entwurfsmittel zugelassen haben, mit denen komplizierte Aufgaben in den Bereichen Geometrie, Wirtschaftlichkeit, Darstellung und Konstruktion gelöst werden, haben wir den Computer zu einem Arbeitsmittel gemacht, das die Kapazität und Fähigkeit des Architekten um ein Vielfaches steigert, so dass er anders nicht lösbare Probleme lösen und anders nicht machbare Formen realisieren kann. Wenn Architekten ihre eigene Computersoftware skripten und programmieren, können sie damit sogar komplizierte Berechnungen nach eigener Erfindung anstellen, wobei das Wissen und die formale Intention des Architekten in der Software abgespeichert – verkapselt – ist.[1]

Dennoch haben sich viele Architekten eine ambivalente, wenn nicht gar antipathische Haltung zur Technologie im Allgemeinen und Computertechnik im Besonderen bewahrt. Die heroische Sicht der Architektur als autonomer, direkter Manifestation des Architektenwillens bleibt ein ebenso allgemein verbreitetes wie persönliches Faszinosum. Selbst technische Innovatoren neigen zu dieser Selbstdarstellung des Berufs, und es fällt ihnen schwer, ihre Tätigkeit im Gegensatz zu den Ingenieurwissenschaften (heute fast schon ein Pejorativum) als Entwerfen hervorzuheben. Eine Technologie, die so leistungsstark, schnell, automatisiert, ja sogar intelligent ist, unterläuft und widerlegt jedoch die Behauptung, dass der autonome Wille und das Fachwissen des Architekten für jeden Entwurf genügen. Die Assoziation des Computers mit exzentrischem Formalismus und unvollständig gelöster baulicher Umsetzung macht ihn umso verdächtiger für alle, die an einer traditionellen Auffassung von Architektur festhalten.[2]

Die Anwendung derartiger Technologien, welche die Praxis und das Selbstverständnis der Architekten so empfindlich stören, haben Auswirkungen auf das postmoderne Projekt der inhaltlichen, theoretischen und historischen Autonomie des architektonischen Entwurfs. Autonomie impliziert die Unabhängigkeit der syntaktischen und rationalen Architekturordnungen von „artfremden" technischen oder ideologischen Bedingungen[3] und bestätigt auch die Bedeutung der Intention des Architekten, dessen syntaktische Entscheidungen ihrerseits das Autonomieprojekt voranbringen.[4] Der wahrhaft autonome Willensakt impliziert eine Art epistemologische Selbstgenügsamkeit: Der entwerfende Architekt besitzt spezifisches Fachwissen über Formgestaltung, und jedes Entwurfsinstrument, das darauf hinzudeuten scheint, dass seine Kenntnisse und Kapazitäten nicht ausreichen, stellt die heroische Deutung von Architektur und Autorschaft in Frage. Deshalb sind die fachlichen Auswirkungen des Computers von Fragen des Wissens abhängig – von der Frage, ob der Computer als intelligentes Arbeitsmittel das Wissen des Architekten mehrt oder mindert. Kann ein Rechner beziehungsweise eine Software Wissen verkapseln, das heißt, speichern (to encapsulate)? Wenn ja, kann man dann auch behaupten, dass ein Nutzer sämtliche in einer solchen Maschine abstrahierten, gespeicherten und automatisierten Prozesse kennt und versteht? Sind solche Maschinen an und für sich so etwas wie verborgene Quellen des Fachwissens?

Der Kern dieser Polemik besteht in der unausgesprochenen Unterscheidung zwischen zwei Arten von Wissen: Entwurfswissen und

---

1 Aranda/Lasch 2006: 9.
2 Mallgrave 2010: 216.
3 Wood 2002: 49.
4 Wood 2002: 50.

Instrumental knowledge is a more narrow understanding of the procedures to successfully operate a certain type of technology, which would include ability to operate a software, program, script, process, tool, instrument, or machine to intended effect. This is in contrast to the way the term "instrumental knowledge" is used in the epistemology of science, for example: as a description of theories of predictive reliability (and thus instrumentality).[7] Instead, in our sense instrumental knowledge is in fact an intentional knowledge of instrument operation. Instrumental knowledge also enables the creation of systems of interrelated technologies intended to facilitate the aims of design. More generally, instrumental knowledge can include the ability to abstract the inverse constraints of these machines onto design with the aim of pre-rationalizing the design itself, as in the case of drawing machines, fabrication machines, or construction machines. This instrumental knowledge is powerful because it makes procedures encapsulated by the technology in question easily accessible, communicable, repeatable, hackable, and transformable.[8]

Architectural knowledge is the combination, in whatever measure or proportion, of design knowledge and instrumental knowledge needed for the intentional practice of architecture. The proportion of this combination, and even the presence or absence of instrumental knowledge in architectural knowledge, becomes the precise problem of the current debate.

Yet the matter at stake is not simply where to draw a particular line in the sand between design knowledge and instrumental knowledge. The machine permeates the relationship between both types of knowledge by being a tool to encapsulate certain operative aspects of design knowledge, including geometric and spatial knowledge. As a result of their fundamental implications for organization knowledge management and productivity, knowledge encapsulation and the reuse of encapsulated knowledge have become key categories in epistemology of economics.[9] Encapsulation preserves complexity without the user needing explicit

7   Boyd 1980: 614.
8   Aranda/Lasch 2006: xi.
9   Langlois 2001: 77.
10 Langlois 2001: 85.
11 Lynn 2000: 11.
12 Iwamoto 2009: 5.

understanding of all this complexity, and software is the paradigmatic case of such encapsulation.[10] An example of encapsulated knowledge in design, as Greg Lynn has pointed out, is calculus-based mathematics encapsulated in computer software,[11] but there are many others. The machine may also encapsulate knowledge not related directly to design—for example, knowledge of the operation of structural or environmental systems, or the knowledge of organizational behavior itself. With the instrumental knowledge of the machine, the user can simulate having the complex knowledge it encapsulates. It is the legitimacy of this simulation and its role in architecture that is ultimately at issue.

These questions of design knowledge and instrumental knowledge with respect to machines directly concern contemporary architects. The use of digital computers for the specification and communication of design and the use of computer-controlled machines for the cutting, forming, and assembling of nonstandard materials and forms is now commonplace.[12] Architects are exploring sophisticated mathematical concepts and material processes through the use of these machines. Increasingly, architects are designing and constructing their own machines toward deliberate design ends, just as they might script their own software. This reinvigorated relationship between architect and machine in both research and practice is placing new importance on instrumental knowledge. Contemporary digital tools continue the trend to abstract and encapsulate knowledge—in particular engineering knowledge—within machines on a new scale, and require new levels of skill and technical virtuosity to operate. Does virtuosic use of these tools form a distinct domain of architectural knowledge?

There are two main camps engaging this debate over the role of instrumental

Instrumentenwissen. *Entwurfswissen (design knowledge)* meint gestalterisches Know-how, meint das spezifische Verständnis des Architekten für die Prinzipien formaler Organisation, etwa der Beziehungen zwischen dem Ganzen und seinen Teilen, der Wechselbezüge zwischen bauprogrammatischen Zwängen, Regeln der Raumgliederung, der Materialwirkungen und der angewandten geometrischen Entwurfsmethode. Das kann ganz unterschiedliche Gliederungsschemata und Diagramme umfassen.[5] Diese Grundprinzipien können in verschiedenen Zusammenhängen eingesetzt werden und sind nicht zwangsläufig von einer bestimmten Arbeitsweise oder von automatisierten Arbeitsmitteln abhängig. In diesem Sinne ist *Geometriewissen* eine besondere Form von Entwurfswissen. Es kann deduktiv und verfahrensorientiert sein, ohne jedoch in Automatismus zu münden. Die Anwendung dieses Spezialwissens erfordert das umfassende und zusammenhängende Verständnis sämtlicher Entwurfszwänge.[6] Entwurfswissen stellt den dauerhaftesten epistemologischen Inhalt der Architektur als Fachdisziplin dar und wird gelegentlich vorschnell mit architektonischem Fachwissen als Ganzes gleichgesetzt.

Der Begriff *Instrumentenwissen (instrumental knowledge)* bezeichnet das Verständnis der für die erfolgreiche Anwendung einer bestimmten Entwurfsmethode erforderlichen Arbeitsschritte einer bestimmten Technologie, sei es die kompetente Handhabung von Software, Programm, Skript, Instrument oder Maschine, um das beabsichtigte Entwurfsergebnis zu erzielen. Diese Auffassung steht im Gegensatz zur Verwendung des Begriffs in der naturwissenschaftlichen Epistemologie, zum Beispiel zur Beschreibung prädiktiver Zuverlässigkeits- und damit Zweckdienlichkeitstheorien.[7] Nach unserer Deutung hingegen handelt es sich bei Instrumentenwissen um die intentionale, zielorientierte Kompetenz in der Handhabung der Instrumente. Mit diesem Wissen ist der Architekt in der Lage, Systeme aus mehreren zueinander in Wechselbeziehung stehenden Technologien zu bilden, die dazu geeignet sind, die jeweiligen Entwurfsziele zu erreichen. Allgemeiner gesagt, kann das die

Fähigkeit umfassen, die den Maschinen eigenen wechselseitigen Restriktionen auf den Entwurf zu übertragen, um diesen im Vorfeld zu rationalisieren, wie das bei der Verwendung von Zeichen-, Produktions- oder Konstruktionsmaschinen geschieht. Dieses Instrumentenwissen überzeugt, weil es die im jeweiligen technischen Arbeitsmittel inhärenten Verfahren leicht zugänglich, vermittelbar, wiederholbar, zerlegbar und veränderbar macht.[8]

Architektonisches Wissen kombiniert, egal in welchem Maß oder Maßverhältnis, Entwurfswissen mit dem für eine intentionale Architektentätigkeit erforderlichen Instrumentenwissen. Die Proportionen innerhalb dieser Kombination und selbst das Vorhanden- oder Nichtvorhandensein von Instrumentenwissen als Teil des Architekturwissens bilden die zentrale Fragestellung der aktuellen Debatte.

Dabei geht es nicht einfach um die Frage, wo genau man die Trennlinie zwischen Entwurfs- und Instrumentenwissen in den Sand zeichnet. Die Maschine durchdringt die Beziehung zwischen beiden Wissensarten als ein Hilfsmittel, das bestimmte operative Aspekte des Entwurfswissens (auch geometrischer und räumlicher Art) speichern oder verkapseln kann. Aufgrund ihrer grundlegenden Rolle im Bereich von Wissensmanagement und Produktivität sind in der Maschine gespeicherte Informationen (*encapsulated knowledge*) und deren Wiederverwendung in der wirtschaftswissenschaftlichen Epistemologie inzwischen zu Schlüsselkategorien avanciert.[9] Die Speicherung bewahrt Komplexität, ohne dass der Nutzer das Speichersystem genau verstehen muss, und Software stellt den paradigmatischen Fall einer solchen Verkapselung des Wissens dar.[10] Wie Greg Lynn ausgeführt hat, ist die in Computerprogramme eingeflossene, auf Differenzial- und Integralrechnung beruhende Mathematik ein Beispiel für diese Verkapselung von Wissen,

5 Kalay/Swerdloff/Maikowski 1990: 50.
6 Kalay/Swerdloff/Maikowski 1990: 51.
7 Boyd 1980: 614.
8 Aranda/Lasch 2006: XI.
9 Langlois 2001: 77.
10 Langlois 2001: 85.

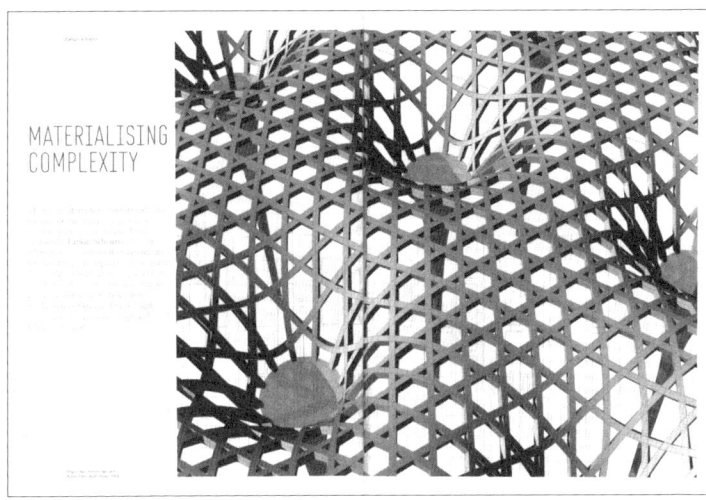

Schlüsselpositionen zur Rolle des Rechners in der Architektur sind in jüngsten Ausgaben der Zeitschrift *Architectural Design (AD)* debattiert worden. „Exuberance in Architecture" (März/April 2010, Marjan Colletti, Herausgeber) macht sich eine ekstatische, lyrische, sogar barocke Vorstellung eines anti-technischen Künstlertums zu eigen. „The New Strukturalism" (Juli/August 2010, Rivka und Robert Oxman, Herausgeber) untersucht eine analytischere und bewusst integrative Herangehensweise, auf der Suche nach gemeinsamen Grundlagen für Architekten und Ingenieure. Die beiden Herangehensweisen stehen in etwa für die beiden aktuellen entgegengesetzten Positionen in Bezug auf das Verhältnis von Entwurfswissen zu Instrumentenwissen.

Key positions in architecture and computation have been advanced in recent issues of *Architectural Design* (AD). "Exuberance in Architecture" (March/April 2010, Marjan Colletti, editor) espouses an ecstatic, lyrical, even baroque notion of techno-skeptical artistry. "The New Structuralism" (July/August 2010, Rivka and Robert Oxman, editors) examines a more analytic and self-consciously integrative approach, seeking common computational frameworks for designers and engineers. The two approaches are broadly representative of two divergent contemporary positions regarding the relationship of design knowledge to instrumental knowledge.

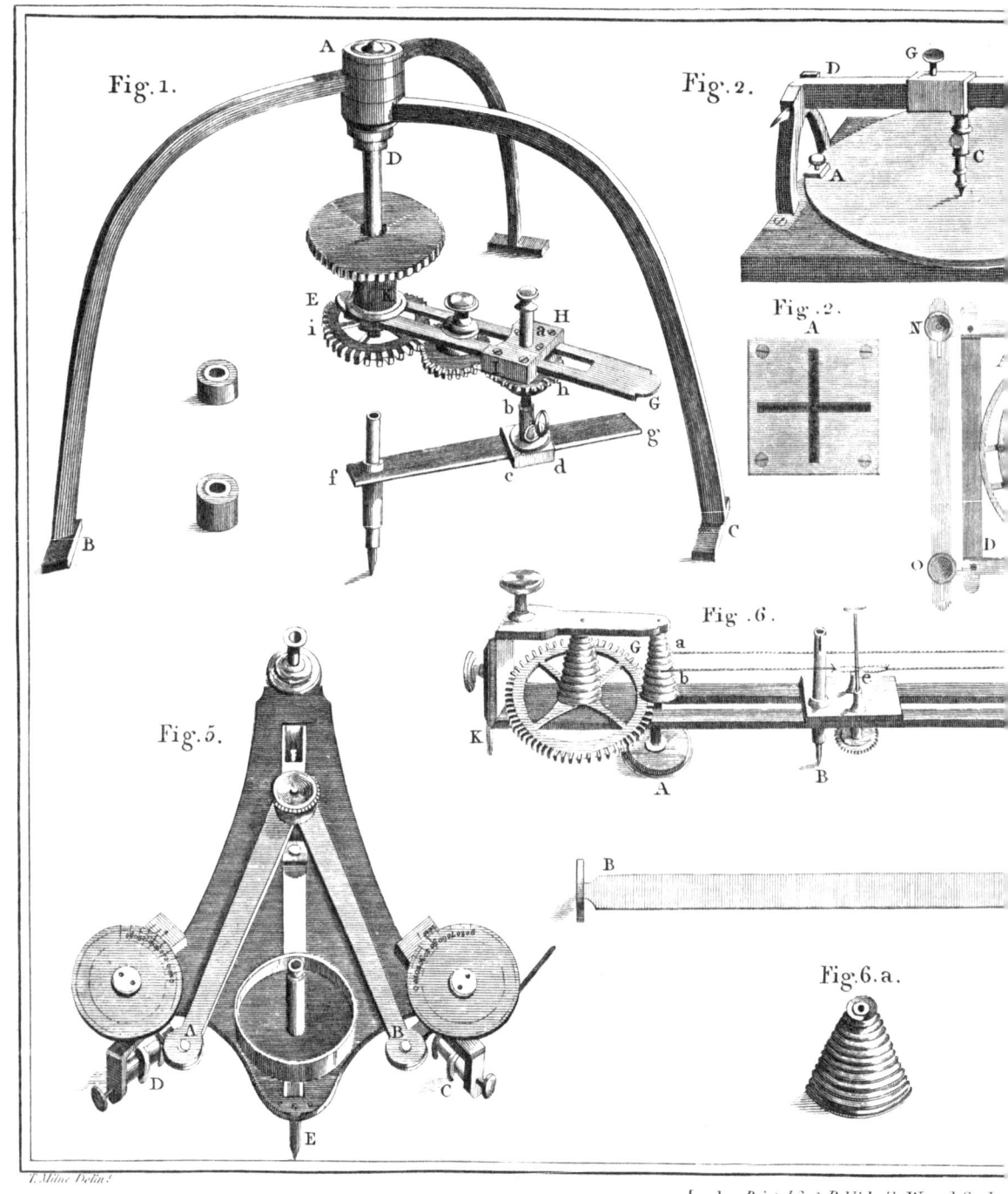

London. Printed för & Published by W. and S. Jo

Die Konstruktion fortgeschrittener Zeicheninstrumente zur Darstellung komplexer Kurven bildete Ende des 19. Jahrhunderts eine eigenständige Disziplin. Mit seinem Werk *Geometrical and Graphical Essays* (1791) stellte George Adams den Lesern im englischen Sprachraum zum ersten Mal zahlreiche fortschrittliche Zeichengeräte vor. Dazu gehörte

Giambattista Suardis „geometrischer Schreiber", ein mehrteiliger Zirkel für die Erstellung von Kreisen, Kegeln sowie komplizierten Epizykloiden und Hypozykloiden. Auf der Bildtafel ist dieses Instrument [Abb. 1] neben einfacheren Geräten wie etwa dem Ellipsografen [Abb. 3] zu sehen.

PLATE XI.

The design of sophisticated instruments for the drawing of complex curves emerged as a dicipline in its own right in the latter part of the nineteenth century. George Adams's *Geometrical and Graphical Essays* (1791) introduced many advanced drawing tools to the English-speaking world for the first time. Among them were Giambattista Suardi's geometrical pen, a compound instrument for the drawing of circles, conics, and more complex epicycles and hypocycles. In the plate, the geometrical pen [figure 1], is placed alongside more prosiac instruments such as the ellipsograph [figure 3].

Plate X

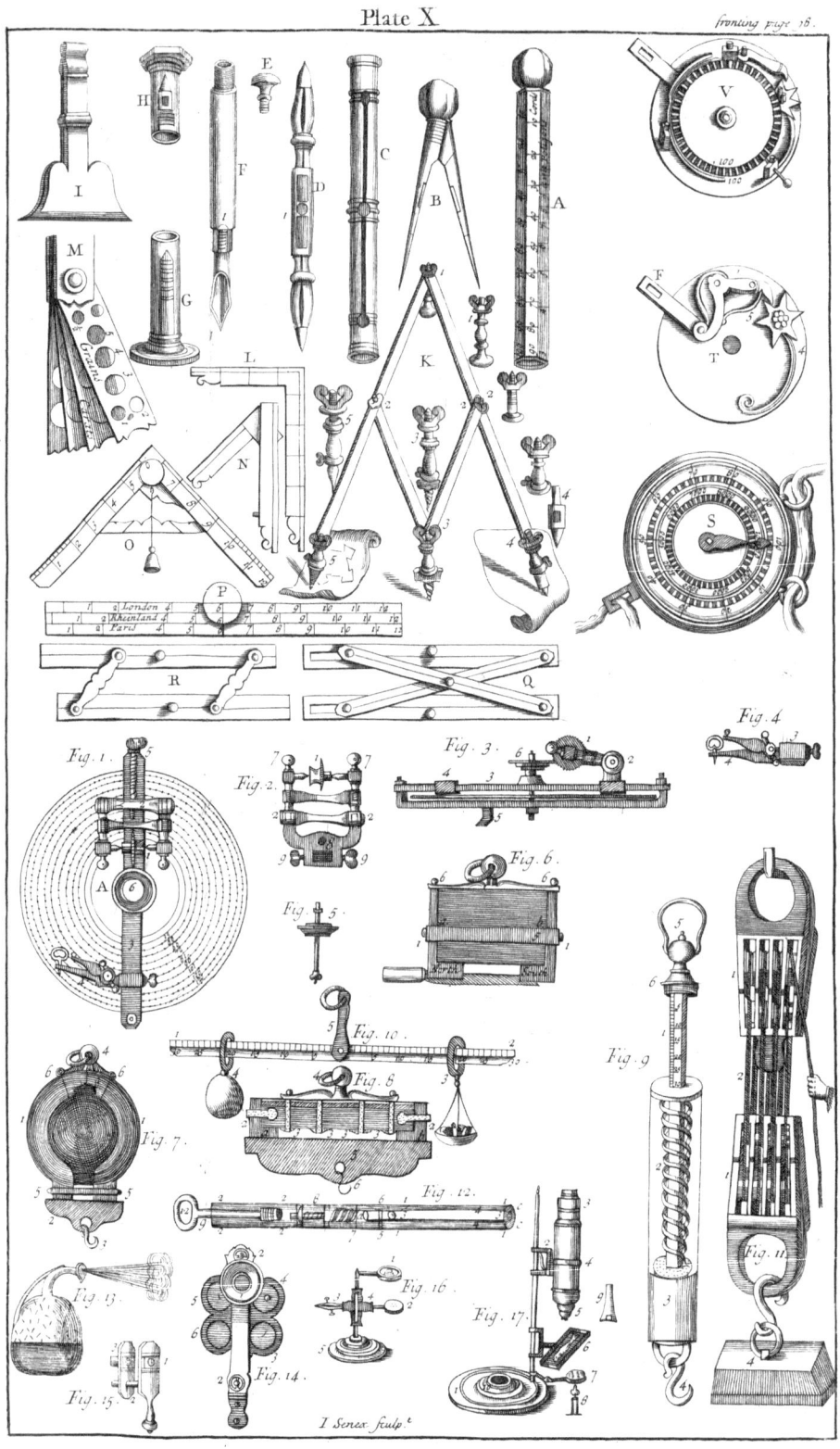

I Senex sculp.t

In seiner Schrift *Traité de la construction et des principaux usages des instruments de mathématiques* (1709) gab Nicolas Bion einen Überblick über die technischen Zeichengeräte des frühen 18. Jahrhunderts.

In his *Traité de la construction et des principaux usages des instruments de mathématiques* (1709), Nicolas Bion provided an overview of the drawing instruments of the early eighteenth century.

knowledge as it relates to the computer in design. A first group sees the new digital formalism, typically associated with complex geometric forms, as a return to a Baroque project deeply connected to a qualitative understanding of design. Terms such as "excess," "elegance," and "exuberance" have become the ideological watchwords of this group and its project of formal transcendence and intensity.[13] This group, while celebrating the design effects of digital virtuosity, maintains a discreet distance between the aesthetic volition of the designer and the instrumental means of its accomplishment. The tendency is rhetorically both anti-technical and anti-epistemic. According to Marjan Colletti, "Neither does exuberance concern the rationalist and epistemological lobby: its barricades crowded and piled high; its manifestos engineering-functionalist, mathematic-descriptive, and neo-*sachlich*. Against this trend, I bring forth the possibility of an empiricist phenomenological counterpart: DigitaAlia—the other digital practice."[14] There is a certain sanctity concerning the epistemic autonomy of design that prohibits such designers from discussing the underlying technical systems with which they are pragmatically preoccupied but cannot, for the sake of design orthodoxy, fully acknowledge. For this group, design knowledge is the true architectural knowledge, instrumental knowledge merely an expedient.

A second group sees both design knowledge and instrumental knowledge as being reciprocal dimensions of architectural knowledge. This camp sees an array of challenges and opportunities bearing on design as being more comprehensive than form-making alone, extending to professional and practical domains of power and control over design execution. While not connected with a particular formal project, this group sees the critical and technical engagement with form as generative of both design and instrumental knowledge. These designers see no conflict in foregrounding instrumental questions as an object of study. In fact, such questions are essential to the reemerging role of the architect as master builder.[15] To them, the computer is a way to access and

13 Colletti 2010.
14 Colletti 2010: 18.
15 Kieren / Timberlake 2004: xi.
16 Kolarevic 2003: 59.
17 Aranda / Lasch 2006.

use domains of knowledge pragmatically, and to extend and organize the capacity of architects.[16] The computer becomes, in effect, a resource for disciplinary organization. This is apparent, for instance, in architects' interest in software for structural analysis or environmental simulation, which are sometimes used as proxies for specialist consultants. Beyond these specialized applications, designers can now embed their knowledge of procedures and processes into software through programming, scripting, and rule-based design, essentially transforming design knowledge into instrumental knowledge. Here there is a strong interest in tool making, tinkering, hacking—and a candor that invention should not be limited to engineering.[17] For this group, instrumental knowledge becomes a powerful way to extend design knowledge, architectural knowledge necessarily encompassing both.

While these polemics extend beyond questions of form, the questions that surround form-making and, more particularly, geometric design knowledge in the creation of complex forms, do bring this polemic into clearer relief. Where does the knowledge required to produce such forms reside? Is this knowledge architectural knowledge? What is the epistemic role of the machine in form-making?

This epistemic debate has implications for contemporary architectural practice, but it may be instructive to shift the context of study away from current controversies toward a distinct historical frame, similar to our own in its fascination for the machine as aid to form-making. The notion of machine-encapsulated design knowledge is germane to the period in nineteenth-century Britain and France characterized by the development of drawing machines for complex curves and projective constructions. These machines expanded the formal vocabulary of architecture by encapsulating as mechanical motions and procedures certain

aber längst nicht die einzige.[11] Die Maschine kann auch Informationen ohne unmittelbare Relevanz für die Entwurfsarbeit enthalten, zum Beispiel Daten zum Betrieb konstruktiver und ökologischer Systeme oder Auskünfte über Organisationsverhalten. Das Instrumentenwissen der Maschine suggeriert dem Nutzer, er verfüge selbst über das komplexe, in ihr gespeicherte Wissen. Letztlich geht es hier also um die Legitimität dieser Simulation und deren Funktion in der Architektur.

Von diesen Aspekten des Entwurfs- und Instrumentenwissens sind zeitgenössische, maschinenbenutzende Architekten unmittelbar betroffen. Die Nutzung digitaler Rechner für Entwurf, Bau- und Leistungsbeschreibungen sowie deren Übermittlung an andere und die Nutzung rechnergesteuerter Maschinen, mit denen Sondermaterialien und -formen zugeschnitten, geformt und montiert werden, ist heute allgemeine Praxis.[12] Mit Hilfe dieser Maschinen untersuchen Architekten komplexe mathematische Konzepte und physisch-physikalische Prozesse. Zunehmend entwickeln und bauen sie eigene Maschinen oder schreiben selber Programme, um gewisse gestalterische Ziele umsetzen zu können. Diese revitalisierte Beziehung zwischen dem Architekten und der Maschine in Lehre und Praxis steigert die Bedeutung von Instrumentenwissen. Die heutigen digitalen Werkzeuge verstärken den Trend zur Abstraktion und Speicherung von Wissen – insbesondere von ingenieurtechnischem Wissen – in Maschinen, und das in großem Umfang. Betrieb und Anwendung dieser digitalen Maschinen erfordern gründlichere Kenntnisse und mehr technische Virtuosität als die früheren Arbeitsmittel des Architekten. Bildet die virtuose Anwendung dieser Werkzeuge ein eigenständiges Gebiet des Architekturwissens?

In der Debatte über die Rolle des Instrumentenwissens in Bezug zum Computer beim Entwurf zeichnen sich zwei große Lager ab. Das eine Lager sieht den typischerweise mit komplexen geometrischen Formen assoziierten, neuen digitalen Formalismus als Rückkehr zu einem barocken Projekt, das tief in einer auf Qualität zielenden Designauffassung verankert ist. Begriffe wie Über-steigerung, Eleganz und Überschwang heißen die ideologischen Parolen dieser Gruppe, die formale Transzendenz und Intensität anstrebt.[13] Während ihre Vertreter die Ergebnisse digitaler Virtuosität preisen, wahren sie diskret den Abstand zwischen der ästhetischen Intention des Entwerfers und den Arbeitsmitteln, mit denen sie verwirklicht wird. Diese Haltung ist rhetorisch sowohl anti-technisch als auch anti-epistemologisch. Laut Marjan Colletti betrifft der Überschwang auch nicht „die Lobby der Rationalisten und Erkenntnistheoretiker. Deren Barrikaden sind umdrängt und hoch aufgetürmt; ihre Manifeste ingenieurtechnisch-funktionalistisch, mathematisch deskriptiv und neo-sachlich. Gegen diesen Trend führe ich die mögliche Existenz eines empirischen phänomenologischen Gegenspielers ins Feld, nämlich DigitaAlia – die andere digitale Praxis."[14] Die erkenntnistheoretische Autonomie der architektonischen Entwurfsarbeit wird gewissermaßen als unantastbar aufgefasst. Sie verbietet es dem Architekten, die seinem kreativen Tun zugrunde liegenden technischen Systeme zu diskutieren, mit denen er sich in der Praxis auseinandersetzen muss, deren Beitrag er aber um der architektonischen Orthodoxie willen nicht voll anerkennen kann. Für diese Gruppe bildet Entwurfswissen das eigentliche architektonische Wissen, Instrumentenwissen hingegen ist nur ein Mittel zum Zweck.

Für die zweite Gruppe sind Entwurfswissen und Instrumentenwissen zwei sich gegenseitig beeinflussende Dimensionen des architektonischen Wissens. In diesem Lager herrscht die Auffassung, dass die den Entwurf prägenden Herausforderungen und Chancen über die Bauformgestaltung hinaus in die fachlichen und praktischen Aufgaben der Leitung und Überwachung der Entwurfsausführung reichen. Die Angehörigen dieses Lagers vertreten zwar kein bestimmtes formales Projekt, verstehen aber die kritisch-theoretische und technisch-praktische

11 Lynn 2000: 11.
12 Iwamoto 2009: 5.
13 Colletti 2010.
14 Colletti 2010: 18 [Dt. Übers.: Annette Wiethüchter].

theoretical and practical advances from projective geometry. Remarkably, this ascendance and diffusion of mechanical drawing was reversed in the early twentieth century, or was at least restricted to disciplines more numerical and analytic than architecture. I argue that the virtual disappearance of these machines in the early modern period led to a regression in the architectural knowledge of geometry that is only now being recovered through the means of digital computation machines. The question of what kind of knowledge superseded this virtuosic machine and geometric knowledge may well reframe how we understand the epistemic consequences of the rise of modernity and the composition of architectural knowledge itself.

Machines and the Mechanical Construction of Curvature

The specific role of geometric drawing devices in the nineteenth century follows from a long tradition of architecture's engagement with the machine, dating at least to the time of Filippo Brunelleschi and Leon Battista Alberti. The work of these men attests to the fundamental role of the machine in the genesis of architecture as discipline.

Brunelleschi's architectural work was remarkable in that he designed not only buildings but also the instruments to construct these buildings: specialized hoists, jigs, and lifts. The dome of Florence Cathedral (completed 1436) is the most spectacular manifestation of this integrated approach, and his burial inscription witnesses this synthetic role: "How Filippo the architect excelled in invention is shown not only by the beautiful shell of his famous temple but also by the various machines that he invented with divine genius."[18] This holistic approach provided an example for architects interested in extending the limits of design through technical invention. For Brunelleschi, architecture encompassed the instrumental knowledge of devices and machines needed to achieve the conceptual aims of design.

Brunelleschi's close contemporary in the latter part of his life, Leon Battista Alberti, provided a description of the architect's role

18 Cited in Prager / Scaglia: 135.
19 Alberti 1988 [1452]: 3.
20 Alberti 1988 [1452]: 3.
21 Carpo 2008: 50.
22 Prager / Scaglia 1970: 97, 105.

that was quite different. Alberti's description of the architect in his influential treatise *De re aedificatoria* (1452) is well known: "Him I consider an architect who, by sure and wonderful reason and method, knows both how to devise through his own mind and energy, and to realize by construction, whatever can be most beautifully fitted out for the noble needs of man, by the movement of weights and the joining and massing of bodies. To do this he must have a knowledge of all the highest and noblest disciplines."[19]

This definition has become foundational to architecture's self-understanding, and definitively acknowledges the role of knowledge in design. Yet Alberti's qualification of this definition has become equally decisive, and fundamental to the current debate over the role of instrumental knowledge by assigning that to a different profession: "I should explain exactly whom I mean by an architect: for it is no carpenter that I would have you compare to the greatest exponents of other disciplines: the carpenter is but an instrument in the hands of the architect."[20] Here we find what is essentially today's distinction between design knowledge and instrumental knowledge. In this simple separation of the architect from the carpenter, intended to elevate the discipline, Alberti calls into question how extensively the architect can or should know the technology of design or of construction.

Of course, Alberti shows a deep respect for those achievements of architecture that today would be considered mechanical engineering. As Mario Carpo has shown, Alberti was profoundly interested in mechanics, particularly for the control and replication of representation.[21] Yet his machines lacked certain key innovations that Brunelleschi had already introduced, leading some critics to assert his incomplete understanding of contemporary mechanics.[22] For Alberti, it seems, design knowledge was distinct from the instrumental knowledge of operative

Auseinandersetzung mit der Form als Quelle jedes Entwurfs- und Instrumentenwissens. Diese Architekten haben kein Problem damit, Fragen der Werkzeuge in den Mittelpunkt ihrer Studien zu stellen. Derartige Fragen sind für sie sogar wesentliche Faktoren für die sich wieder neu abzeichnende Rolle des Architekten als Baumeister.[15] Der Computer bietet ihnen die Chance, diverse Wissensgebiete zu erschließen sowie praktisch zu nutzen und die Arbeitsleistung des Architekten zu steigern und zu organisieren.[16] So wird der Computer de facto eine Ressource fachlich-beruflicher Organisation. Das zeigt sich etwa am wachsenden Interesse an Baustatikprogrammen oder Simulationssoftware, mit der sich ökologische Zusammenhänge darstellen lassen, die unter Umständen einen externen Fachberater überflüssig machen. Darüber hinaus können Entwerfer heutzutage ihre verfahrenstechnischen Kenntnisse durch Programmieren, Skripten und regelbasierte Entwürfe in Softwareprogramme einfügen, wodurch sie Entwurfswissen in Instrumentenwissen umwandeln. Hier besteht ein starkes Interesse am digitalen Werkzeugbau, an Basteleien und Hacking – und am offenen Eingeständnis, dass Erfindungen nicht dem Ingenieurwesen vorbehalten sein sollten.[17] Für diese Gruppe wird Instrumentenwissen zu einem leistungsstarken Mittel Entwurfswissen zu erweitern; Architekturwissen umfasst notwendigerweise beide Formen.

Auch wenn es in dieser Auseinandersetzung um mehr als nur formale Fragen geht, wird sie verschärft durch Fragen zur Formgebung und insbesondere durch die Frage nach der Rolle des geometrischen Fachwissens bei der Gestaltung komplexer Formen. Wo sitzt das zur Erzeugung derartiger Formen erforderliche Wissen? Handelt es sich dabei um Architekturwissen? Welche erkenntnistheoretische Rolle spielt die Maschine bei der Entwicklung und Herstellung der Form?

Diese epistemologische Debatte hat Auswirkungen auf die zeitgenössische Architekturpraxis. Es könnte aber lehrreich sein, sich nicht länger darüber zu streiten, sondern das Augenmerk auf einen bestimmten historischen Kontext zu richten, der dem gegenwärtigen insofern ähnlich ist, als er von der Maschine als Hilfsmittel der Formgebung fasziniert war. Die Vorstellung von dem in einer Maschine gespeicherten, verkapselten Wissen war im 19. Jahrhundert in Großbritannien und Frankreich von großer Bedeutung und führte zur Entwicklung mechanischer Zeichengeräte für komplexe Kurven und projektive Konstruktionen, die das Formenvokabular der Architektur vergrößerten, indem sie bestimmte theoretische und praktische Weiterentwicklungen der projektiven Geometrie in die mechanischen Bewegungen und Prozesse von Maschinen umsetzten. Erstaunlicherweise kam es Anfang des 20. Jahrhunderts zu einer Rückentwicklung in der Verbreitung des mechanischen Zeichnens oder zumindest zu deren Beschränkung auf analytischere Fachgebiete außerhalb der Architektur. Meiner Meinung nach führte das nahezu vollständige Verschwinden dieser mechanischen Zeichengeräte zu Beginn der Klassischen Moderne dazu, dass das geometrische Wissen der Architektur weitgehend verloren ging und erst jetzt über die digitalen Rechner zurückgewonnen wird. Die Frage, welche Art von Wissen dieses virtuose Maschinen- und Geometriewissen ersetzte, könnte sehr wohl unser heutiges Verständnis der erkenntnistheoretischen Konsequenzen der Moderne und auch unser Verständnis des Architekturwissens selbst neu definieren.

Maschinen und die mechanische Konstruktion der Kurvatur

Die besondere Rolle der geometrischen Zeichengeräte im 19. Jahrhunderts kam nicht von ungefähr: Maschinen im Sinne von Arbeitsgeräten des Architekten blickten auf eine lange Tradition zurück, die mindestens bis in die Zeit von Filippo Brunelleschi und Leon Battista Alberti zurückreichte. Das Schaffen dieser beiden Männer belegt die zentrale Rolle der Maschine in der Genese der Architektur als Fachdisziplin.

---

15 Kieren/Timberlake 2004: xi.
16 Kolarevic 2003: 59.
17 Aranda/Lasch 2006.

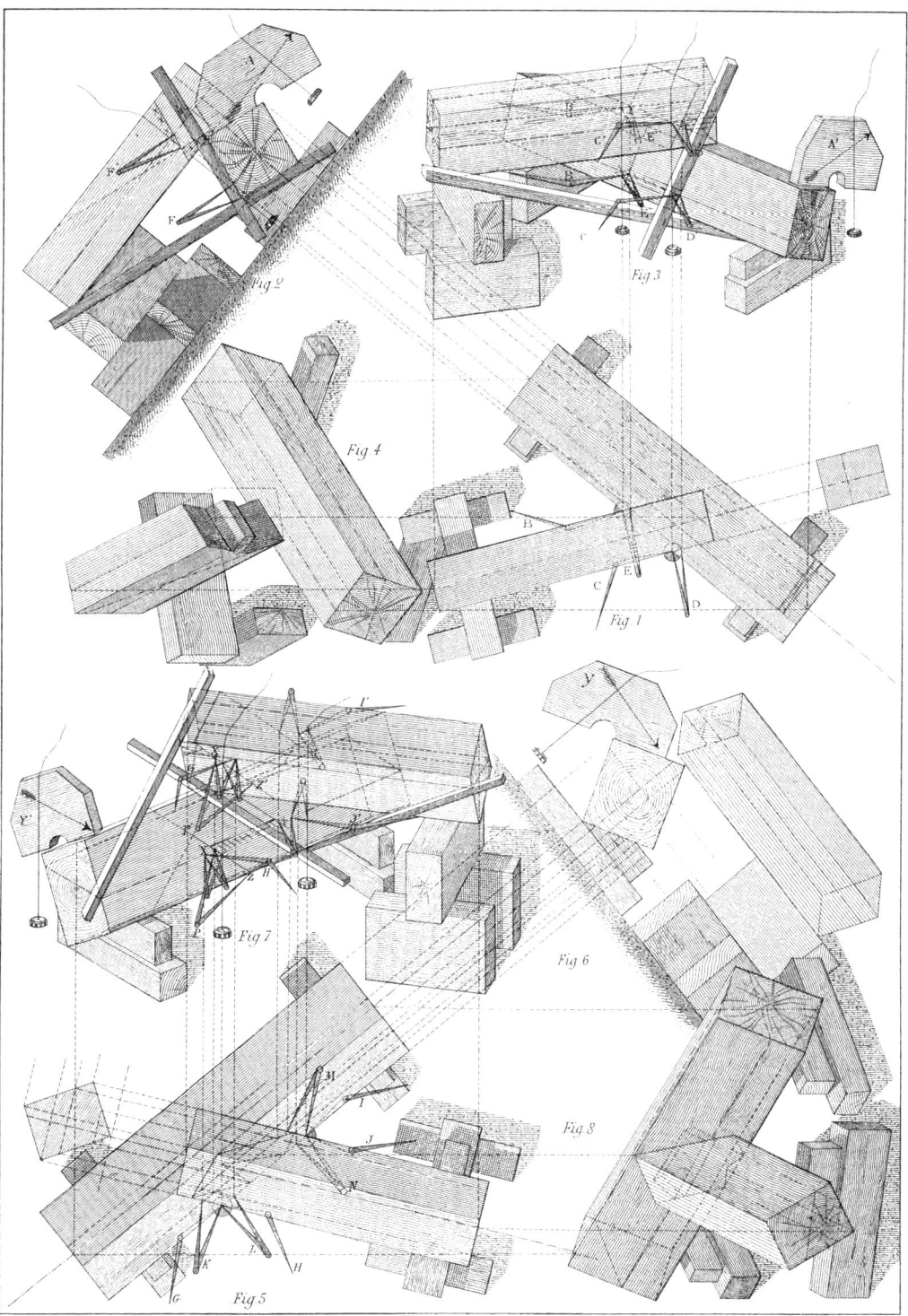

PIQUÉ DES BOIS À DEVERS ET À TOUT DEVERS.

Andrew J. Witt
A Machine Epistemology

Candide No. 3, 12/2010
Essay

Mit seinem Werk *Traité théorique et pratique de charpente* (1895) fasste Louis Mazerolle die Anwendung projektiver Geometrie auf den Holzbau zusammen. Die Herstellung komplexer Holzformen erforderte präzise mechanische Messungen. In dieser Zeichnung werden neben den Holzformen die dafür benötigten Messinstrumente mit abgebildet.

With his *Traité théorique et pratique de charpente* (1895), Louis Mazerolle synthesized the application of projective geometry to carpentry. The fabrication of complex wood pieces required precise mechanical measurement. Here the mechanical tools necessary for the measurement of these members are indicated in the drawing itself.

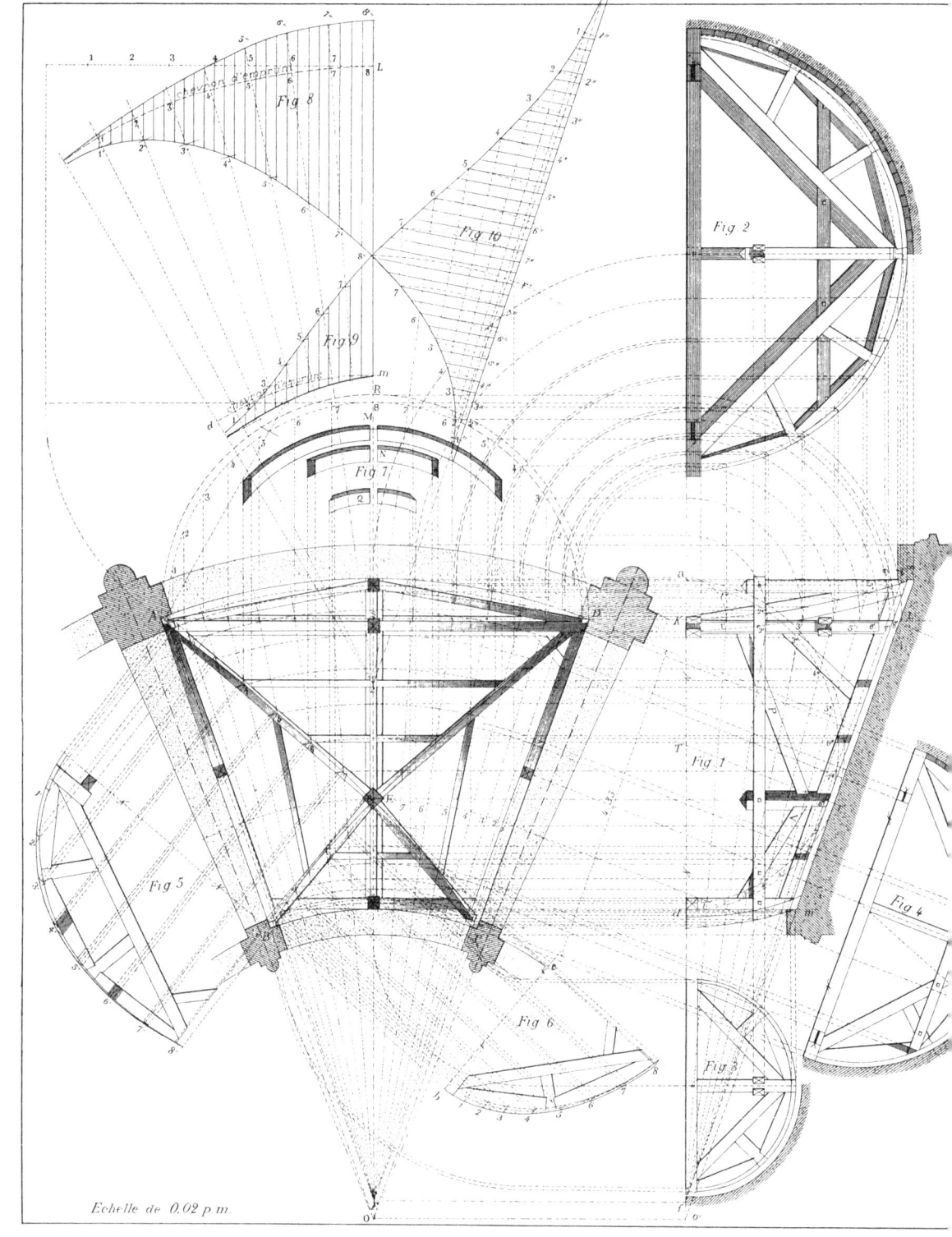

CINTRES POUR VOÛTE D'ARÊTES CIRCULAIRE ET CONIQU

Die Konstruktion komplexer Holzgewölbe erforderte die räumliche Entwicklung und Bemessung von Korbbögen, einschließlich der Berechnung komplexer abgewickelter Formen.

The framing of complex wooden vaults required the spatial development and measurement of compound curvature, including the calculation of complex unrolled shapes.

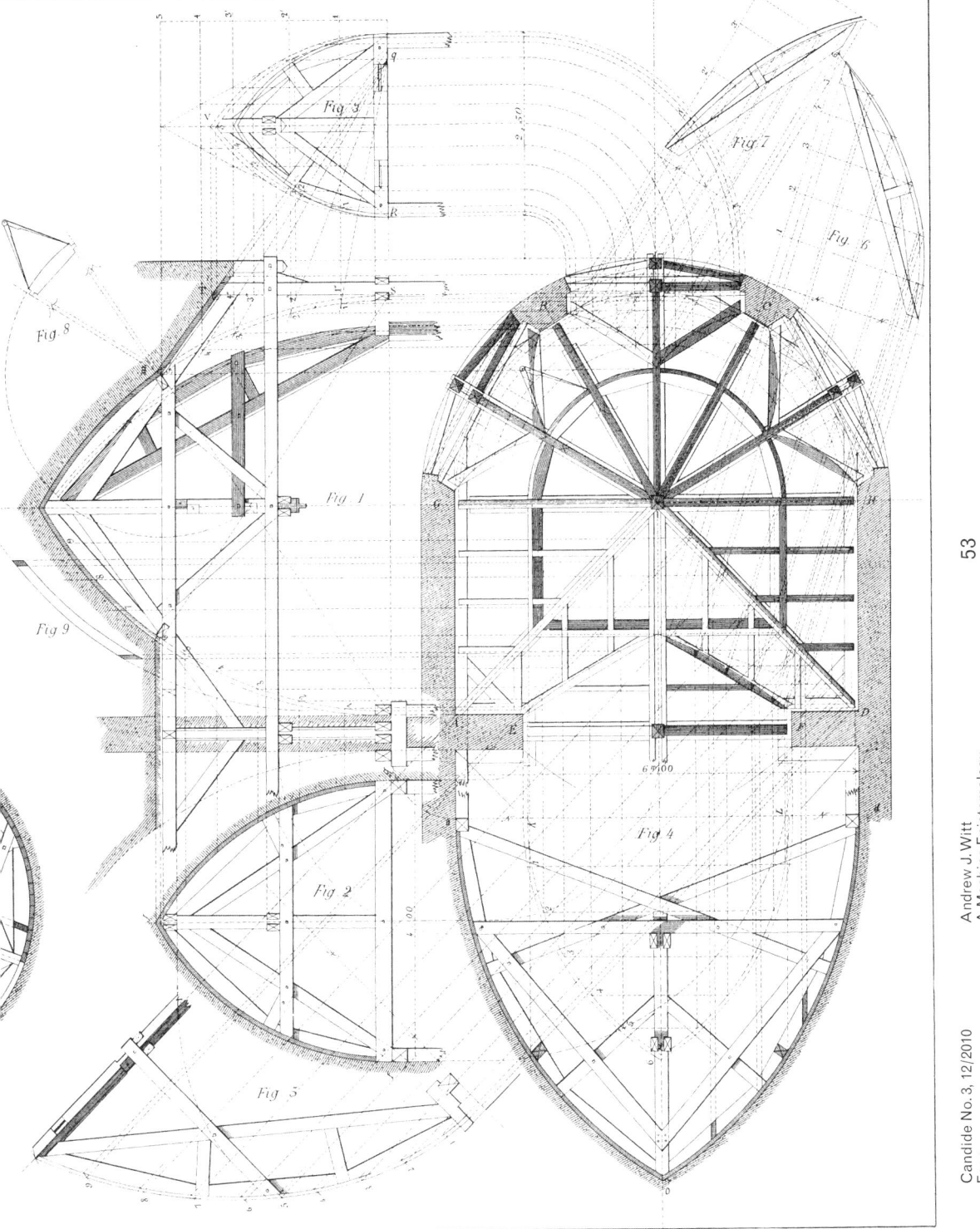

NTRES POUR VOUSSURE EN ARC DE CLOÎTRE PÉNÉTRÉE.

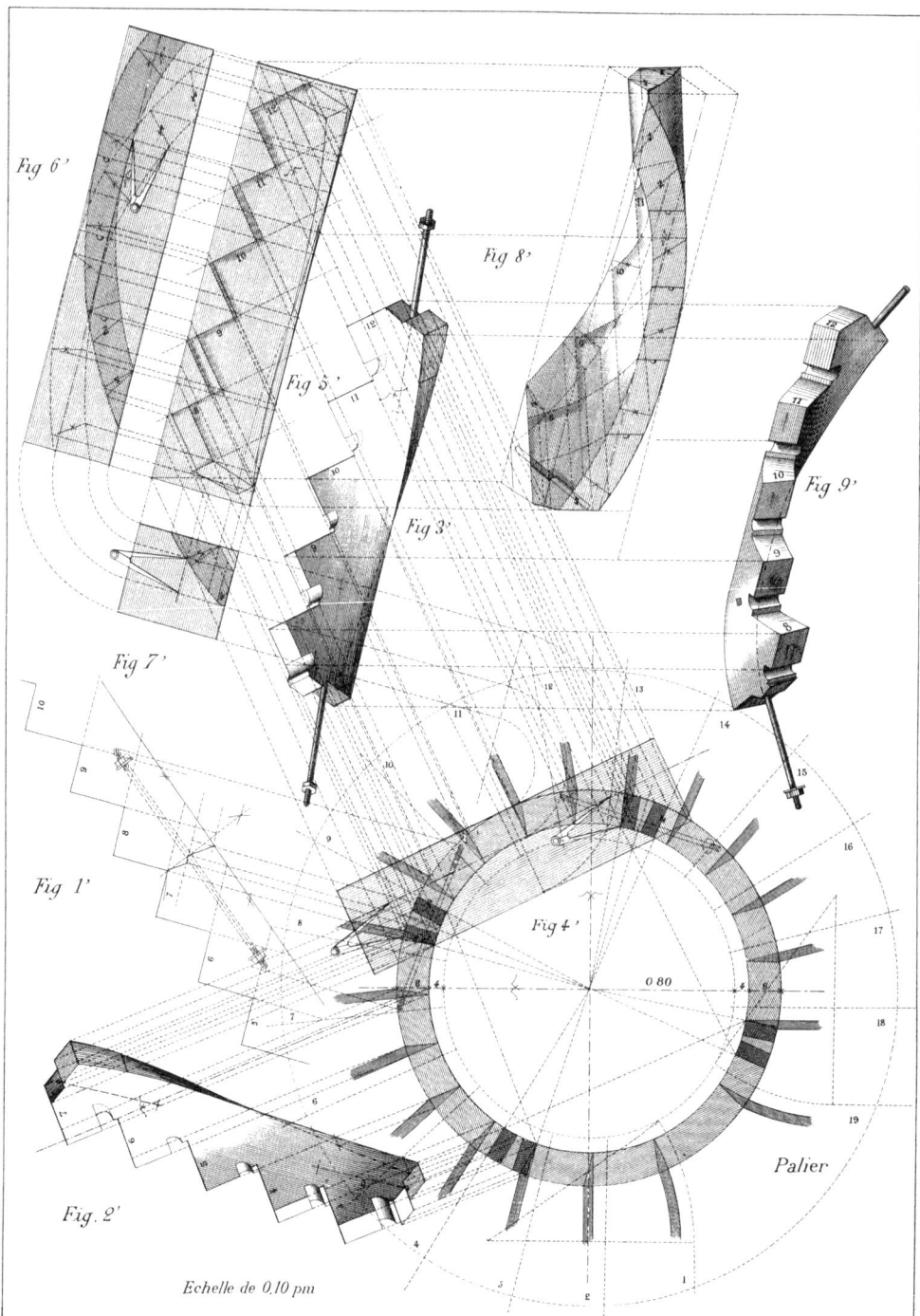

Fig 6'

Fig 8'

Fig 5'

Fig 9'

Fig 3'

Fig 7'

Fig 1'

Fig 4'

0 80

Palier

Fig. 2'

Echelle de 0,10 pm

DÉTAILS DE L'ESCALIER À JOUR ROND.

Die Virtuosität der Architekten und Handwerker des 19. Jahrhunderts mit komplexer, zweifach gekrümmter Geometrie umzugehen, wird in dieser Zeichnung deutlich, in der die minimal umgebenden Rechtecke von gedreh-ten, gekrümmten Bauteilen dargestellt werden. Diese Rahmen waren notwendig, um das Volumen der Holzleeren für das Geländer einer gedrehten Treppe zu berechnen. In manchen Fällen konnten Zeichenmaschinen, die zu die-ser Zeit entstanden, bei der Berechnung helfen.

The virtuosity of nineteenth-century designers and crafts-men with even complex double-curved geometry is apparent from this drawing, in which the minimum bounding boxes of twisted curved members are represented. These bounding boxes were necessary to calculate the volume of wood blanks for the railing of a twisted staircase. In some cases these calculations could be aided by drawing machines that emerged during this period.

machines. The difference in the way Brunelleschi and Alberti approached the machine demonstrates that the role of instrumentality in design knowledge has been a subtext in architecture at least since the Renaissance.

Theoretical distinctions are often overtaken by practical concerns, however, and in the following centuries practical concerns very often involved resolving how to design and build complex geometric forms such as doubly-curved vaults, complex squinches, and intersecting arches. The need to supplement the architect's design knowledge with precise geometrical and mathematical procedures became especially pressing with the curved distortions, deformations, and projections of the Baroque. Initially this additional design knowledge was generated by architects themselves. Robin Evans has written extensively of the developments in architecture that enabled perspective and projection to be employed to design apparent and actual spatial distortions.[23] In the mid-sixteenth century, the work of the French architect Philibert de l'Orme, who applied such techniques of distortion to design and stonecutting, was particularly influential.[24] One focus of interest was the ellipse, a conic section that results when a circle is projected onto a ramp or an oblique plane. During the Baroque period, the ellipse took on its most recognizable role as a frequent trope of ornament. Gradually, however, architects realized that the construction of an ellipse could be one in a longer procedural sequence of formal moves that ultimately went beyond motif to define a space itself. For example, the ellipse appears as the intersection of two cylinders of equal radii, and thus as the rib of a vault; or as the intersection of a single cylinder with an oblique wall or ceiling, and thus as an embrasure. This understanding of the conic sections as being spatial constructs changed the status of curved geometry from something essentially flat and merely decorative to something inherently spatial.

The drawing procedures required by de l'Orme and others to represent curved forms were sophisticated and time consuming, and resembled cartographic operations in their intricacy. The complexity of these design

23 Evans 2000 [1995]: 187.
24 Potie 1996: 9.
25 Horsburgh 1996: 256.
26 George Adams's *Geometrical and Graphical Essays* (1791) first introduced Suardi's work to an English-speaking audience. Adams's work was first published in German in 1795.
27 Adams 1797 [1791]: 152.

operations required knowledgeable and skilled practitioners. Some of these architects, engineers, and cartographers turned to toolmakers to encapsulate the knowledge of these geometric operations into specific drawing machines, thereby instrumentalizing this aspect of design knowledge. In this instrumentalization, the toolmakers deployed various methods of mechanical construction of conics developed by mathematicians such as René Descartes, Isaac Newton, and Colin Maclaurin, including methods for the design of ellipses, parabolas, and hyperbolas.[25] By the eighteenth century advanced tool making to support the design of more complex curves had become a discipline in itself, with its own encyclopedic references and disciplinary projects. Nicolas Bion's *Traité de la construction et des principaux usages des instruments de mathématiques* (1709) provides a catalog of the state-of-the-art of tool making during this period. The work begins with the typical compasses and dividers but moves to more ambitious implements such as trisectors and elliptical trammels, which were applicable in architectural contexts.

Eighteenth-century toolmakers proposed a host of methods for the construction of complex curves that exploited a new mechanical understanding of motion. The Italian Giambattista Suardi's work in particular is remarkable for its range and advances in this domain. In his *Nuovi istromenti per la descrizione di diverse curve antiche e moderne e di molte altre* (1752),[26] Suardi proposed two instruments of particular note: the first was a conchoidograph for the drawing of conchoid curves, and the second was a sophisticated "geometrical pen."[27] This "pen" was actually a compound machine designed by Suardi to mechanically draw curves ranging from ellipses to complex epicycloids. The geometrical pen exploited the combinatorial variety of curves that could be generated by

Brunelleschis Bauten sind insofern bemerkenswert, als er nicht nur die Gebäude entwarf, sondern auch die technischen Geräte, mit deren Hilfe sie errichtet wurden: spezielle Flaschenzüge, Lehren und Hubwerke. Die Kuppel des Florentiner Doms (1436 vollendet) ist das spektakulärste Zeugnis dieses integrierten Ansatzes, und die Inschrift auf Brunelleschis Epitaph belegt seine Kunst der Synthese aller architektonischen Künste: „Wie viel der Architekt Filippo mit dädalischer Kunst vermochte, davon können sowohl das wundersame Gewölbe dieser so berühmten Kirche als auch die von ihm mit göttlichem Geist erfundenen Maschinen Zeugnis ablegen."[18] Dieser holistische Ansatz wurde zum Vorbild für diejenigen Architekten, welche die Grenzen des architektonischen Entwerfens durch technische Erfindungen überwinden wollten. Für Brunelleschi umfasste Architektur auch die genaue Kenntnis der Instrumente, Geräte und Maschinen, mit denen sich das architektonische Konzept ausführen lässt.

Leon Battista Alberti, Kollege Brunelleschis in dessen zweiter Lebenshälfte, dagegen lieferte in seiner Abhandlung *De re aedificatora* (*Zehn Bücher über die Baukunst*, 1452) eine ganz andere bekannte Definition der Aufgabe des Baumeisters: „Ein Architekt wird der sein, behaupte ich, der gelernt hat, mittels eines bestimmten und bewundernswerten Planes und Weges sowohl in Gedanken und Gefühl zu bestimmen, als auch in der Tat auszuführen, was unter der Bewegung von Lasten und der Vereinigung und Zusammenfügung von Körpern den hervorragendsten menschlichen Bedürfnissen am ehesten entspricht und dessen (möglichste) Erwerbung und Kenntnis unter allen wertvollen und besten Sachen nötig ist, derart wird also ein Architekt sein."[19] Albertis berühmte Definition würdigt die Rolle des Wissens bei der architektonischen Entwurfsarbeit und ist zur Grundlage des baumeisterlichen Selbstverständnisses geworden. Sie beginnt allerdings mit einer Einschränkung, die für die heutige Debatte zur Rolle des Instrumentenwissens in der Architektur von zentraler Bedeutung

ist, weil sie die Kenntnis der Werkzeuge einem anderen Beruf zuweist: „Doch glaube ich auseinandersetzen zu müssen, wen ich für einen Architekten gehalten wissen will. Denn ich werde Dir keinen Zimmermann bringen, den Du mit den hervorragendsten Männern anderer Fächer vergleichen sollst. Die Hand des Arbeiters dient ja dem Architekten nur als Werkzeug."[20] Hier steht also, was den eigentlichen Unterschied zwischen Entwurfswissen und Instrumentenwissen bis heute ausmacht. Mit der simplen Unterscheidung zwischen Architekt und Zimmerer wollte Alberti den Architektenberuf adeln; gleichzeitig warf er damit aber auch die Frage auf, inwieweit der Architekt die für Entwurf und Bauausführung nötige Technik kennen und beherrschen sollte.

Natürlich zollte Alberti denjenigen Leistungen der Architektur, die wir heute dem Maschinenbau zuordnen würden, höchste Anerkennung. Wie Mario Carpo nachgewiesen hat, interessierte sich Alberti sehr für Mechanik, speziell für die präzise Ausführung und Vervielfältigung von Darstellungen.[21] Seinen Maschinen fehlten aber wichtige Innovationen, die Brunelleschi bereits eingeführt hatte, weshalb einige Kritiker behauptet haben, Albertis Wissen auf dem Gebiet der damaligen Mechanik sei lückenhaft gewesen.[22] Alberti selbst unterschied offenbar zwischen Entwurfswissen und einem Instrumentenwissen, das den Betrieb von Geräten und Maschinen umfasste. Brunelleschis und Albertis unterschiedliche Auffassungen von Maschinen zeigen, dass die Frage nach der Rolle des Instrumentenwissen im Entwurfswissen spätestens seit der Renaissance ein unterschwelliges Thema der Architektur ist.

Theoretische Unterscheidungen werden allerdings häufig durch die Praxis überholt, und in den folgenden Jahrhunderten ging es bei der Lösung konkreter Bauaufgaben

---

18 Zitiert nach Prager/Scaglia 1970: 135 [Dt. Übers.: Annette Wiethüchter].
19 Alberti 1991 [1452]: 9.
20 Alberti 1991 [1452]: 9.
21 Carpo 2008: 50.
22 Prager/Scaglia 1970: 97, 105.

the compound motion of two or more circles rolling along each other's circumferences. The construction of the pen made it possible to vary the radii, tracing speed, and length of the drawing arm to produce hundreds of distinct curve types. By this method one could produce straight lines, circles, ellipses, and many other higher-order compound cycloids.[28] In many ways the geometrical pen became a standard by which later nineteenth-century machines would be judged. Indeed some of the notable ellipsograph designs employ only slightly altered methods.

These instruments could obviate the need for the user to possess the geometric design knowledge encapsulated in the instruments, for instance concerning the construction of complex figures, particularly conic sections such as the ellipse. As a consequence of this encapsulation, the stage was set for an even more profound mechanization of form to follow.

New Domains of Geometric Knowledge

The encapsulation of design knowledge, or, more specifically, geometric knowledge, into machines accelerated markedly in the nineteenth century, driven both by developments in the geometry of curves and curved surfaces and by the emergence of more exact and scalable machine reproduction technologies. In particular, projective geometry opened up new avenues of mechanical investigation: "It was natural that with the further development of projective geometry, which lends itself easily to geometrical constructions, other methods of generating conics should arise."[29] These developments had a reciprocal relationship with each other: the requirements of precise geometric drawings drove the development of particular instruments, while the availability of exact instruments facilitated new types of drawings and thus approaches to geometry.

In mathematics, some remarkable theoretical developments illuminated the possibilities and limitations of mechanical instrumentation for the representation of curves and surfaces. In the late 1820s, the French mathematician Évariste Galois

28 Adams 1797 [1791]: 151.
29 Horsburgh 1914: 256.
30 Monge 1989 [1799]: 4.

proposed a remarkable abstract algebraic approach to geometry that ultimately proved that some basic curves and figures could not be constructed by compass alone. This demonstrated that compound motion of more sophisticated machines would be necessary in order to design a broad lexicon of curved forms.

A second major theoretical development was the codification of descriptive geometry through the work of the French mathematician and physicist Gaspard Monge. Monge's *Géometrie descriptive* (1799) systematized the conceptual and pedagogical approach he had developed over the previous years for the mathematical description of spatial forms as complexes of projections. His new approach to representing curves and curved surfaces in space provided a much more general and flexible system than typical orthographic projection, and his pedagogical propagation of these practices (above all at the École Polytechnique in Paris) enabled more sophisticated spatial representations in design and engineering in the early nineteenth century. Particularly remarkable were Monge's solution of certain general conic intersections as they pertained to vaults. He demonstrated a method to derive, by drawing, the intersections of general extrusion surfaces, and pointed the way to a more ambitious and thoroughly spatial understanding of curved geometries. He also explicitly affirmed the problems of machine operation as central to the subject matter of geometry, and a belief that mastery of spatial geometry was a key element of the national evolution of French machine industry.[30]

These developments had immediate impacts on the practical craft of stereotomy (the stone cutting of complex three-dimensional shapes) as well as on the more theoretical discourse of projective geometry (the description of spatial form through linear or planar projection). Monge's methods encouraged his contemporaries and successors to explore the relationship of geometric design knowledge to all parts of the technical

vielfach um die Frage, wie man komplexe geometrische Gebilde – zum Beispiel Doppelgewölbe, Eckkragbögen oder einander durchdringende Bögen – zu konstruieren hatte. Der Architekt musste sein gestalterisches Wissen also um gründliche Kenntnisse auf den Gebieten der Geometrie und Mathematik erweitern, wenn er die verzerrten Schwünge, Verformungen sowie Projektionen des Barockstils erzeugen wollte. Ursprünglich eigneten sich Architekten dieses Entwurfswissen autodidaktisch an. Robin Evans hat die architektonischen Neuentwicklungen in perspektivischer Darstellung und Projektion, mit denen es gelang, scheinbare und tatsächliche räumliche Verzerrungen zu entwerfen, ausführlich beschrieben.[23] Mitte des 16. Jahrhunderts wandte der französische Baumeister Philibert de l'Orme diese Verzerrungstechniken auf Entwurf und Steinschnitt an und übte damit großen Einfluss auf andere Architekten aus.[24] Besonderes Interesse galt der Ellipse, einem Kegelschnitt, der entsteht, wenn ein Kreis auf eine Rampe oder eine andere geneigte Fläche projiziert wird. Im Barock spielte die Ellipse die größte, offensichtlichste Rolle als Ornament. Allmählich erkannten Architekten jedoch, dass die Konstruktion einer Ellipse Teil einer längeren Reihung formaler Elemente sein könnte, mit der man schließlich nicht nur dekorative Muster schaffen, sondern ganze Räume umreißen würde. Zum Beispiel trat die Ellipse als Überschneidung zweier Zylinder mit gleichem Radius und somit als Gewölberippe, oder als Schnittfläche zwischen einem einzigen Zylinder und einer schrägen Wand oder Decke, und somit als nach innen abgeschrägte Fenster- oder Obergadenlaibung in Erscheinung. Diese Interpretation von Kegelschnitten als Raumkonstrukte erhob die Kurvengeometrie aus dem Bereich eher flacher Dekoration zur dreidimensionalen architektonischen Form.

Die von de l'Orme und anderen angewandten Zeichentechniken der Darstellung gekrümmter Formen waren anspruchsvoll und erforderten großen Zeitaufwand. In ihrer ausgefeilten Präzision ähnelten sie kartografischen Arbeiten und konnten nur von geschickten, kenntnisreichen Zeichnern

ausgeführt werden. Einige Architekten, Ingenieure und Kartografen ließen sich von Werkzeugmachern spezielle Zeichengeräte anfertigen, in die ihre geometrischen Kenntnisse sozusagen eingebaut wurden. Auf diese Weise instrumentalisierten sie diese Aspekte des Entwurfswissens. Im Zuge dieser Instrumentalisierung setzten die Werkzeugmacher verschiedene Methoden der mechanischen Konstruktion von Kegeln ein, die von Mathematikern wie René Descartes, Isaac Newton und Colin Maclaurin entwickelt worden waren, darunter Methoden zum Entwurf von Ellipsen, Parabeln und Hyperbeln.[25] Ende des 18. Jahrhunderts hatte sich dann die Herstellung von Zeichengeräten für die Darstellung komplexer Kurven bereits zu einem eigenen Zweig der Werkzeugmacherei mit eigenen technischen Lehrbüchern und Erfindungen entwickelt. Der Franzose Nicolas Bion zum Beispiel veröffentlichte 1709 die Abhandlung *Traité de la construction et des principaux usages des instruments de mathématiques*, das einen Katalog zum Stand der Technik in der Kunst des Instrumentenbaus zu Beginn des 18. Jahrhunderts umfasst. Es beginnt mit den herkömmlichen Kompassen und Zirkeln, um sich dann komplizierteren Geräten wie Dreiteilern und Ellipsenzirkeln zu widmen, die alle auch in der Architektur Verwendung fanden.

Die Werkzeugmacher des 18. Jahrhunderts entwickelten eine ganze Reihe an Methoden zur Konstruktion komplexer Kurven auf der Basis eines neuen mechanischen Verständnisses von Bewegung. Insbesondere die Arbeiten des Italieners Giambattista Suardi stechen durch ihre Vielfalt und Fortschritte in diesem Bereich hervor. In seinem Werk *Nuovi istromenti per la descrizione di diverse curve antiche e moderne e di molte altre* (1752),[26] schlägt Suardi zwei

23 Evans 2000 [1995]: 187.
24 Potie 1996: 9.
25 Horsburgh 1996: 256.
26 George Adams' *Geometrical and Graphical Essays containing a General Description of the Mathematical Instruments used in Geometry, Civil and Military Surveying, Levelling, and Perspective* (1791) führte als erstes Suardis Arbeiten einer englischsprachigen Leserschaft vor. Auf Deutsch wurde Adams' Werk 1795 erstmals veröffentlicht.

process of architecture and fabrication, particularly carpentry and stonecutting. During the nineteenth century several technical professors who were also master craftsmen, such as Jean Paul Douliot, Charles-François-Antoine Leroy, Louis Monduit, and Louis Mazerolle, published practical works on both stereotomy and projective geometry. Architects took particular interest in the new formal possibilities offered by these projective classes of surfaces, and made these developments of surface geometry an object of design knowledge.

Douliot's *Traité speciale de coupe des pierres* (1825) takes a specifically taxonomic approach: he classifies the types of surfaces he judges most appropriate to construction, including particularly the ruled surfaces, that is, the surfaces generated by the movement of a generatrix line through space. He goes on to classify single and double curvature surfaces, and cylindrical, conic, ellipsoidal, and other types of more complex surfaces. But since this is all a treatise on construction, he proceeds immediately to the types of new surfaces most appropriate for a wall, whether right, cylindrically oblique, or conic, and its decomposition into stones of the appropriate geometric typology.[31] Again, considerable time is devoted to the resolution of conic vaults.[32] It provides a remarkable synthesis of design, geometric, and architectural knowledge in one work.

As the century progressed a continuous and reciprocal evolution of conceptual techniques of geometry and material techniques of irregular stone and wood cutting enriched the formal range of architecture. Manuals particularly for architects abound, such as C. Protot's *Cours spécial d'architecture, ou Leçons particulières de géométrie descriptive* (1838). In some cases encyclopedic compendiums such as *La Science des artistes* (1844) compiled contributions by many geometers and architects, summarizing the theoretical state of the art of descriptive geometry. Other works were intended more for craftsmen. For example, Charles-François-Antoine Leroy's *Traité de stéréotomie, comprenant les applications de la géométrie descriptive* (1844) presents all the key

31 Douliot 1825: 59.
32 Douliot 1825: 149.
33 Leroy 1844: 64.

stonecutting and carpentry techniques to construct complex geometries of the period, including complex doubly-curved spiral vaults.[33]

By the latter quarter of the nineteenth century, these techniques had been completely assimilated at the technical level of architectural construction, and with the techniques fully settled the publications of this period became graphic showpieces. Monduit's *Traité théorique et pratique de stéréotomie* (1889) presents the canonical constructive and discretized solutions to many fundamental geometric problems, including the intersections of generalized cylinders and cones. Perhaps this treatise is the most compelling example of the extent of geometric sophistication required to execute certain nineteenth-century designs, particularly vaults. Mazerolle's *Traité théoretique et pratique de charpente* (1895) complemented in many ways Monduit's work. In it Mazerolle records the standard yet intricate projective and stereotomic methods to manipulate wood planks, using methods of volumetric intersection to derive planking diagrams for complex roof structures. He also provided rigorous methods for the description of curved wood beams, which were often the necessary results of volumetric intersections. In some ways these constructions were even more technically sophisticated than the stereotomic ones; considered together, these works on carpentry and stonecutting represent the pinnacle of geometric understanding in nineteenth-century craft.

This expanded geometric knowledge had a direct and profound impact on architecture in the nineteenth century. Perhaps no architect used the projective and surface methods to greater effect than Antoni Gaudí on his Sagrada Família cathedral in Barcelona (1882–present). Gaudí's instructor in projective geometry had been a student and disciple of the mathematical approach of Monge, and he in turn introduced his

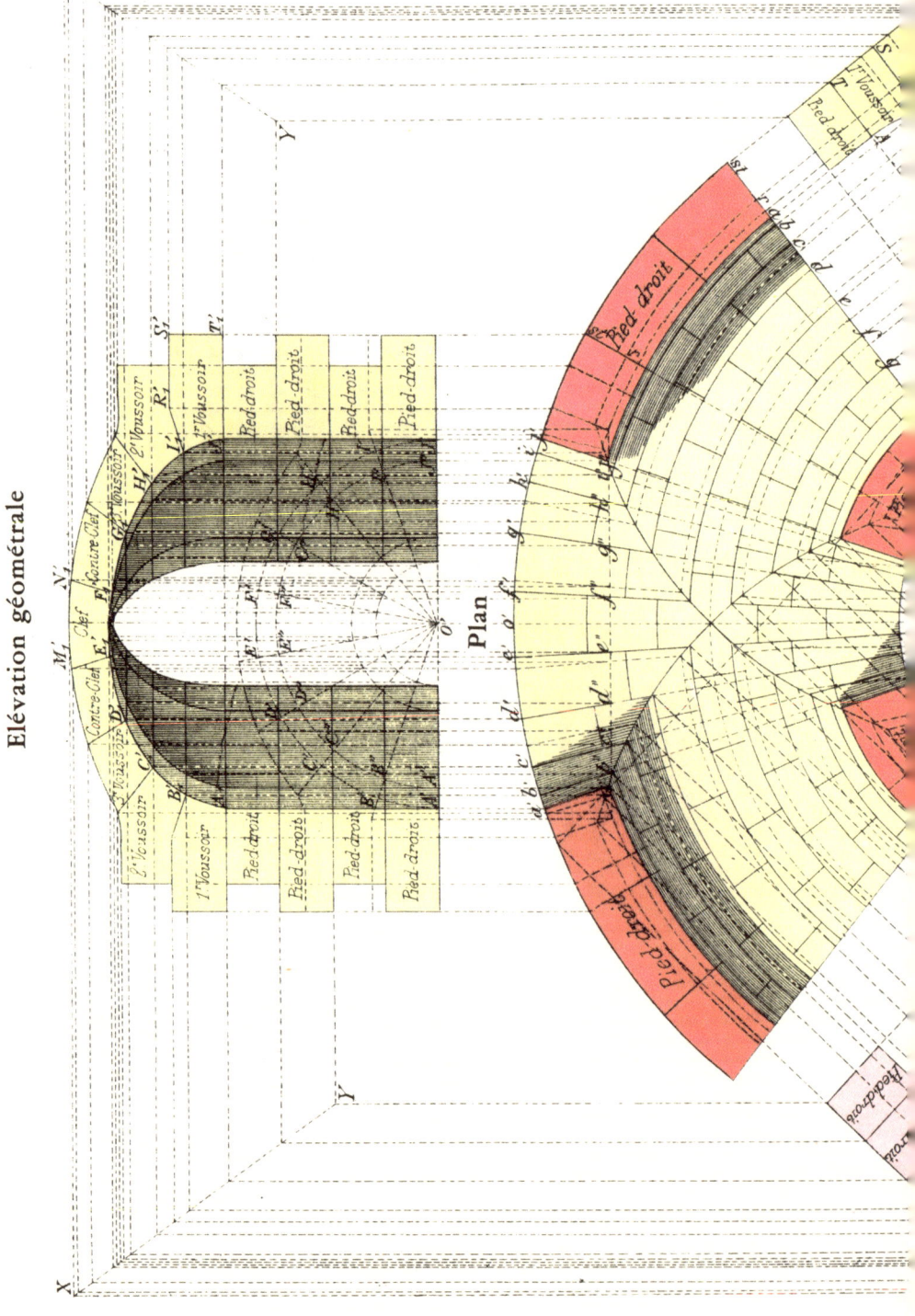

VOÛTE D'ARÊTE DANS UNE VOÛTE ANNULAIRE

Elévation géométrale

Plan

Louis Monduits *Traité théorique et pratique de stéréotomie* (1889) präsentierte Lösungen zahlreicher grundlegender geometrischer Aufgabenstellungen. Dieses verzerrte Gewölbe – eine Verschneidung von einem Zylinder und einem Torus – zeigt, welche komplizierten geometrischen Operationen Architekten und Bauhandwerker im 19. Jahrhundert ausführten. Dies beinhaltete auch die Entwicklung abwickelbarer Formen für die Diskretisierung nicht genormter, gekrümmter Verschneidungen. Bei den Bogenüberschneidungen handelte es sich oft um Kegelschnitte oder deren Ableitungen, von denen viele mechanisch konstruierbar sind.

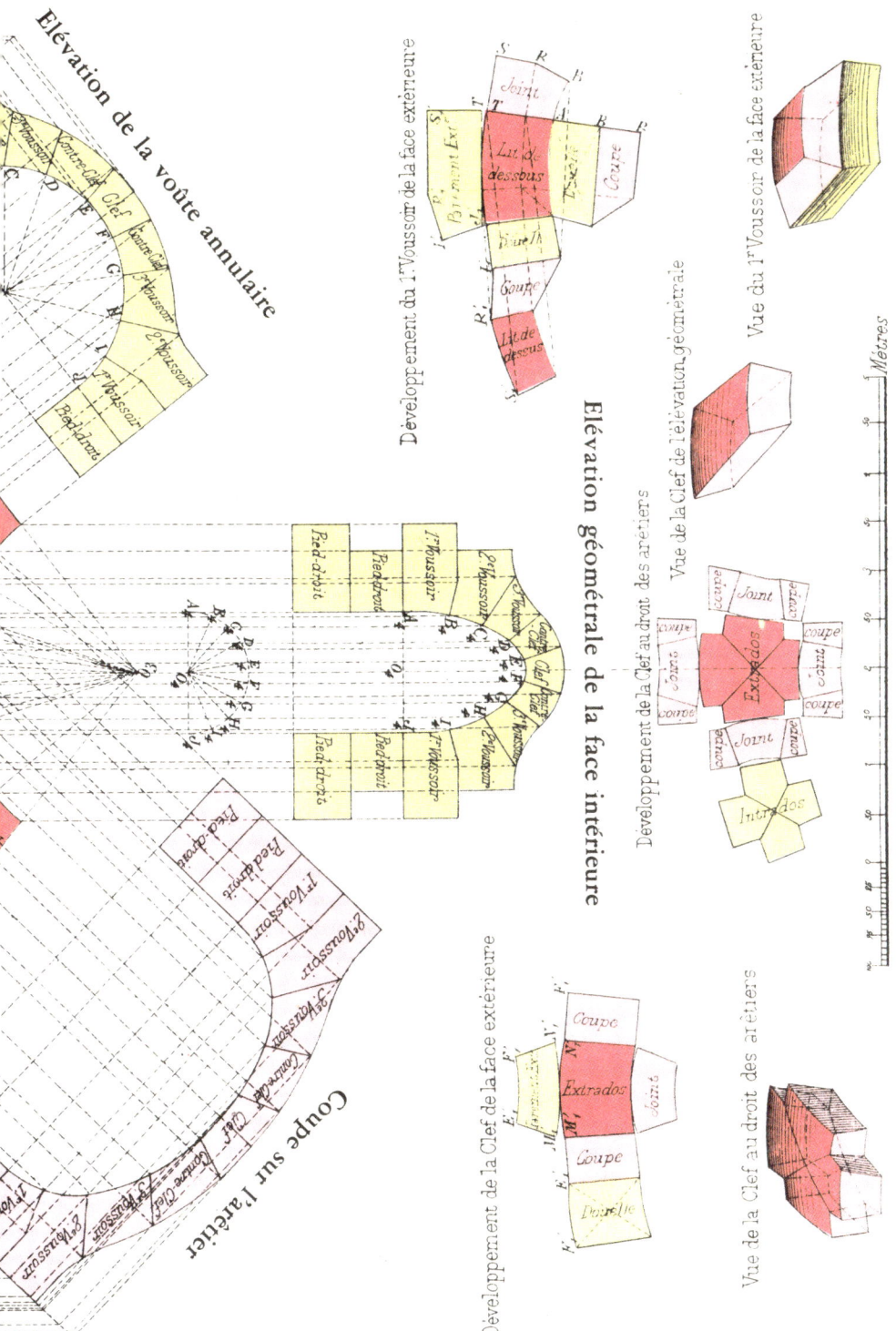

Élévation de la voûte annulaire

Coupe sur l'arcier

Développement du 1.ᵉʳ Voussoir de la face extérieure

Élévation géométrale de la face intérieure

Développement de la Clef de la face extérieure

Développement de la Clef au droit des arétiers

Vue de la Clef au droit des arétiers

Vue du 1.ᵉʳ Voussoir de la face extérieure

Vue de la Clef de l'élévation géométrale

Vue de la Clef au droit des arétiers

Mètres

Louis Monduit's *Traité théorique et pratique de stéréotomie* (1889) presented solutions to many fundamental geometric problems. This distorted vault, an intersection between a cylinder and a torus, illustrates the more sophisticated types of geometric operations architects and craftsmen undertook during the nineteenth century, including the development of unfolded shapes in the discretization of nonstandard curved intersections. These intersections were often conic sections or their derivatives, many of which are mechanically constructible.

besonders erwähnenswerte Instrumente vor. Das erste war ein Konchoidograf für das Zeichnen von konchoiden Kurven, das zweite war ein fortgeschrittener „geometrischer Schreiber".[27] Dieser „Schreiber" war eine von Suardi konstruierte Maschine mit mehrfachen Operationen, die Kurven – von Ellipsen bis hin zu komplexen Epizykloiden – zeichnen konnte. Das Gerät nutzte die kombinatorische Vielfalt von Kurven, die durch Teilbewegungen von zwei oder mehr Kreisen gebildet werden, die sich entlang ihrer Kreislinien abrollen. Der geometrische Schreiber ist so konstruiert, dass sich die Radien, Rollgeschwindigkeiten und Längen der Fahrstifthalter verschieden einstellen lassen, so dass mit dem Gerät Hunderte von geraden Linien und Kurvenformen wie Kreise, Ellipsen sowie gewöhnliche, verkürzte oder verlängerte Zykloide erzeugt werden können.[28] In vielerlei Hinsicht wurde Suardis geometrischer Schreiber zum Standard, an dem später entwickelte technische Zeichengeräte des 19. Jahrhunderts gemessen wurden. Tatsächlich weisen etliche der besten Ellipsografen nur leicht veränderte Methoden auf.

Das in diese Instrumente gewissermaßen eingebaute Wissen machte unter Umständen den Erwerb des geometrischen Entwurfswissens durch den Zeichner überflüssig, so zum Beispiel wenn es um die Konstruktion komplexer Figuren ging, insbesondere von Kegelschnitten wie etwa Ellipsen. Infolge dieser Verkapselung war der Weg frei für die spätere noch weiter gehende Mechanisierung der Form.

Neue Bereiche des Geometriewissens

Die Speicherung von Entwurfswissen, speziell des Geometriewissens, in mechanischen Zeichengeräten nahm im Laufe des 19. Jahrhunderts rasch zu. Dies wurde sowohl durch neue Erkenntnisse zur Geometrie von Kurven und gekrümmten Flächen und durch die Entwicklung präziserer, skalierbarer Techniken im Maschinenbau vorangetrieben. Insbesondere eröffnete die projektive Geometrie neue Wege für mechanische Entwicklungen: „Es war natürlich, dass mit der Weiterentwicklung der projektiven Geometrie, die sich der geometrischen Konstruktion geradezu anbietet, andere Methoden zur Konstruktion von Kegelschnitten entstehen sollten."[29] Diese Entwicklung verlief wechselseitig: Der Bedarf an präzisen Bauzeichnungen förderte die Entwicklung von Präzisionsinstrumenten, während die Verfügbarkeit dieser Instrumente neue Arten von Zeichnungen – und damit neue geometrische Ansätze – ermöglichte.

In der Mathematik erklärten einige erstaunliche neue Theorien die Möglichkeiten und Grenzen mechanischer Instrumente bei der Darstellung von Kurven und gekrümmten Flächen. Ende der 1820er Jahre schlug der französische Mathematiker Évariste Galois eine bemerkenswerte, abstrakte algebraische Herangehensweise zur geometrischen Kalkulation vor, die schließlich bewies, dass für die Konstruktion bestimmter Grundkurven und -figuren der Kompass allein nicht ausreicht. Damit zeigte sich, dass höher entwickelte Maschinen nötig sein würden, die in der Lage wären, gleichzeitig mehrere Teilbewegungen auszuführen, um ein breites Spektrum geschwungener Formen zu entwerfen.

Eine weitere wichtige Theorie entwickelte der französische Mathematiker und Physiker Gaspard Monge mit seinem Werk zur darstellenden Geometrie, *Géométrie descriptive* (1799). Darin systematisierte er die mathematische Darstellung dreidimensionaler Objekte auf einer zweidimensionalen Darstellungsebene, mit deren Prinzipien und Didaktik er sich in den Jahren zuvor beschäftigt hatte. Seine neue Methode, Kurven und gekrümmte Flächen im Raum darzustellen, lieferte ein wesentlich umfassenderes und flexibleres System als die typische orthografische Projektion, und da Monge sie (unter anderem an der Pariser École Polytechnique) lehrte, ermöglichte seine darstellende Geometrie bereits zu Beginn des 19. Jahrhunderts anspruchsvolle Darstellungen in Architektur und Ingenieurwissenschaften.

27 Adams 1795 [1791]: 152.
28 Adams 1795 [1791]: 151.
29 Horsburgh 1914: 256 [Dt. Übers.: Susanne Schindler].

34 Burry/Coll Grifoll/Gomez Serrano 2008: 18.
35 Burry/Coll Grifoll/Gomez Serrano 2008: 70.
36 Piedmont-Palladino 2007: 42.
37 Stanley 1878: 77; ICE 1851: 245.
38 Stanley 1878: 85.
39 Stanley 1878: 72.
40 Ein herausragendes Beispiel einer solchen Maschine befindet sich in der Harvard Collection of Historical Scientific Instruments, Inventory 5120.

students to the use of ruled surfaces and surface intersections in the design of spaces.[34] In the Sagrada Família the result is that the deployment of ruled surfaces for spatial design is pervasive. One particularly striking example is in the frames of certain windows, which are themselves hyperbolas of revolution, and whose intersections then may be constructed as projected ellipses.[35] Though exceptional, Gaudi's work is characteristic of the prevalent use of advanced geometric knowledge in the design of space toward the end of the nineteenth century.

The work of Monge and his successors greatly expanded design knowledge, but also created new technical requirements for architects hoping to deploy his methods. Monge's approach had a mathematical rigor, and without the aid of mechanical tools, production of the requisite drawings was intricate and time-consuming work. Projective methods required extensive use of auxiliary views at irregular or oblique angles, which in turn required mechanical compasses. The development of curved geometries was even more labor intensive: point-by-point projection and interpolation was often required for even the simplest of curves. In addition, many of the distorted shapes or intersections between shapes derived through projective constructions were ideally drawn by machine, which was quicker and more accurate than point-by-point projections. The complexity of design ambition in the nineteenth century thus contributed to the need for machines that could encapsulate these geometric operations in a simple and repeatable way. Ultimately, it led to the need to transform design knowledge into instrumental knowledge by way of the machine.

Nineteenth-Century Knowledge Machines

The new geometric methods created more urgent requirements for tools that could encapsulate complex geometric operations to rapidly—almost algorithmically—assist the designer in generating these projections or intersections. The construction of conic sections—ellipses, parabolas, hyperbolas—was particularly key, since these frequently occur-

ring sections are the surface intersections and projected images of more sophisticated figures. The English geologist and writer John Farey proposed one of the first influential mechanical tools for the construction of ellipses in 1813.[36] Known as ellipsographs, they provided more regularity and controlled variability than previous methods of ellipse construction. In particular, they allowed the construction of figures with a greater range of major and minor axes than the classical elliptical trammel. Soon tools began to emerge to represent other, more complex curves as well, often with specifically architectural applications. Various types of helicographs for the drawing of logarithmic spirals, the volutes of Ionic columns, and the traces of spiral staircases were introduced and patented by F. C. Penrose in 1850.[37] English machinist William Ford Stanley's conchoidograph for the representation of the profile of classical columns followed, although based on principles detailed by Suardi a century before.[38] Stanley was particularly prolific, designing ellipsographs, conchoidographs, and various spirographs for the production of complex curves, as well as pantographs for the interactive mechanical replication of drawings. Architects also designed their own instruments: In 1871, the Englishman Edward Burstow designed a complex ellipsograph that was considered by contemporaries among the best.[39] Stanley adapted Bustow's design for his own ellipsographs, produced later.[40]

Perhaps the most sophisticated of such machines was the clampylograph, designed by the physicist and meteorologist Marc Dechevrens around 1900. This intricate device featured several compound motions but could replicate a vast range of curves, over 979 distinct types, including all of the conic sections and a range of cycloids and epicycloids.

Besonders bemerkenswert war Monges Lösung für bestimmte Kegelschnitte von Gewölbeverschneidungen. Er zeigte damit, wie man in Handzeichnungen die Überschneidungen allgemeiner Prismen- und Zylinderflächen (Extrusionsflächen) darstellt, und wies den Weg zu einem voll und ganz räumlichen Verständnis komplizierterer Kurvengeometrien. Außerdem stellte er ausdrücklich fest, dass die korrekte Handhabung von Maschinen in der Geometrie unabdingbar ist, und vertrat die Überzeugung, dass die Beherrschung der räumlichen Geometrie ein Schlüsselfaktor für die Entwicklung der französischen Maschinenindustrie sei.[30]

Alle diese Erkenntnisse hatten unmittelbare Auswirkungen auf die Stereotomie (den Steinschnitt komplexer dreidimensionaler Körper) und auf den theoretischen Diskurs der projektiven Geometrie (die Darstellung dreidimensionaler Körper mittels linearer oder ebenflächiger Projektion). Monges Methoden ermutigten seine Zeitgenossen und Nachfolger dazu, die Beziehungen zwischen dem geometrischen Entwurfswissen und sämtlichen praktischen Arbeitsschritten im Bauwesen vom architektonischen Entwurf bis zur Konstruktion von Gebäuden, insbesondere beim Zimmern und Natursteinschneiden zu untersuchen. Im 19. Jahrhundert veröffentlichten Professoren, die zugleich Handwerksmeister waren – darunter Jean-Paul Douliot, Charles-François-Antoine Leroy, Louis Monduit und Louis Mazerolle – praktische Lehrbücher über Steinschnitt und projektive Geometrie. Architekten interessierten sich besonders für die gestalterischen Möglichkeiten, die ihnen diese neuartigen projektiven Oberflächen eröffneten, und machten die Oberflächengeometrie zu einem Gegenstand des Entwurfswissens.

Douliots *Traité spécial de coupe des pierres* (1825) verfolgt einen spezifisch taxonomischen Ansatz. Er klassifiziert darin die Arten von Oberflächen, die er für das Bauen am besten geeignet hält, darunter Regelflächen, das heißt Flächen, die durch die Bewegung einer erzeugenden Linie im Raum entstehen. Des Weiteren klassifiziert er einfach und

doppelt gekrümmte Flächen, Oberflächen von Zylindern und Kegeln, ellipsoide sowie andere, noch komplexer geformte Arten von Flächen. Da sein *Traité* aber als praktisches Lehrbuch über das Bauen gedacht war, beschreibt er darin ausführlich auch die für Wände geeigneten Flächen – ob lotrecht, zylindrisch geneigt oder konisch – und deren Zerlegung in Steine der jeweils geeigneten geometrischen Typologie.[31] Ebenso ausführlich widmet er sich den Lösungen für die Erstellung von Kegelgewölben.[32] Das Buch bietet eine bemerkenswerte Synthese der Grundlagen der Architektur im Hinblick auf Entwurf, Geometrie und Konstruktion. Im weiteren Verlauf des 19. Jahrhunderts bereicherten fortschrittliche konzeptuelle Techniken sowohl in der Geometrie als auch in der Technik des unregelmäßigen Natursteinschnitts und der Herstellung unregelmäßig geformter Holzteile das Formenvokabular der Architektur. Außerdem erschienen zahlreiche Lehr- und Handbücher für Architekten, darunter *Cours spécial d'architecture, ou Leçons particulières de géométrie descriptive* von C. Protot (1838). Etliche einschlägige Enzyklopädien wie *La science des artistes* (1844) enthalten Beiträge von Geometern und Architekten, die darin den damaligen Wissensstand der darstellenden Geometrie zusammenfassen. Andere Lehrbücher wurden speziell für Bauhandwerker geschrieben. Charles-François-Antoine Leroys *Traité de stéréotomie, comprenant des applications de la géométrie descriptive* (1844) erklärt zum Beispiel alle wesentlichen Steinschnitt- und Zimmerertechniken der Konstruktion komplexer Bauformen, einschließlich sogenannter Spiral- oder Spindelgewölbe.[33]

Im letzten Viertel des 19. Jahrhunderts waren diese Techniken im Bauwesen bereits allgemeine Praxis, und bei den Publikationen jener Zeit handelt es sich zumeist um grafische Vorzeigeobjekte. Monduits *Traité théorique et pratique de stéréométrie* (1889) präsentiert die anerkannten konstruktiven und

---

30 Monge 1989 [1799]: 4.
31 Douliot 1825: 59.
32 Douliot 1825: 149.
33 Leroy 1844: 64.

[Whitaker 2001: 175.] It probably represented the pinnacle of sophstication in the nine-teenth-century construction of curve-gener-ating devices. The Institut Poincaré in Paris archives one of the few known models.

With such machines, for the first time, calculating and drawing certain types of complex curves—such as the conic intersec-tions between certain solid volumes, or the intersection of certain ruled surfaces—was a matter of simple mechanical operation. Of course, the historical emergence of these machines was enabled by material develop-ments of the industrial revolution in the nine-teenth century; while some of the geometric principles underlying these machines had been articulated before, their precision reproduction required industrialization. Three manufacturing advances in particular made such machines possible. First, the industrial revolution precipitated a host of improve-ments in accuracy, repeatability, and scale that afforded a new level of complexity to machine instruments of all types. Artisanal machine tools from watch making were generalized to large-scale metal manufactur-ing, dramatically increasing the precision of the machining process. This repeatability made it possible for instrument makers to move beyond hand tools and embrace more automated instruments.[41] This most basic repeatability was achieved only at the turn of the nineteenth century, however; a lathe to accurately and reliably thread screws was only invented in 1797.[42] The further standard-ization of machine screws, essential to the development of precise compound machinery, was not substantially underway until the 1830s.

Second, the new precision in mechani-cal components enabled the compound motions necessary for the construction of more complex second-order machines. An example of a first-order machine is a com-pass. Once the radius is fixed, the compass has one degree of freedom, its angle of rotation. An example of a second-order machine is an ellipsograph, or more generally a spirograph. In such machines there are two interrelated compound motions, for instance when a primary rotation moves the

41 Morrison-Low 2007: 187.
42 Morrison-Low 2007: 188.
43 Morrison-Low 2007: 188.

stationary point for a second rotation. This second motion increases the required machi-ning accuracy exponentially, since errors in the first motion will be magnified by the second. Higher-order machines of three or more interlocking motions are also possible, Suardi's geometrical pen being perhaps the clearest example. With the advent of accurate screws to control motion, a second com-pound motion dependent on the results of a first primary motion became precise and reliable. This compounding of motions can be repeated and amplified, but the application of such motions in a nested and recursive way to construct a new range of instruments was a technical leap.

Third, drawing instruments became increasingly associated with calculation and not only conception. They became devices to analyze design, not simply to record de-sign. New machines to calculate quantities directly from drawings afforded new control over sophisticated designs. These machines became a sort of encapsulated knowledge base, able to rapidly follow the rules of cer-tain calculations without the full compre-hension of these rules by the user. The new emphasis on heuristics meant that a whole series of allied disciplines could benefit from the solution of related problems in another, through the use of machines. As Alison Morrison-Low writes: "As problems were solved in one industry, it was immediately realized that the solution was applicable in another where there was a close technical relationship; and it was transmitted to them through the machine tool industry, which 'may be looked upon as constituting a pool or reservoir of skills and technical knowledge which are employed throughout the entire machine-using sectors of the economy.'"[43]

A particularly fascinating example of this type of calculating machine is a series of instruments that translated ideas from differ-ential calculus, such as polar integration, into the mechanical motions of tools. This class of tools, known collectively as planimeters, was invented by the Swiss mathematician

diskretisierten Lösungen zahlreicher grundlegender geometrischer Aufgabenstellungen, einschließlich der Verschneidung von Zylindern und Kegeln. Vielleicht stellt diese Abhandlung das überzeugendste Beispiel für das Ausmaß geometrischer Raffinesse dar, die im 19. Jahrhundert für die Berechnung und Errichtung bautechnisch und künstlerisch anspruchsvoller Konstruktionen (speziell Gewölbe) erforderlich war. Mazerolles *Traité théorique et pratique de charpente* (1895) ergänzt Monduits Werk in vielerlei Hinsicht. Er führt darin die standardmäßigen, aber komplizierten projektiven und stereotomen Verfahren der Verformung von Schalungsbrettern auf der Basis volumetrischer Überschneidungen auf, aus denen sich Schalungsdiagramme für komplexe Dachkonstruktionen ableiten lassen. Mazerolle beschrieb außerdem schlüssige Methoden der Darstellung gebogener Holzbalken, die vielfach das unvermeidliche Ergebnis volumetrischer Überschneidungen sind. In gewisser Weise sind seine Konstruktionen aus Holz noch raffinierter als die aus Naturstein. Insgesamt betrachtet, entsprechen die genannten Publikationen über Zimmerer- und Steinschnitt den Höhepunkt des geometrischen Wissens im Handwerk des 19. Jahrhundert.

Die Erweiterung des Geometriewissens hatte direkte, weitreichende Auswirkungen auf das Bauen des 19. Jahrhunderts. Wohl kein anderer Architekt hat die projektiven und flächenbasierten Methoden mit eindrucksvollerer Wirkung angewandt als Antoni Gaudí beim Entwurf der heute noch unvollendeten Kirche Sagrada Família in Barcelona (Baubeginn: 1882). Gaudís Lehrer in projektiver Geometrie hatte bei Monge studiert, war Anhänger von dessen mathematischer Entwurfslehre und brachte demgemäß seinen Studenten bei, wie man Regelflächen und Flächenüberschneidungen für den Entwurf von Räumen nutzt.[34] Fast alle Räume der Sagrada Família hat Gaudí daher unter Einsatz von Regelflächen gebildet. Ein besonders eindrucksvolles Beispiel ist eine Reihe von Fensteröffnungen: Sie sind von Laibungen in Form von Rotationshyperbeln eingerahmt, deren Überschneidungen zu projizierten Ellipsen zusammengefügt werden können.[35]

Gaudís Werk ist zwar einerseits außergewöhnlich, andererseits aber auch charakteristisch für den Einsatz eines höheren Geometriewissens, das im ausgehenden 19. Jahrhundert in der Architektur zur Anwendung kam.

Die Werke von Monge und seinen Nachfolgern erweiterten das Architekturwissen um ein Vielfaches, erzeugten aber auch Bedarf an neuen technischen Geräten für Architekten, die deren Methoden anwenden wollten. Die von Monge propagierten Entwurfsverfahren erforderten mathematische Genauigkeit, und die Anfertigung der entsprechenden Zeichnungen wäre ohne mechanische Zeichengeräte sehr schwierig und zeitaufwendig gewesen. Die geometrische Projektion erforderte immer wieder zahlreiche zusätzliche Ansichten aus verschiedenen, auch schrägen Blickwinkeln, und dazu brauchte man mechanische Kompasse. Das Zeichnen von Kurvengeometrien war noch arbeitsintensiver und erforderte häufig Punkt-für-Punkt-Projektionen und Interpolationen – selbst für einfachste Kurven. Außerdem ließen sich viele der gekrümmten oder überschnittenen Formen, die durch Projektionen entstanden waren, viel besser maschinell zeichnen, was schneller ging und präziser war als Punkt-für-Punkt-Projektionen. Komplexe Ansprüche an den Entwurf trugen im 19. Jahrhundert also zum Bedarf an Maschinen bei, die diese geometrischen Arbeitsschritte auf einfache und wiederholbare Weise ausführen konnten. Letzten Endes führte dies zur Notwendigkeit, mittels der Maschine Entwurfswissen in Instrumentenwissen umzuwandeln.

Wissens-Maschinen des 19. Jahrhunderts

Neuentwicklungen auf dem Gebiet geometrischer Darstellungsweisen verursachten also den dringenden Bedarf an Werkzeugen, mit denen entwerfende Architekten komplexe geometrische Darstellungen wie Perspektiven oder Überschneidungen rasch – fast algorithmisch – anfertigen konnten. Die Konstruktion von Kegelschnitten (Ellipsen, Parabeln,

34 Burry/Coll Grifoll/Gomez Serrano 2008: 18.
35 Burry/Coll Grifoll/Gomez Serrano 2008: 70.

Jakob Amsler-Laffon in 1854, and was based on certain boundary line integrals.[44] Amsler's planimeter could be used to mechanize the process of determining the area of non-standard figures by simply tracing the outline of a curve and calculating the area through a series of interrelated counting dials.[45] Planimeters enjoyed robust sales among engineers, architects, and planners into the early twentieth century, Amsler himself selling many thousands of units.[46] Amsler went on to develop more sophisticated iterations of this planimeter, including a version that could calculate spherical areas. So compelling were these new mechanical instruments for integration that in the second half of the nineteenth century even the illustrious physicist James Clerk Maxwell, author of the synthetic electromagnetic theory, was proposing his own variations on it.[47] Just as differential calculus had sublimated arithmetic operations to continuous analysis, these new machines allowed the control and analysis of a new scope of nonstandard forms and volumes.

The result of these three technological developments was a range of machines that each encapsulated specific advanced geometric procedures, with particular implications for design. Devices such as elliptical and semi-elliptical trammels automated the design of eccentric arches.[48] The ellipsograph encapsulated design knowledge that provided an exact way to represent the intersection of cylinders of equal radii. Such machines became standard enough that technical treatises began to recommend the use of the ellipsograph in design.[49] Some of the most sophisticated instruments addressed design problems from antiquity. The precise proportions and curves that describe the classical orders, for example, were a matter of rigorous and laborious precision.[50] As such, they were ideal for mechanization. Helicographs encapsulated the surprisingly complex design rules of ionic columns and certain types of staircases. And conchoidographs captured the equally complex design knowledge needed to describe exactly classically proportioned columns. In a sense, these tools were like

44 Stanley 1878: 249.
45 Stanley 1878: 249.
46 Murray 1898: 188.
47 Thomson 1875/76: 262.
48 Stanley 1878: 68.
49 Ashpitel 1867: 183.
50 Carpo 2003: 448.
51 Lee 1995: 171.
52 Hambly 1988: 91.
53 Lee 1995: 173.

custom software applications for each of these specific design problems. They augmented the forms conceivable by the architect, and systematized the use of complex curves within design.

The knowledge underlying geometric constructions as well as the mechanical means for their execution evolved profoundly during the nineteenth century. Through the expansion of geometric understanding of second-degree curves, such as conic sections, and of surfaces, such as ruled and extrusion surfaces, architects, engineers, scientists, and draftsmen created new demand for what were essentially computation machines for the calculation of spatial forms. Design and geometric knowledge was encapsulated in instruments, and this encapsulated knowledge enabled the more facile articulation of complex projective forms. Increasingly sophisticated machines in turn were put to use in the drawing machine industry itself, elevated the industry that created them, making new applications possible and allowing the design of yet more sophisticated machines.

The porosity between drafting and scientific instrumentation and their interdependence in cycles of innovation is exemplified by Joseph Clement, a well-known draftsman and one of the foremost makers of precision instruments in nineteenth-century Britain.[51] Clement won national recognition for the design of mechanical drawing instruments, particularly those for the construction of ellipses, and worked extensively on the manufacture of automatic machine tools.[52] But his most remarkable collaboration was in the construction of Charles Babbage's difference engine, the first large-scale mechanical computation device, between 1824 and 1833.[53] As the principal engineer behind its execution, Clement drafted and planned the

Andrew J. Witt
A Machine Epistemology

Candide No. 3, 12/2010
Essay

Hyperbeln) war von besonderer Bedeutung, da diese überall vorkommen und die Flächenüberschneidungen und Projektionen von noch viel komplizierteren Gebilden darstellen. Der englische Geologe und Schriftsteller John Farey erfand 1813 eines der ersten bahnbrechenden mechanischen Instrumente für das Zeichnen von Ellipsen,[36] das als Ellipsograf bekannt wurden und eine regelmäßigere, geregeltere Abänderung von Ellipsen ermöglichte als frühere Verfahren. Insbesondere erlaubten sie die Konstruktion von Figuren mit einer größeren Bandbreite an Haupt- und Nebenachsen als die klassischen Ellipsenzirkel es ermöglichten. Schon bald kamen weitere Instrumente auf, mit denen andere, komplexere Kurven erzeugt werden konnten, von denen viele in der Architektur zum Einsatz kamen. F. C. Penrose führte 1850 verschiedene Varianten des Helikografen zur Darstellung logarithmischer Spiralen (zum Beispiel Voluten ionischer Säulen oder Spirallinien einer Wendeltreppe) ein und ließ sie patentieren.[37] Im Folgenden erfand der englische Mechaniker William Ford Stanley seinen *conchoidograph* zur Darstellung des Profils klassischer Säulen, wobei das Instrument auf den Prinzipien beruhte, die Suardi bereits ein Jahrhundert früher ausgeführt hatte.[38] Stanley war besonders produktiv und entwickelte Ellipsografen, Konchoidografen (Muschelkurvenzirkel) und verschiedene Spirografen für komplexe Kurven sowie Pantografen für die interaktive mechanische Vervielfältigung von Zeichnungen. Auch Architekten bauten Instrumente, zum Beispiel der Engländer Edward Burstow, der 1871 einen hoch leistungsfähigen Ellipsografen konstruierte, den Zeitgenossen für den besten hielten.[39] Stanley passte Bustows Entwurf für seine eigenen Ellipsografen an, die er später herstellen ließ.[40]

Die vielleicht fortgeschrittenste dieser Maschinen war der *clampylograph*, der um 1900 von dem Physiker und Meteorologen Marc Dechevrens entwickelt wurde. Dieses Gerät verband mehrere Teilbewegungen aber konnte eine großes Spektrum an Kurven, über 979 verschiedene Formen, inklusive aller konischen Schnitte und eine Reihe von Zykloiden und Epizykloiden, replizieren. [Whitaker 2001: 175.] Das Gerät stellte möglicherweise den Höhepunkt der Verfeinerung im Bau von kurvengenerierenden Geräten im 19. Jahrhundert dar. Das Institut Poincaré in Paris verfügt über eines der wenigen bekannten Exemplare.

Derartige Maschinen machten die Berechnung und Anfertigung von Zeichnungen bestimmter komplexer Kurven, zum Beispiel der Überschneidungskurven von massiven Körpern oder bestimmter Regelflächen, zu einer einfachen mechanischen Arbeit. Natürlich war der Siegeszug dieser Geräte erst durch die Industrialisierung des 19. Jahrhunderts möglich geworden. Während einige der geometrischen Prinzipien, die diesen Maschinen zu Grunde lagen, schon früher benannt worden waren, ermöglichte erst die Industrialisierung deren präzise Vervielfältigung. Besonders drei fortschrittliche Entwicklungen waren dafür verantwortlich. Erstens beschleunigte die Industrialisierung eine Fülle von Verbesserungen im Hinblick auf Präzision, Wiederholbarkeit und Produktionsmengen, was zur Folge hatte, dass mechanische Geräte aller Art wesentlich komplexer wurden. Uhrmacherwerkzeuge wurden für die Massenfertigung von Metallwaren in Produktionsmaschinen „übersetzt“, was die Präzision der maschinellen Fertigung erheblich steigerte. Die Wiederholbarkeit machte es möglich, dass Werkzeugmacher und Gerätebauer nun nicht nur Handwerkzeuge sondern auch mechanisch-automatische Werkzeuge einsetzen konnten.[41] In ihrer Grundform setzte sich die serielle Fertigung allerdings erst um die Wende zum 19. Jahrhundert allgemein durch. Eine Drehbank, auf der man Schraubengewinde präzise schneiden konnte, wurde zum Beispiel erst 1797 erfunden.[42]

36 Piedmont-Palladino 2007: 42.
37 Stanley 1878: 77; ICE 1851: 245.
38 Stanley 1878: 85.
39 Stanley 1878: 72.
40 Ein herausragendes Beispiel einer solchen Maschine befindet sich in der Harvard Collection of Historical Scientific Instruments, Inventory 5120.
41 Morrison-Low 2007: 187.
42 Morrison-Low 2007: 188.

interworkings of hundreds of high-precision machined components. Babbage's project to create a machine for the automatic mechanical calculation of logarithm tables marks the most ambitious and systematic attempt at automatic computation, and prefigures in many ways the digital computers of today. It is remarkable that at the center of the project was a draftsman who was intimately involved in the creation of drawing machines for complex curves.

In this way, the development of complex drawing instruments in the early nineteenth century enabled the design of the first mechanical computer. This mechanical computer was part of a larger trend, exemplified among others by Amsler's planimeters, of simultaneously mechanizing and spatializing calculus-based computation. Although Babbage's machine is perhaps the most spectacular example, it is interesting to note that many contemporaries also saw the value of mechanizing computation, and that some of the resulting devices functioned in the service of design, planning, and architecture. It is not an exaggeration to say that the impulse to design ever more complex curves and develop the related drawing machines engendered the knowledge required to design a large-scale mechanical computation device.

Conclusion: Machine Epistemology and its Disruptions

The nineteenth century saw an explosion of design knowledge in the form of new geometric methods, which in turn were enabled by geometric knowledge encapsulated in particular drawing and analytic machines. Encapsulated within these machines, this geometric knowledge could be simulated by the user through the instrumental knowledge of machine use. This created a much more efficient and reliable way to access this knowledge, but also created a certain reliance on the machine itself.

The case of the nineteenth-century drawing machines illustrates that advances in design knowledge and instrumental knowledge are often complementary, even symbiotic: one enables the understanding and expansion of the other. Design knowledge and, more particularly, geometric knowledge, drive the need for new tools, and these new tools in turn allow the discovery or creation of more advanced design knowledge. Similarly, in our time, advanced geometry software has been the catalyst for the introduction of many particular concepts that were once considered outside the realm of design: surface geometry, mathematical parametrics, even aspects of process control and automation. In effect this dialog between geometry and machine has fundamentally expanded design knowledge.

Of course a potential risk of this view is that once design knowledge has been encapsulated in a machine process, access to it becomes dependant on both instrumental knowledge of the machine and on the machine itself. The tool and the knowledge that it encapsulates enable or disable the designer in the act of design. A loss of knowledge about a particular instrumental machine operation could very well mean loss of access to the utility of the underlying knowledge, particularly if this knowledge is highly specialized and not readily available in the architectural community itself. This is the case with some particularly complex geometric constructions, which are the purview of mathematical specialists; if the instrumental knowledge were lost, there would be no comparably advanced geometric knowledge to replace the loss. In short, after its transition from design knowledge to instrumental knowledge, instrumental knowledge becomes fundamental to the process of design itself and thus integral to architectural knowledge.

A loss of instrumental knowledge can be induced in many ways, not the least of which is a change in designers' attitudes and tastes. I argue that the advent of early twentieth-century modernism induced just such a change. It marginalized the remarkable nineteenth-century developments of complex drawing instruments by understanding the value of the machine in architecture in a fundamentally altered way.

Andrew J. Witt
A Machine Epistemology

Candide No. 3, 12/2010
Essay

Die mechanische Vorgeschichte des computergestützten Entwerfens

The Mechanical Prehistory of Design Computation

1752
Giambattista Suardi entwickelt einen „geometrischen Schreiber", der durch den Einsatz mehrerer miteinander verbundener Teilbewegungen komplexe Kurven zeichnen kann.

1791
George Adams veröffentlicht *Geometrical and Graphical Essays*, in denen die erste englischsprachige Beschreibung von Suardis Maschine erscheint. Die deutsche Ausgabe von Adams' Werk folgt 1795.

1799
Gaspard Monge veröffentlicht mit *Géométrie descriptive* einen systematischen Zugang zur grafischen Kalkulation von Kurven, Oberflächen und deren Überschneidungen.

1813
John Farey stellt einen mechanischen Ellipsografen vor.

1822
Charles Babbage beginnt seine Arbeit an der *difference engine*.

1838
C. Protot veröffentlicht *Cours spécial d'architecture, ou Leçons particulières de géométrie descriptive*.

1850
F.C. Penrose stellt einen Helikografen vor.

1871
Edward Burstow, Architekt, entwickelt einen fortgeschrittenen Ellipsografen.

1883
Antoni Gaudí beginnt mit den Entwürfen für Sagrada Família auf der Grundlage von Regelflächen und projektiven Oberflächen.

1884
Hermann Holerith kreiert einen Rechner auf elektromechanischer Grundlage. Das Zeitalter mechanischer Rechenmaschinen ist damit abgeschlossen.

1889
Louis Monduit veröffentlicht *Traité théorique et pratique de stéréometrie*.

1900
Marc Dechevrens erfindet den *campylograph* für die Erzeugung von Lissajous-Kurven.

1915
William F. Rigge erfindet die Creighton Compound Harmonic Motion Machine, eine der fortgeschrittensten Instrumente für die mechanische Produktion von Kurven. Sie ähnelt Babbages *difference engine*, einer allgemeinen Rechenmaschine für Kurven.

1958
Le Corbusier und Iannis Xenakis entwerfen den Philips-Pavillon, der aus hyperbolischen Paraboloiden zusammengesetzt ist.

1959
Paul de Casteljau beschreibt eine Kurve, die sich für rechnerbasierte Applikationen gut eignet. Diese Kurve entspricht im Wesentlichen der Bezier-Kurve, der Vorläuferin heutiger NURBS-Kurven.

1962
Desmond Paul Henry stellt seine erste rechnerbasierte Zeichenmaschine aus, die teilweise von Suardis Arbeiten inspiriert ist.

1962
Miguel Fisac entwirft die Laboratorios JORBA, eines der ersten Beispiele einer neuen Generation von Experimenten mit Regelflächen in der Architektur.

1963
Das DAC-1 (Design Augmented by Computer), von IBM und GM entwickelt, ist eines der ersten Systeme, das eine digitale Visualisierung im Entwurfsprozess ermöglicht.

1968
Die Ausstellung Cybernetic Serendipity in London versammelt Vorreiter des rechnerbasierten Entwerfens, darunter Desmond Paul Henry sowie Architekten, die den Computer für generative Fassadenmuster einsetzen.

1997
Frank O. Gehry wird mit dem Guggenheim-Museum Bilbao beauftragt, einem der ersten Bauten, bei denen eine umfassend von Entwurf bis Umsetzung eine 3D-CAD-Technologie eingesetzt wird.

1752. Giambattista Suardi proposes a geometrical pen for the design of curves from the compound motion of several gears.

1791. George Adams publishes his *Geometrical and Graphical Essays*, including the first description of Suardi's machine in English.

1799. Gaspard Monge publishes *Géométrie descriptive*, a systematic approach to the visual calculation of curves, surfaces, and their intersections.

1813. John Farey introduces his mechanical ellipsograph.

1822. Charles Babbage begins work on his difference engine.

1838. C. Protot publishes his *Cours spécial d'architecture, ou Leçons particulières de géométrie descriptive*.

1850. F.C. Penrose introduces his helicograph.

1871. Edward Burstow, an architect, designs an advanced ellipsograph.

1883. Antoni Gaudí begins his designs for Sagrada Família, with pervasive use of ruled and projective surfaces.

1884. Hermann Holerith creates a computer based on electromechanical principles, ending the age of mechanical calculating machines.

1889. Louis Monduit publishes his *Traité théorique et pratique de stéréotomie*.

1900. Marc Dechevrens invents the campylograph for the production of compound Lissajous curves.

1915. William F. Rigge invents the Creighton Compound Harmonic Motion Machine, one of the most sophisticated instruments for the mechanical production of curves. Superficially, it resembles Babbage's difference engine, a general calculation machine for curves.

1958. Le Corbusier and Iannis Xenakis design the Philips Pavilion, composed of hyperbolic paraboloids.

1959. Paul de Casteljau describes a type of curve particularly well suited to computation applications. It is essentially the Bezier curve, forerunner of today's NURBS curves.

1962. Desmond Paul Henry exhibits his first computational drawing machine, partially inspired by Suardi's work.

1962. Miguel Fisac designs the Laboratorios JORBA, one of the first examples of a new generation of architectural experiments with ruled surfaces.

1963. The DAC-1 (Design Augmented by Computer), one of the first systems to use digital visualization for design, is developed by IBM and GM.

1968. The Cybernetic Serendipity exhibition in London gathers those working in design computation, including Desmond Paul Henry and architects using the computer for generative façade patterns.

1997. Frank O. Gehry is commissioned with the Guggenheim Museum Bilbao, one of the first buildings to comprehensively use 3D CAD technology from design through assembly.

1800   1900   2000

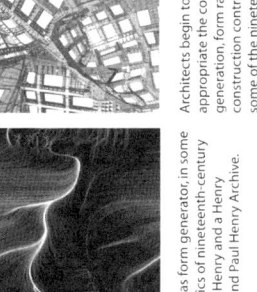
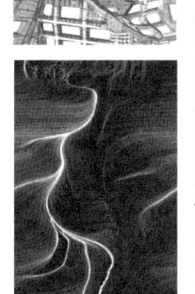
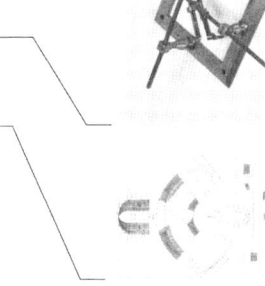
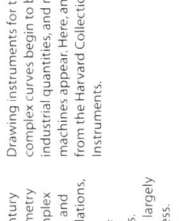
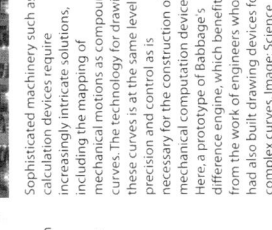

Nineteenth-century projective geometry introduces complex new geometric and spatial manipulations, including the construction of complex curves. Construction is largely a manual process. Here, a plate from Monduit's treatise.

Drawing instruments for the design of complex curves begin to be produced in industrial quantities, and new types of machines appear. Here, an ellipsograph from the Harvard Collection of Scientific Instruments.

Sophisticated machinery such as calculation devices require increasingly intricate solutions, including the mapping of mechanical motions as compound curves. The technology for drawing these curves is at the same level of precision and control as is necessary for the construction of mechanical computation devices. Here, a prototype of Babbage's difference engine, which benefited from the work of engineers who had also built drawing devices for complex curves. Image: Science Museum, London.

Mechanical computers evolve into electromechanical devices, and the first CAD systems for internalizing graphic representation emerge. Engineers engage the computer as a form rationalization tool. Here, the GM.IBM DAC-1, one of the first such graphical interfaces for design. Image: Krull 2004.

At the same time, artists engage the computer as form generator, in some cases repurposing the mechanical drawing logics of nineteenth-century instruments. Here, a machine of Desmond Paul Henry and a Henry drawing produced by machine. Images: Desmond Paul Henry Archive.

Architects begin to comprehensively appropriate the computer for form generation, form rationalization, and construction control, reclaiming some of the nineteenth-century interest in precise geometry and the epistemic consequences of mechanical operations of design. Here, an image from the Lou Ruvo Brain Institute, a Gehry Partners project.

Die projektive Geometrie des 19. Jahrhunderts umfasst komplexe geometrische und räumliche Manipulationen. Diese beinhalten die Konstruktion komplexer Kurven, die hauptsächlich von Hand ausgeführt werden. Hier: eine Tafel aus Louis Monduits Lehrbuch.

Zeicheninstrumente für den Entwurf komplexer Kurven werden industriell und in großen Mengen gefertigt. Neue Maschinen entstehen. Hier: ein Ellipsograf aus der Harvard Collection of Scientific Instruments.

Hochentwickelte Maschinen wie Rechengeräte verlangen nach zunehmend komplexen Lösungen, unter anderem für die Darstellung von mechanischen Bewegungen als zusammengesetzte Kurven. Die Technologie, um diese Kurven zu zeichnen, verlangt den gleichen Grad an Präzision und Kontrolle wie die Konstruktion mechanischer Rechenmaschinen. Hier: ein Prototyp von Babbages *difference engine*, die wesentlich von der Arbeit von Ingenieuren profitierte, die auch Zeichengeräte für komplexe Kurven entwickelt hatten. Abbildung: Science Museum, London.

Mechanische Computer werden durch elektromechanische Apparate abgelöst. Die ersten CAD-Systeme zur integrierten grafischen Darstellung entstehen. Ingenieure setzen den Computer als Werkzeug zur Formrationalisierung ein. Hier: ein Bild des GM.IBM DAC-1, einer der ersten solchen für den Entwurfsprozess geeigneten Schnittstellen. Abbildung: Krull 2004.

Zeitgleich benutzen Künstler den Rechner als Formgenerator. In manchen Fällen werden die Logiken der mechanischen Zeicheninstrumente des 19. Jahrhunderts dafür neu eingesetzt. Hier: eine Maschine von Desmond Paul Henry und eine maschinengenerierte Zeichnung Henrys. Abbildungen: Desmond Paul Henry Archive.

Architekten beginnen, den Computer umfassend zur Formgenerierung und -rationalisierung sowie zur Kontrolle der Bauausführung einzusetzen. Dabei knüpfen sie an das im 19. Jahrhundert gewachsene Interesse an präziser Geometrie und an den epistemischen Konsequenzen mechanischer Operationen im Entwurf an. Hier: eine Darstellung des Lou Ruvo Brain Institute, ein Projekt von Gehry Partners.

Ellipsenzeichner
Seit der Antike

Dieses Instrument zeichnet Ellipsen, deren Haupt-
und Nebenachsen nicht kleiner sind als die
Kreuzform des Instrumentenfußes. Dieser Ellip-
senzeichner lässt in verschiedenen Varianten ohne
Einsatz von Maschinenwerkzeugen anfertigen.
Mit Ellipsen werden Gewölbeverschneidungen
sowie Überschneidungen von zylindrischen Extrusionen und Flächen sowie bestimmte Bogen-
formen dargestellt.

Elliptical Trammel
Since antiquity

This instrument traces an ellipse whose major and
minor axes are no smaller than the cross frame that
forms the base of the instrument. Variations of
this instrument can be readily constructed without
machine tools. Ellipses are used to describe vault
intersections and intersections of cylindrical
extrusions with planes, as well as certain types of
arches.

Ellipsograf
1813 (hier John Fareys Modell)

Mit diesem Gerät zeichnet man Ellipsen, deren
Haupt- und Nebenachsen unendlich klein sein
können. Ellipsografen (auch Elliptografen genannt)
wurden im 19. Jahrhundert ständig weiter entwickelt. Mit Ellipsen werden Gewölbeverschneidungen sowie Überschneidungen von zylindrischen
Extrusionen und Flächen sowie bestimmte Bogen-
formen dargestellt.

Ellipsograph
1813 (Farey model shown)

This instrument traces an ellipse whose major and
minor axes may be infinitely small. Ellipsographs
(or alternatively, elliptographs) were under constant
evolution during the nineteenth century. Ellipses
are used to describe vault intersections and
intersections of cylindrical extrusions with planes,
as well as certain types of arches.

Helikograf
1850 (hier Penrose und Bennets Modell)

Dieses Instrument zeichnet Nicomedische Spiralen, bei denen die sich nach außen bewegenden
Spirallinien immer im gleichen Abstand vom
nächstinneren Zykel verlaufen. Mit Hilfe dieses
Geräts ließen sich die Spiralkurven ionischer
Säulenkapitelle darstellen. Helikografen waren
spätestens seit 1791 in Gebrauch, wurden aber im
19. Jahrhundert ständig weiter entwickelt.

Helicograph
1850 (Penrose and Bennet model shown)

This instrument traces a spiral of Nicomedes. This
spiral is such that each successive outward cycle
of the spiral is equidistant from the next interior
cycle. These curves are used to describe the traces
of Ionic column capitals. Such instruments existed
since at least 1791, although they also evolved
continuously during the nineteenth century.

Planimeter
1854 (hier Jakob Amsler-Laffons Modell)

Mit diesem Instrument werden die Flächeninhalte
unregelmäßig begrenzter Areale berechnet.
Wenn man mit dem Fahrstift eine geschlossene
Kurve zieht, wird die davon umschlossene Fläche
zeitgleich vom Messrad mechanisch integriert.

Planimeter
1854 (Jakob Amsler-Laffon model shown)

This instrument calculates the area of a planar
region with an irregular boundary. Through the
tracing of a closed curve with the planimeter, an
accumulator wheel mechanically integrates the
area bounded by the closed curve.

Konchoidograf
1866 (hier Fabrikat von William Ford Stanley)

Mit diesem Muschelkurvenzirkel werden Nicomedische Konchoide gezeichnet. Konchoide werden
unter anderem dazu benutzt, vertikale Profile
und zum Beispiel die Kannellierung klassischer
Säulen darzustellen. Laut Nicomedes haben die
Säulen des Pantheons konchoide Profile.

Conchoidograph
1866 (William Ford Stanley model shown)

This instrument traces a conchoid of Nicomedes.
Conchoids are used in the description of the vertical
profiles of classical columns or their fluting, among
other uses. According to Nicomedes, the columns
of the Pantheon have profiles which are conchoids.

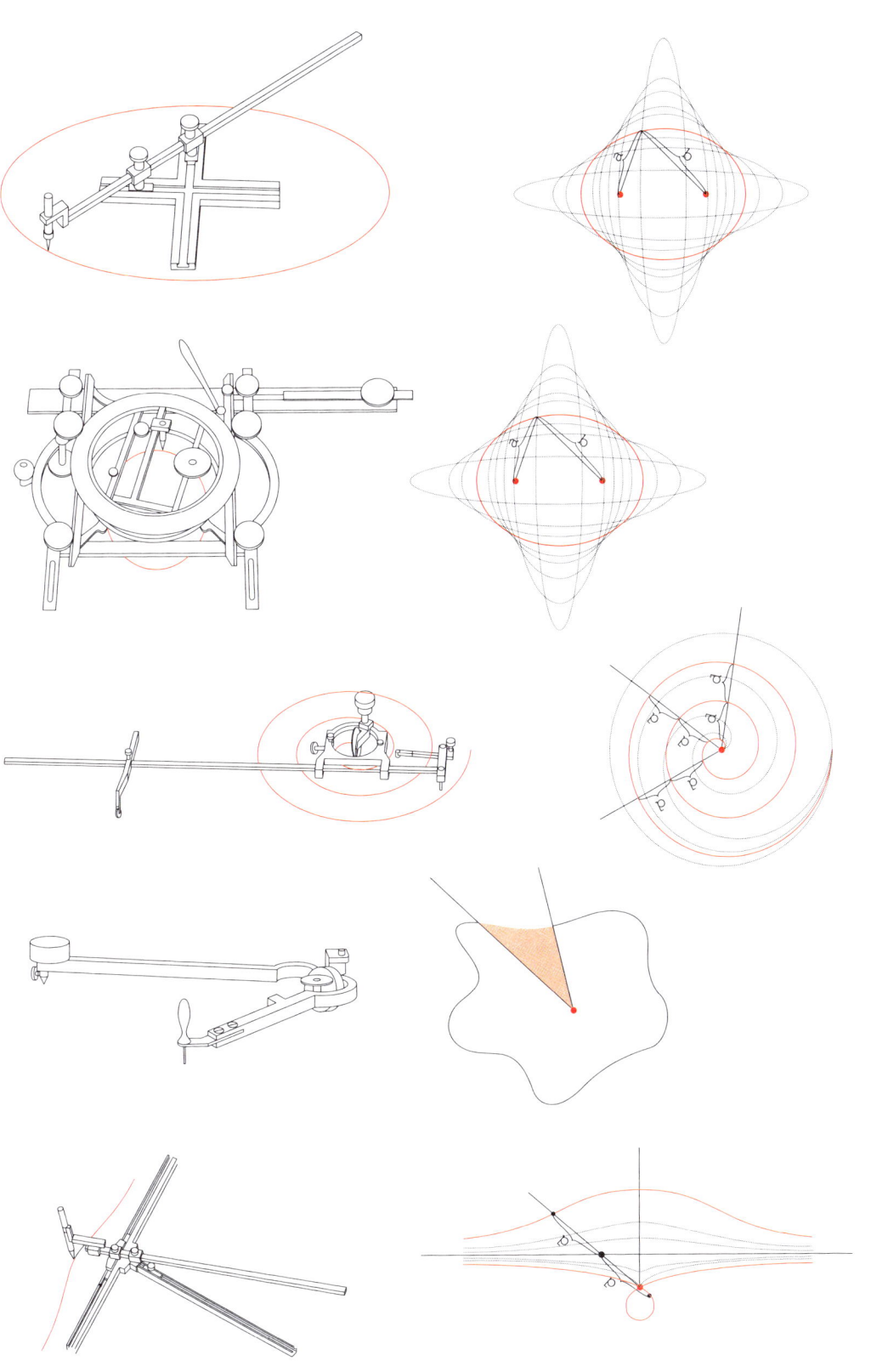

Candide No. 3, 12/2010
Essay

Andrew J. Witt
A Machine Epistemology

Suardis „geometrischer Schreiber"

Der „geometrische Schreiber" wurde 1750 vom Italiener
Giambattista Suardi entwickelt und ist ein Vorläufer zahlreicher späterer Zeichengeräte für komplexe Kurven,
insbesondere für den Einsatz mehrerer miteinander verbundener Teilbewegungen. Siehe auch Seite 79.

Suardi's Geometrical Pen

The geometrical pen (1750) was in instrument designed by
the Italian Giambattista Suardi. This geometrical pen antici-
pated many of the later developments in instruments for
drawing complex curves, including notably the employment
of compound motion. See also page 79.

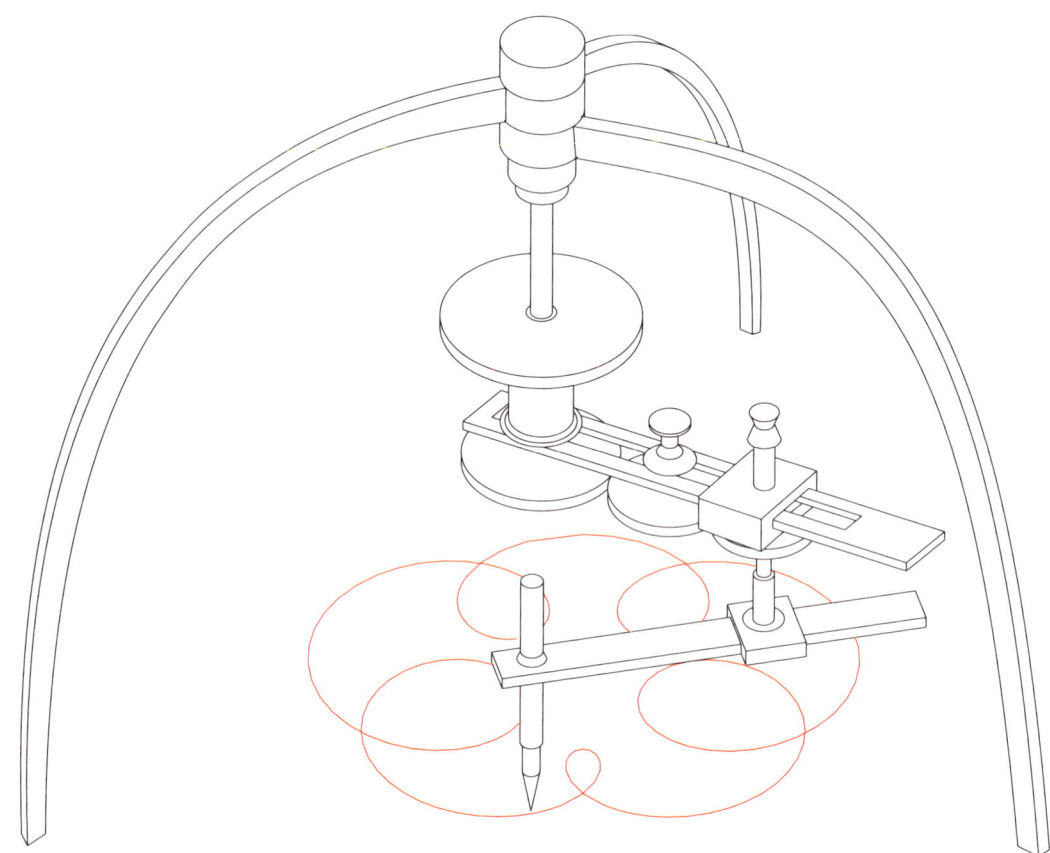

Bei den vom „geometrischen Schreiber" gezogenen Kurven handelt es sich um Verallgemeinerungen einer Kurvenfamilie, die man Zykloide nennt. Im Allgemeinen ist eine Zykloide (oder zyklische Kurve) die Spur, die ein auf einem Kreis festgelegter Punkt hinterlässt, wenn der Kreis etwa – wie unten dargestellt – auf einer geraden Linie entlang rollt. Die abgebildete, einfachste zyklische Kurve nennt man eine gewöhnliche Zykloide.

The curves traced by the geometrical pen are generalizations of the family of curves called cycloids. In general, a cycloid is the trace of a fixed point on the radius of a circle as it rolls continuously along a second curve. Below is the simplest cycloid, traced by a point on the circumference of a curve as it rolls along a line. This simplest cycloid is known as the right cycloid.

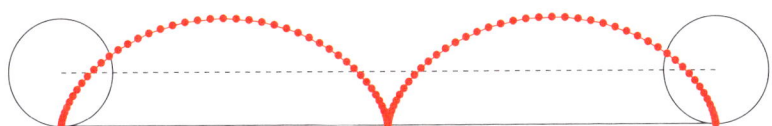

Verschiedene Einstellungen des „geometrischen Schreibers". Weitere Einstellungen mit verschiedenen Radien sind möglich. Mit jeder Einstellung lässt sich eine andere Kurve zeichnen. Laut Suardi gibt es 1200 Kombinationsmöglichkeiten.

1   Zwei Einstellungen mit gleichem Radius: Gerade
2   Zwei Einstellungen mit ungleichen Radien: Ellipse
3   Drei Einstellungen: Zykloide und verschiedene Epizykloide

Below, the distinct gear configurations of the geometrical pen. The number of gears and the gear radii may be modified. Each gear configuration produces a different curve; Suardi claims over 1200 distinct combinatorial possibilities.

1   Two gears of equal radii: line
2   Two gears of unequal radii: ellipse
3   Three gears: cycloids and assorted epicycloids

1

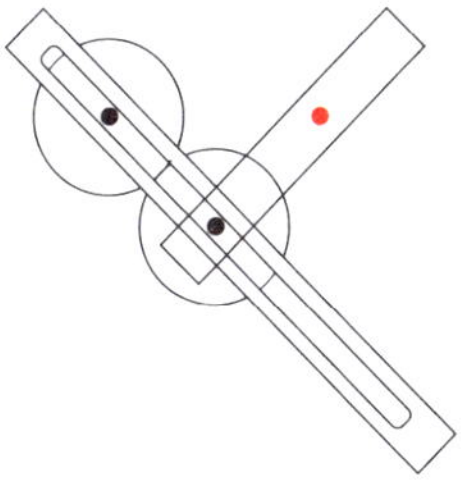

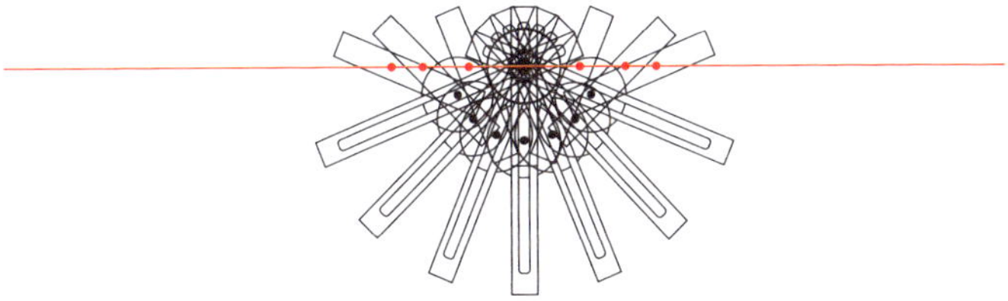

2

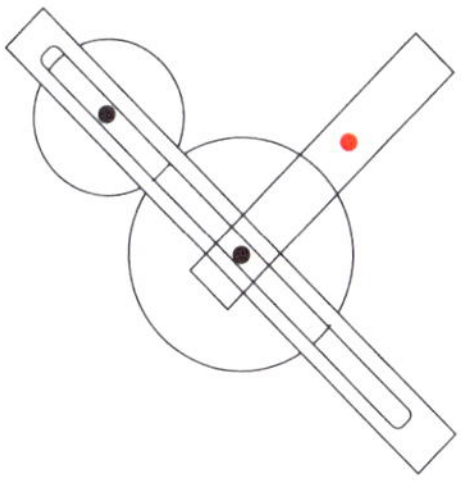

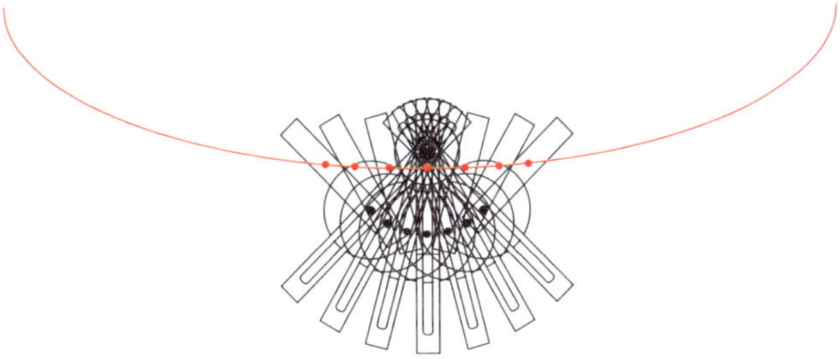

3

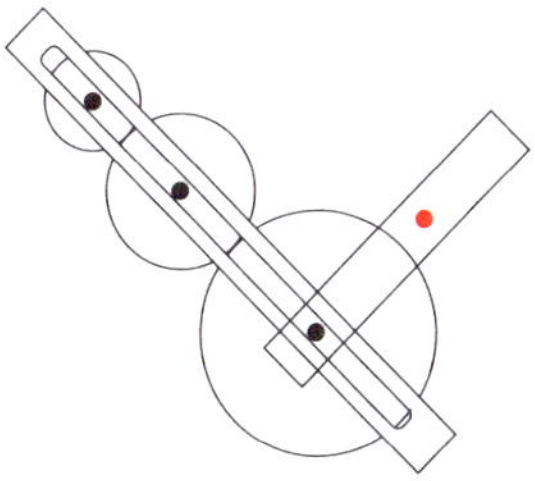

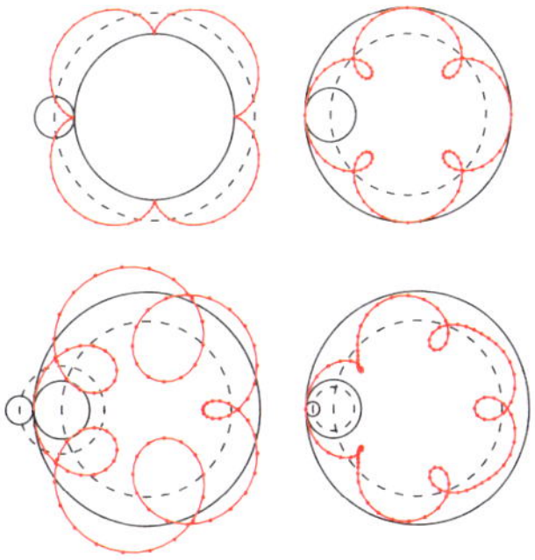

Ellipsograf eines Architekten

Architekten waren nicht nur Benutzer komplexer Zeicheninstrumente, sondern auch deren Designer. Dieser vom Architekten Edward Burstow entwickelte Ellipsograf von 1873 wurde serienmäßig von William Ford Stanleys Instrumentenfabrik hergestellt.

Um es zu benutzen, muss der Kurbelgriff oben auf dem Gerät erst um 360° – einmal ganz um die eigene Achse – gedreht werden. Je nach Winkelstellung der weiteren verstellbaren Teile zeichnet das Gerät verschiedene Ellipsenformen. Rechts: Beispiele der dynamischen Bewegungen dieses Ellipsografen. Siehe auch Seite 81.

An Architect's Ellipsograph

Architects were not only consumers of complex drawing instruments but designers of them as well. This design, dating to 1873, by the architect Edward Burstow, was produced commercially by William Ford Stanley's instruments company.

To operate, the user turns the topmost handle through 360 degrees, a full rotation. Various adjustable travels allow a continuous range of ellipses to be produced. At right, an example of the dynamic motion of this ellipsograph. See also page 81.

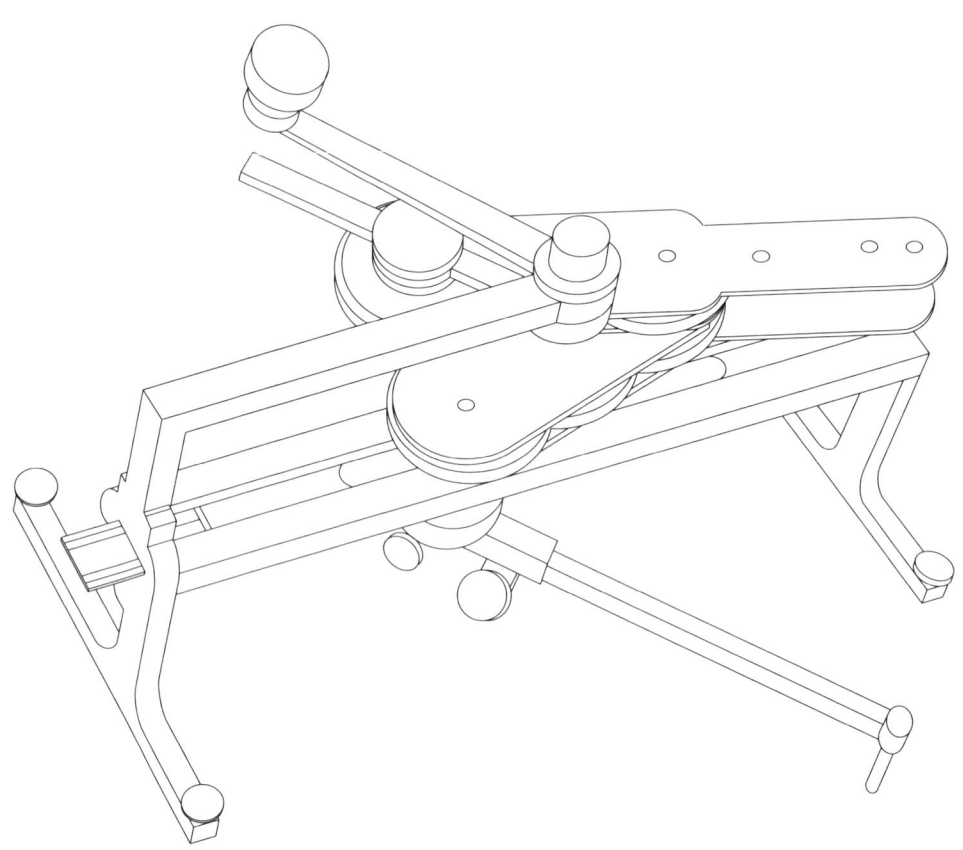

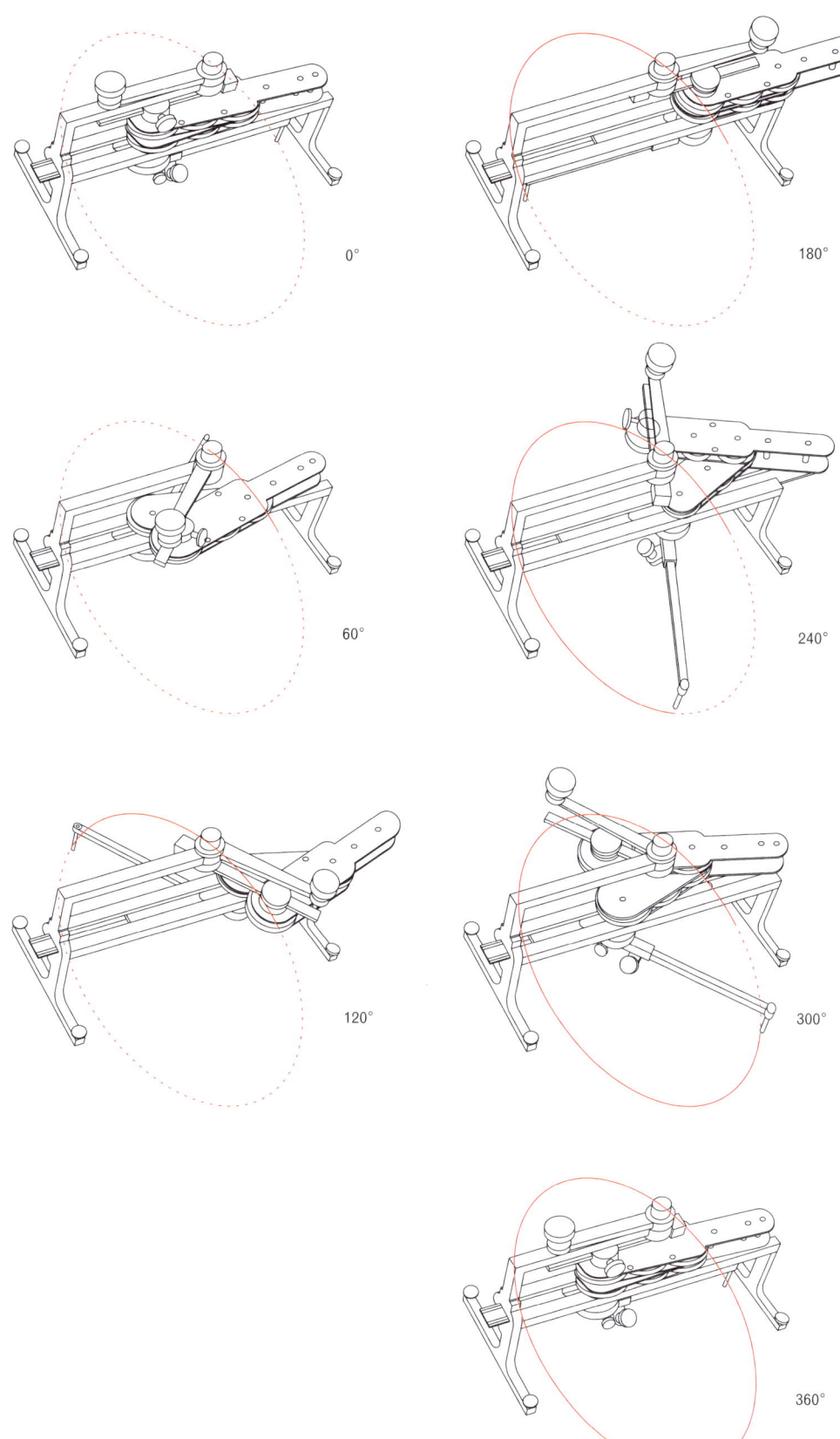

0°

60°

120°

180°

240°

300°

360°

Andrew J. Witt
A Machine Epistemology

Candide No. 3, 12/2010
Essay

Die Standardisierung von Maschinenschrauben – eine unverzichtbare Maßnahme für die Entwicklung von Maschinen, die mehrere Operationen ausführten – erfolgte dagegen in beträchtlichem Umfang erst in den 1830er Jahren.

Zweitens ermöglichte die neue Präzision mechanischer Komponenten die Teilbewegungen, die eine Voraussetzung für den Bau komplexer Maschinen zweiter Ordnung darstellten. Ein Kompass ist zum Beispiel eine Maschine erster Ordnung. Wenn die Windrose erst einmal eingebaut und der Radius fixiert ist, kann die Kompassnadel sich nur auf dieser einen Ebene drehen, hat einen Freiheitsgrad, den Rotationswinkel. Beispiel für eine Maschine zweiter Ordnung ist der Ellipsograf beziehungsweise der Spirograf, weil er zwei voneinander abhängige Teilbewegungen ausführt, wenn eine primäre Drehbewegung den stationären Punkt verschiebt, um eine zweite Rotation zu erzeugen. Diese erhöht die erforderliche Präzision der Fertigung exponentiell, da Fehler in der ersten Bewegung von der zweiten deutlich vergrößert werden. Maschinen noch höherer Ordnung mit drei oder mehr verschränkten Bewegungen sind auch möglich; Suardis geometrischer Stift ist dafür möglicherweise das deutlichste Beispiel. Die Herstellung präziser Schrauben zur Regelung der Bewegungen führte dazu, dass die zweite Teilbewegung des Spirografen (die von der primären abhängig war) mit zuverlässiger Präzision erfolgen konnte. Die Verknüpfung von Bewegungen ließ sich wiederholen und amplifizieren, aber erst die Umsetzung mechanischer Teilbewegungen in geschachtelte, berechenbare Takteinheiten ermöglichte die Konstruktion ganz neuer Instrumente – was eine Revolution in der Entwicklung mechanischer Zeichengeräte auslöste.

Drittens verwandelten sich Zeichengeräte zunehmend in Bemessungshilfen, im Gegensatz zu früher, als sie konzeptionelle Arbeitsmittel waren. Mit den mechanischen Instrumenten konnte man Entwürfe nicht nur aufzeichnen, sondern auch auswerten, und mit den neuen Maschinen für die Ableitung von Mengenberechnungen aus Bauplä-

nen konnten anspruchsvolle Entwürfe besser geprüft werden. Entwurfs- und Zeichengeräte entwickelten sich demnach zu so etwas wie Datenbanken, die in der Lage waren, die Regeln bestimmter Rechenverfahren rasch zu befolgen, ohne dass der Benutzer diese Regeln voll verstehen musste. Eine neue Betonung der Heuristik bedeutete, dass eine ganze Reihe verwandter Disziplinen davon profitieren konnte, wenn ein gemeinsames oder analoges Problem in einem anderen Fachgebiet gelöst wurde, und zwar durch den Einsatz von Maschinen. Alison Morrison-Low schreibt: „Wenn in einem Industriezweig Lösungen für bestimmte Probleme gefunden wurden, erkannte man sofort, dass sie in einem anderen ebenfalls anwendbar waren, wenn zwischen beiden eine enge technische Beziehung bestand. Die Lösung wurde durch die Werkzeugmaschinenindustrie vermittelt, die als Reservoir an fachlichen Qualifikationen und technischen Kenntnissen gelten kann, welche in sämtlichen Wirtschaftszweigen, die Maschinen einsetzen, angewandt werden."[43]

Besonders faszinierende Beispiele dieser Art Rechenmaschinen ist eine Reihe von Instrumenten, welche die Konzepte der Differenzialrechnung (wie etwa die Integration von Polarkoordinaten) in die mechanischen Bewegungen von Werkzeugen übertragen. Diese Art Präzisionsinstrumente werden als Planimeter bezeichnet und basieren auf bestimmten Grenzlinienintegralen.[44] 1854 entwickelte der Schweizer Mathematiker Jakob Amsler-Laffon seinen sogenannten Polarplanimeter, mit dem sich der Flächeninhalt selbst ungewöhnlicher ebener Figuren durch Nachziehen der Grenzlinie mit einem „Fahrstift" mittels einer Reihe zusammenhängender Zählscheiben an einer Skala ablesen ließ.[45] Bis ins frühe 20. Jahrhundert wurden Polarplanimeter von Ingenieuren, Architekten und Stadtplanern gerne gekauft. Amsler wurde Fabrikant und produzierte und verkaufte selbst viele Tausend Stück.[46]

43 Morrison-Low 2007: 188
   [Dt. Übers.: Annette Wiethüchter].
44 Stanley 1878: 249.
45 Stanley 1878: 249.
46 Murray 1898: 188.

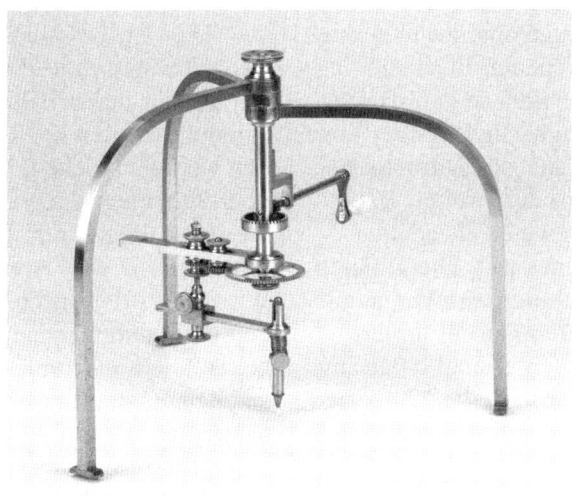

Dieser Ellipsograf, der um 1813 hergestellt wurde, mit dem sich Kurven durch mechanische Teilbewegungen darstellen lassen, hat große Ähnlichkeit mit Giambattista Suardis „geometrischem Schreiber".

This ellipsograph, dating to circa 1813, resembles closely the design proposed by Giambattista Suardi for a geometrical pen, capable of the description of curves of compound mechanical motion.

Dieser Ellipsograf, hergestellt zwischen 1850 und 1870, beruht auf einer relativ standardmäßigen Konstruktionsweise, die für serienmäßig produzierte Instrumente typisch gewesen wäre.

This ellipsograph, fabricated between 1850 and 1870, has a relatively standard design that would have been typical of large-scale production instruments.

Später entwickelte er seinen Polarplanimeter noch weiter und konstruierte unter anderem einen, mit dem sich Kugeloberflächengrößen ermitteln ließen. Diese neuen Flächenbemessungsinstrumente waren so gut, dass selbst der berühmte englische Physiker James Clerk Maxwell, Entdecker des synthetischen Elektromagnetismus, in der zweiten Hälfte des 19. Jahrhunderts seine eigenen, abgewandelten Versionen entwarf.[47] Die Differenzialrechnung hatte arithmetische Vorgänge in fortlaufende Berechnungen sublimiert, und die neuen Maschinen ermöglichten in ähnlicher Weise die Kontrolle und Analyse einer neuen Gruppe unregelmäßiger Flächen- und Rauminhalte.

Diese drei technischen Entwicklungen führten zur Entwicklung einer Reihe von Maschinen, die verschiedene fortschrittliche, spezifische geometrische Mess- und Darstellungstechniken ermöglichten, die sich auf die architektonische Entwurfsarbeit auswirkten. Instrumente wie Ellipsen- und Halbellipsenzirkel erleichterten zum Beispiel die Entwicklung außermittiger Bögen[48] und der Ellipsograf verkörperte das Entwurfswissen über die genaue Darstellungsweise der Überschneidung von Zylindern mit gleichen Radien. Derartige Maschinen setzten sich weitgehend als Standard durch, und technische Abhandlungen empfahlen in der Folge den Einsatz von Ellipsografen bei der Entwurfsarbeit.[49] Mit Hilfe einiger höher entwickelter Instrumente ließen sich Entwurfsaufgaben lösen, die schon die antiken Baumeister beschäftigt hatten, zum Beispiel die mühevolle Bemessung der Proportionen und Kurven der klassischen Ordnungen, die absolute Präzision erforderte.[50] Von daher bot sich für diese Aufgabe die Mechanisierung an. Helikografen „enthielten" die erstaunlich komplexen Regeln der Bemessung ionischer Säulen sowie bestimmter Treppenformen, und Konchoidografen das für den Entwurf klassischer Säulenproportionen erforderliche mathematische Wissen. Diese Instrumente entsprachen also in etwa unseren heutigen maßgeschneiderten Computeranwendungen für die genannten Entwurfsaufgaben. Sie erhöhten die Zahl der Formen, die der Architekt überhaupt entwer-

fen konnte, und systematisierten die Berechnung komplexer Kurven in der Architektur.

Das den Bauwerken innewohnende Geometriewissen und die mechanischen Geräte, mit deren Hilfe es konkrete Gestalt annahm, wurden im 19. Jahrhundert erheblich weiterentwickelt. Neue Erkenntnisse über Kurven zweiten Grades (etwa bei Kegelschnitten, Regel- und Extrusionsflächen) führten dazu, dass Architekten, Ingenieure, Wissenschaftler und technische Zeichner den Bedarf an mechanischen Geräten ankurbelten, die im Grunde Rechenmaschinen zur Bemessung dreidimensionaler Formen darstellten. Das in diesen Instrumenten gespeicherte Entwurfs- und Geometriewissen erleichterte die Gliederung komplexer architektonischer Projektionen. Auch die für die Fertigung höher entwickelter mechanischer Zeichengeräte erforderlichen Produktionsmaschinen wurden immer komplexer. Sie adelten den feinmechanischen Zweig der Maschinenbauindustrie und förderten neue Entwurfsmethoden und die Entwicklung immer komplizierterer Maschinen.

Joseph Clement, bekannter englischer technischer Zeichner und führender Präzisionswerkzeugmacher des 19. Jahrhunderts, steht für das Ineinandergreifen von architektonischem Entwurf und wissenschaftlichen Instrumenten sowie deren wechselseitige Abhängigkeit in Innovationszyklen.[51] Clement machte sich einen Namen als Erfinder mechanischer Zeichengeräte, speziell für die Konstruktion von Ellipsen, und befasste sich eingehend mit der Entwicklung und Herstellung automatischer Maschinenwerkzeuge.[52] Am bekanntesten wurde er jedoch durch seine Mitarbeit (von 1824 bis 1833) an Charles Babbages *difference engine*, der ersten mechanischen Rechenmaschine.[53] Als Chefingenieur der Fabrikation entwarf und zeichnete Clement hierfür Hunderte der hoch präzisen maschinell gefertigten Komponenten. Babbages Projekt eines

47 Thomson 1875/76: 262.
48 Stanley 1878: 68.
49 Ashpitel 1867: 183.
50 Carpo 2003: 448.
51 Lee 1995: 171.
52 Hambly 1988: 91.
53 Lee 1995: 173.

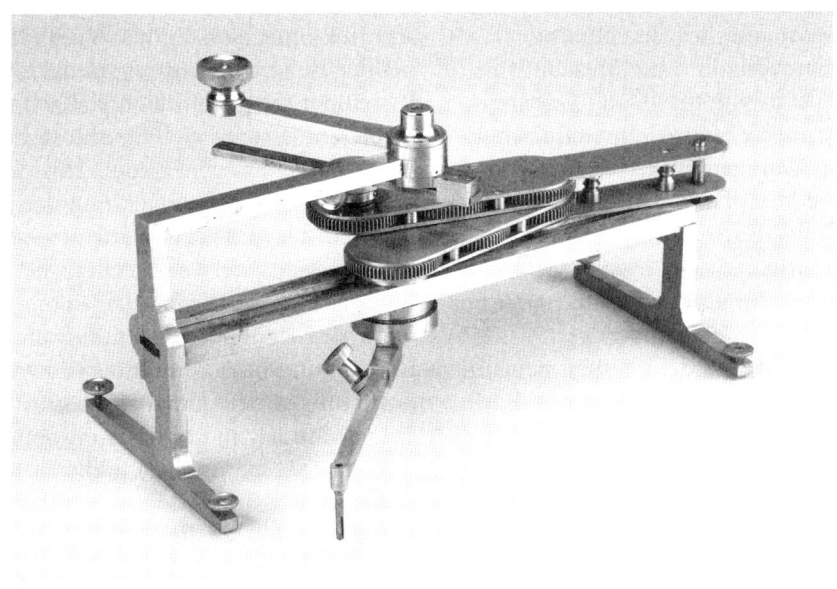

Die Abbildung zeigt einen typischen Bustow'schen Ellipsografen, der nach 1873 in der Fabrik von William Ford Stanley hergestellt wurde.

This is a typical example of Bustow's ellipsograph, produced by William Ford Stanley after 1873.

It was the repeatability, speed, and mass productivity of machines, not the precision handling of calculation and geometric complexity, that captivated many architects of the interwar period. Le Corbusier's writing is only the most obvious example: "The lesson of the airplane is not primarily in the forms it has created, and above all we must learn to see in an airplane not a bird or a dragon-fly, but a machine for flying; the lesson of the airplane lies in the logic which governed the enunciation of the problem and which led to its successful realization."[54] It was the economic law of the machine even more than the formal one that was decisive.[55] While they adopted a certain economic or social ethic of progress through mechanization, an undeniably primitive formal tendency marginalized forms that architects assumed could not be easily reproduced, such as complex curves or hyperbolic and spherical forms. Since the forms themselves become the object of modern reaction, the tools used for their creation—this array of instruments that encap-

54 Le Corbusier 1986 [1923]: 110.
55 Le Corbusier 1986 [1923]: 227.

sulated fundamental geometric knowledge and ability—were superfluous to the aims of modernism. Thus the geometric knowledge embodied and encapsulated in these instruments was essentially lost to the profession.

This epistemic, formal, and technical rupture had lasting consequences. In fact there was a palpable absence of true curved geometric experimentation in the mainstream of design for essentially half a century. Ruled surfaces, subjects of explicit architectural study by Douliot as early as 1825, did not re-emerge in the architectural vocabulary until the 1950s with the work of Miguel Fisac, Marcel Breuer, and others, and then without the aid of advanced geometric drawing machines. Even sophisticated operations such as the subdivision of Buckminster Fuller's geodesic domes were undertaken largely without mechanical aid. These architects found themselves reinventing the notion of

Automaten zur Berechnung von Logarithmentafeln stellt den ehrgeizigsten systematischen Versuch in automatischer Berechnung seiner Zeit dar, weshalb seine Maschine als Vorläufer des heutigen digitalen Computers gilt. Interessanterweise war ein technischer Zeichner und Werkzeugmacher von Geräten zur Erstellung komplexer Kurven entscheidend an der Entstehung von Babbages Maschine beteiligt.

Die Entwicklung präziser mechanischer Zeicheninstrumente zu Beginn des 19. Jahrhunderts hatte also dem ersten mechanischen Computer den Weg gebahnt, und zwar als Teil der umfassenderen Entwicklung mechanisierender und zugleich raumbildender Bemessungen auf der Basis der Differenzial- und Integralrechnung, wie sie mit Amslers Planimetern ausgeführt werden konnten. Die *difference engine* von Charles Babbage ist zwar möglicherweise das spektakulärste Beispiel derartiger Erfindungen, viele seiner Zeitgenossen hatten aber ebenfalls den Wert automatischer Rechengeräte erkannt, und einige der resultierenden Geräte dienten planerischen und architektonischen Zwecken. Es ist nicht übertrieben zu behaupten, dass der Impuls, immer noch komplexere Kurven zu entwerfen und die dafür notwendigen Zeichenmaschinen zu entwickeln, das Wissen erzeugte, das für die Entwicklung großer mechanischer Rechenmaschinen nötig war.

Fazit: Die Epistemologie der Maschine und ihre Brüche

Man kann sagen, dass im 19. Jahrhundert das Wissen über geometrisch-gestalterische Vorgänge und neue Bemessungsmethoden geradezu explodierte und in den Bau spezieller Zeichen- und Berechnungsmaschinen einfloss. Das in diesen Instrumenten gespeicherte Geometriewissen konnte vom Benutzer aufgrund seines Instrumentenwissens – das heißt seiner Kenntnis der Maschinenfunktion und -handhabung – erschlossen werden (er konnte simulieren, das Wissen selbst zu haben), was ihm einen effizienteren und zuverlässigeren Zugang zu diesem Wissen verschaffte, ihn aber auch bewog, sich auf die Maschine zu verlassen.

Die mechanischen Zeichengeräte des 19. Jahrhunderts belegen, dass Fortschritte in architektonischem Entwurfswissen und bei der Beherrschung des dazugehörigen Instrumentenwissens sich vielfach gegenseitig ergänzen, ja sogar eine Symbiose eingehen. Beide Wissensarten ermöglichen das Verständnis und die Entwicklung der jeweils anderen. Das Entwurfswissen (speziell die Beherrschung der Geometrie) weckt den Bedarf an neuen Entwurfsinstrumenten, und diese Werkzeuge wiederum führen zur Entdeckung oder Schaffung von weiter fortgeschrittenem Entwurfswissen. In ähnlicher Weise hat in unserer Zeit Software für fortgeschrittene Geometrie die Einführung zahlreicher Konzepte beschleunigt, die früher nicht zum Bereich des architektonischen Entwurfs zählten, nämlich Oberflächengeometrien, mathematische Parametrien, ja sogar bestimmte Aspekte der Prozesssteuerung und -automation. Die Wechselbeziehung zwischen Geometrie und Maschine hat das Entwurfswissen grundlegend verändert und erweitert.

Natürlich birgt das auch ein Risiko: Ab dem Moment, in dem dieses Entwurfswissen in die Maschine eingespeichert wird, ist es nur noch den Nutzern zugänglich, die sowohl über das Instrumentenwissen in der Handhabung der Maschine als auch über die Maschine selbst verfügen. Das Werkzeug und das darin gespeicherte Wissen versetzen den Entwerfer in die Lage (oder eben auch nicht) zu gestalten. Verloren gegangenes Wissen über bestimmte maschinelle Vorgänge könnte sehr wohl den praktischen Nutzen des mechanischen Instruments beziehungsweise des in ihm enthaltenen Wissens zunichte machen, besonders wenn dieses hoch spezialisiert und ansonsten unter Architekten nicht allgemein verfügbar ist. Das ist bei etlichen hoch komplexen geometrischen Konstruktionen der Fall, die in den Bereich spezialisierter Mathematiker fallen. Wenn das Instrumentenwissen verloren ginge, gäbe es keinen vergleichbaren aktuellen Wissensstand in der Geometrie, mit dem der Verlust kompensiert werden könnte. Kurzum: Mit der Umwandlung von Entwurfswissen zu Instrumentenwissen wird Instrumentenwissen zur

56 Whitehead 1911: 61.

the curved form in architecture, inventing geometric design knowledge that would have been enabled by a forgotten technology.

This rupture of continuity and loss of knowledge was avoidable. If instrumental knowledge and its formal implications had been understood as ideologically independent from formal design agendas, and instead had been candidly embraced as part of the knowledge culture of architecture, the formal limits of twentieth-century modernism would have been mitigated by an unbroken evolution of technical innovation through instrumental innovation. In other words, if instrumental knowledge had been seen as a fundamental part of architectural knowledge, the machine culture of architecture we see today could be properly understood as a part of a continuous evolution of the instrumental dimension of architectural knowledge. Our current epistemic debate would be fundamentally different.

Contemporary architects are again increasingly mechanizing and automating their approach to design. The pervasive use of digital technology in the conception and execution of buildings dramatically increases our reliance on representational and operational systems of which we have incomplete understanding but that we nevertheless trust implicitly. In this way there is a strong parallel to the developments of the nineteenth century: the facilitation and even diffusion of design by mechanical instrumentation opened rigorous formal possibilities partially through a mastery of instrumental mechanical methods, which required a reorganization of design pedagogy and ultimately, architectural knowledge.

The machine, particularly the computer, calls into question the self-understanding of architecture and its self-imposed alienation from technical processes. There is a strong tendency, arguably beginning with Alberti, to dichotomize design knowledge and instrumental knowledge, and to relegate technical or mechanical expertise to the domain of specialists or operators. Perhaps this can be explained by a mistrust of the architect's need to rely on mechanical, electrical, computational, or conceptual operations of which

the architect cannot have complete understanding. This trust in machines, however, far from being an innocent conceit, represents an implicit belief in the possibility that collective memory and design knowledge can be instrumentally encapsulated in machines. It represents not a barrier to advancement of architectural knowledge but a great opportunity. The power of knowledge encapsulation and automation is aptly summarized by mathematician Alfred North Whitehead when he claims: "It is a profoundly erroneous truism, repeated by all copy-books and by eminent people when they are making speeches, that we should cultivate the habit of thinking what we are doing. The precise opposite is the case. Civilization advances by extending the number of important operations which we can perform without thinking about them."[56]

This understanding is of fundamental importance for the advancement of architectural epistemology: it implies that some design knowledge is ultimately modular, something that can be abstracted, encapsulated, trusted, mechanically represented, and propagated. To some extent design knowledge may be simulated by the use of instrumental knowledge of machines that can produce the same effects as the original design knowledge. In fact, the fluent use of machinery can produce architectural effects that may not come by any other form of design knowledge alone. Thus instrumental knowledge constitutes a positive and essential component of architectural knowledge. As a particular dimension of architectural knowledge, its loss, as in the first half of the twentieth century, is conversely a loss of architectural knowledge.

A new synthesis of design and instrumentality seems imminent within architecture: one that acknowledges the centrality of technique, geometry, and machine to design. We should properly welcome this shift as a new formal opportunity, a candid synthesis, and a new epistemic paradigm for architecture.

Andrew J. Witt
A Machine Epistemology

Candide No. 3, 12/2010
Essay

Grundlage des Entwurfsprozesses und somit zum integralen Bestandteil des Architekturwissens als Ganzes.

Dieses Instrumentenwissen kann auf vielerlei Weise verloren gehen, nicht zuletzt aufgrund veränderter Haltungen und ästhetischer Vorlieben der Architekten. Ich behaupte, dass das Neue Bauen zu Beginn des 20. Jahrhunderts einen solchen Verlust bewirkte. Mit ihrer grundlegend anderen Auffassung vom Wert der Maschine in der Architektur verdrängte und veränderte die Moderne die bemerkenswerten Entwicklungen des 19. Jahrhunderts auf dem Gebiet präziser mechanischer Zeichengeräte. Es waren die durch Maschinen möglich gewordene schnelle Reproduzierbarkeit und hohe Produktivität, die zahlreiche Architekten in der Zeit zwischen den beiden Weltkriegen faszinierten. Der folgende Text von Le Corbusier ist nur das bekannteste Beispiel: „Die Lehre des Flugzeugs liegt nicht so sehr in den gestalteten Formen, und zuerst muß man lernen, in einem Flugzeug nicht einen Vogel oder eine Libelle zu sehen; es ist eine Maschine zum Fliegen. Die Lektion, die uns das Flugzeug erteilt, liegt in der Logik, aus der die Stellung des Problems erfolgte, und die Erfolg und Verwirklichung geleitet hat."[54] Mehr noch als die formalen Gesetze waren die ökonomischen Gesetze der Maschine für Le Corbusier entscheidend.[55] Während sie bestimmte Aspekte des Glaubens an den wirtschaftlichen und sozialen Fortschritt durch die Mechanisierung übernahmen, verdrängten die Vertreter der Architekturmoderne mit ihren unverkennbar primitiven formalen Tendenzen andere Figuren und Formen, die sich ihrer Meinung nach nicht rationell serienmäßig reproduzieren ließen, nämlich komplexe Kurven, Hyperbeln oder gar Kugeln. Die Tatsache, dass Formen an sich zum Gegenstand der modernen Reaktion wurden, führte dazu, dass dem Berufsstand des Architekten die Mittel zu ihrer Erzeugung – das heißt, die vielen Instrumente, in denen die theoretischen Grundlagen und praktischen Anwendungen der Geometrie gespeichert waren – abhanden kamen.

Dieser erkenntnistheoretische, formale und technische Bruch hatte weitreichende Folgen: Während fast eines halben Jahrhunderts gab es im architektonischen Mainstream keine ernsthaften kurvengeometrischen Experimente mehr. Regelflächen, die bereits 1825 Douliots Forschungsgegenstand gewesen waren, tauchten erst in den 1950er Jahren in den Projekten von Miguel Fisac, Marcel Breuer und anderen wieder auf, dann aber ohne Einsatz moderner mechanischer Zeichengeräte. Selbst die Strukturierung so hoch komplexer Oberflächen wie Buckminster Fullers geodätischer Kuppeln erfolgte weitgehend ohne mechanische Hilfsmittel. Diese Architekten mussten das Konzept der geschwungenen architektonischen Form also sozusagen ganz neu erfinden – einschließlich des geometrischen Wissens, das eine vergessene Technik ermöglicht hätte.

Dieser Bruch und Wissensverlust hätte vermieden werden können. Wenn das Instrumentenwissen und dessen formale Auswirkungen als ideologisch unabhängig von formalen Dogmen aufgefasst und offen als Teil der spezifisch architektonischen Wissenskultur anerkannt worden wären, hätte die formale Begrenztheit der Moderne des 20. Jahrhunderts durch die kontinuierliche Entwicklung bautechnischer Innovationen mit Hilfe instrumententechnischer Innovationen gemildert werden können. Anders gesagt: Wenn instrumentelles Wissen als fundamentaler Bestandteil des Architekturwissens gegolten hätte, könnte man die heutige Maschinenkultur der Architektur als Teil einer kontinuierlichen Entwicklung der instrumentellen Dimension des Architekturwissens richtig verstehen – und die aktuelle epistemologische Debatte sähe grundlegend anders aus.

Zunehmend mechanisieren und automatisieren zeitgenössische Architekten erneut die Entwurfsarbeit. Die Nutzung der digitalen Technologie bei der Konzeption und Ausführung von Gebäuden aller Art hat dazu geführt, dass Architekten sich heute in erheblichem Maße auf darstellende und

54 Le Corbusier 1963 [1923]: 89.
55 Le Corbusier 1963 [1923]: 166.

ausführende Systeme verlassen, die sie zwar nicht völlig verstehen, denen sie aber trotzdem unhinterfragt vertrauen. Das stellt eine starke Parallele zu den Entwicklungen mechanischer Zeichen- und Bemessungsinstrumente im 19. Jahrhundert dar, welche die Entwurfsarbeit erleichterten und neue Entwurfsmethoden förderten, indem sie dem entwerfenden Architekten neue formgebende Möglichkeiten eröffneten, wenn er die Instrumente kennen und handhaben lernte. Das erforderte Umstellungen der Lehre und – letztlich – des Architekturwissens.

Die Maschine – speziell der Computer – stellt das Selbstverständnis der Architektur und ihre selbstauferlegte Entfremdung von technischen Prozessen in Frage. Die Tendenz, das Entwurfswissen und das Instrumentenwissen auseinander zu dividieren und das Wissen auf dem Gebiet der Mechanik den Technikspezialisten und Bauausführenden zu überlassen, besteht seit Langem, möglicherweise schon seit Alberti. Das lässt sich vielleicht damit erklären, dass Architekten im Allgemeinen einer Abhängigkeit von mechanischen, elektrischen, rechnerischen oder konzeptionellen Verfahren, die sie nicht voll verstehen können, misstrauen. Weit davon entfernt, eine harmlose Einbildung zu sein, entspricht der Verlass auf die Maschine dem impliziten Glauben an die Möglichkeit, dass das kollektive entwerferische Gedächtnis und Wissen sich instrumentell in Maschinen speichern lässt. Das ist kein Hemmnis, sondern eine große Chance für die Weiterentwicklung des Architekturwissens. Alfred North Whitehead hat die Macht des in Maschinen gespeicherten und automatisierten Wissens treffend beschrieben: „Es ist eine weit verbreitete, aber völlig irrige Auffassung, die sich in allen Anleitungen findet und durch hervorragende Leute in Reden wiederholt wird, daß wir die Denkgewöhnung bei allem, was wir tun, pflegen müssen. Das genaue Gegenteil ist der Fall. Die Zivilisation schreitet vorwärts, indem sie die Zahl der wichtigen Operationen erhöht, die wir ohne zu denken ausführen können."[56]

Diese Auffassung ist von grundlegender Bedeutung für die Weiterentwicklung der architektonischen Epistemologie. Sie impli-

ziert, dass ein bestimmter Teil des Entwurfswissens letztlich modular ist, dass man es abstrahieren, speichern, mechanisch darstellen und vermehren kann und dass es verlässlich ist. Bis zu einem gewissen Grad lässt sich das Entwurfswissen simulieren, und zwar mittels der eigenen Kenntnis der zu dessen Anwendung erforderlichen Maschinen, so dass man damit die gleichen Resultate erzielen kann, die man auch ohne maschinelle Hilfsmittel erzielt hätte. Die theoretische und praktische Beherrschung von Maschinen kann in der Tat architektonische Effekte herbeiführen, die mit keiner anderen Form von Entwurfswissen erzeugt werden könnten. Instrumentenwissen stellt daher einen wesentlichen und positiven Aspekt des Architekturwissens dar. Der Verlust dieses Teilwissens – wie er in der ersten Hälfte des 20. Jahrhunderts erfolgte – ist zugleich ein Verlust an Architekturwissen.

Heute scheint sich eine neue Synthese aus gestalterischer Kompetenz und Beherrschung der hierfür erforderlichen Instrumente abzuzeichnen, welche die zentrale Bedeutung von Arbeitsverfahren, Geometrie und Maschine für den architektonischen Entwurf anerkennt. Diese Entwicklung sollten wir als neue formale Chance und echte Synthese begreifen – und als neues epistemologisches Paradigma für die Architektur.

56 Whitehead 1958 [1911]: 35f.

Andrew J. Witt ist Architekt. Er arbeitet derzeit im Pariser Büro von Gehry Technologies, wo er mit parametrischen und geometrischen Entwurfsmethoden, neuen Konstruktions- und Bautechniken und der Integration aller beteiligten Fachdisziplinen für verschiedene internationale Auftraggeber befasst ist. Witt ist nicht nur Architekt, sondern auch studierter Mathematiker. Sein spezielles Interesse gilt daher der technischen Synthese und logischen Stringenz der architektonischen Form. Neben der Praxis lehrt er an der Harvard University Graduate School of Design, an der er sein Studium mit einem MArch und einem MDes (in Geschichte und Theorie der Architektur) abgeschlossen hat.

Deutsche Übersetzung:
Annette Wiethüchter.

Andrew J. Witt is a designer currently based in Paris, France. He is a director at the Paris office of Gehry Technologies, where he consults on parametric design, geometric approaches, new technologies, and integrated practice for a diverse range of international clients. Trained as both an architect and mathematician, Witt has a particular interest in a technically synthetic and logically rigorous approach to form. He currently lectures at Harvard University Graduate School of Design, where he completed an MArch and an MDes (History and Theory).

References

Alberti, Leon Battista. 1452. *De re aedificatoria.*
ENGLISH: 1988. *On The Art of Building in Ten Books.* Joseph Rykwert with Neil Leach and Robert Tavernor, trans. and ed. Cambridge, Mass: MIT Press.
DEUTSCH: 1991 [1912] *Zehn Bücher über die Baukunst.* Max Theurer, Übers. und Hrsg. Darmstadt: Wissenschaftliche Buchgesellschaft.

Adams, George. 1797 [1791]. *Geometrical and graphical essays containing a general description of the mathematical instruments used in geometry, civil and military surveying, levelling, and perspective.* London: J. Dillon and Co.
DEUTSCH: 1795. *Geometrische und graphische Versuche oder Beschreibung der mathematischen Instrumente, deren man sich in der Geometrie, der Civil- und Militair-Vermessung, beim Nivellieren und in der Perspektive bedient.* Johann Gottlieb Geißler, Übers. Leipzig: Siegfried Lebrecht Crusius. Neuauflage: 1985. Peter Damerow und Wolfgang Lefèvre, Hrsg. Darmstadt: Wissenschaftliche Buchgesellschaft.

Aranda, Benjamin/Chris Lasch. 2006. *Tooling.* New York: Princeton Architectural Press.

Ashpitel, Arthur. 1867. *Treatise on Architecture, including the Arts of Construction, Building, Stone-Masonry, Arch, Carpentry, Roof, Joinery, and Strength of Materials.* Edinburgh: Adam and Charles Black.

Bion, Nicolas. 1709. *Traité de la construction et des principaux usages des instrumens de mathématique.* Paris.
DEUTSCH: 1712. *Neu-eröffnete mathematische werck-schule.* Doppelmayr, Johann Gabriel, Übers. Frankfurt, Leipzig, Nürnberg: im Hoffmännischen Buchladen.
ENGLISH: 1723. *The construction and principal uses of mathematical instruments.* Edmund Stone, trans. London.

Boyd, Richard. 1980. "Scientific Realism and Naturalistic Epistemology". *Proceedings of the Biennial Meeting of the Philosophy of Science Association.* Volume Two: Symposia and Invited Papers: 613–662.

Browne, H. F. 1942, July. "1598. Amsler's Planimeter." *The Mathematical Gazette.* Vol. 26, No. 270: 135–137.

Burry, Mark/Jordi Coll Grifoll/Josep Gomez Serrano. 2008. *Sagrada Familia s. XXI.* Barcelona: Edicions UPC.

Carpo, Mario. 2003, December. "Drawing with Numbers: Geometry and Numeracy in Early Modern Architectural Design." *Journal of the Society of Architectural Historians.* Vol. 62, No. 4: 448–469.

———. 2008. *Perspective, Projections, and Design.* London: Routledge.

Colletti, Marjan, ed. 2010, March/April. "Exuberance: New Virtuosity in Contemporary Architecture." *Architectural Design.* London: Wiley.

Douliot, Jean Paul. 1825. *Traité spécial de coupe des pierres.* Paris: Imprimerie de Richomme.

Evans, Robin. 2000 [1995]. *The Projective Cast: Architecture and its Three Geometries.* Cambridge, MA: MIT Press.
DEUTSCH [auszugsweise Übersetzung]: 1997, Juni. „Die Anfänge moderner Raumkonzeptionen." Fritz Schneider, Übers. 137 *ARCH+.*

Hambly, Maya. 1988. *Drawing Instruments, 1580–1980.* London: Sotheby's Publications.

Horsburgh, E. M. 1914. *Modern Instruments and Methods of Calculation.* London: G. Bell and Sons.

Institution of Civil Engineers. 1851. *Minutes of Proceedings of the Institution of Civil Engineers.* Vol. 10. London: Institution of Civil Engineers.

Iwamoto, Lisa. 2009. *Digital Fabrications: Architectural and Material Techniques.* New York: Princeton Architectural Press.

Kalay, Yehuda/Lucien Swerdloff/ Bruce Majkowski. 1990, Winter. "Process and Knowledge in Design Computation." *Journal of Architectural Education.* Vol. 43, No. 2: 47–53.

Kieren, Stephen/James Timberlake. 2004. *Refabricating Architecture.* New York: McGraw-Hill Professional.

Kolarevic, Branko. 2003. *Architecture in the Digital Age: Design and Manufacturing.* London: Taylor & Francis.

Krull, F. N. 1994, Fall. "The Origin of Computer Graphics within General Motors." *Annals of the History of Computing, IEEE*. Vol. 16, No. 3: 40–56.

Langlois, Richard N. 2001. "Knowledge, Consumption, and Endogenous growth." *The Journal of Evolutionary Economics* 11: 77–93.

Le Corbusier. 1923. *Vers une architecture*. Paris: G. Cres.
ENGLISH: 1986 [1931]. *Towards a New Architecture*. Frederick Etchells, trans. New York: Dover Publications.
DEUTSCH: 1963 [1926]. *Ausblick auf eine Architektur*. [Bauwelt-Fundamente 2.] Hans Hildebrandt/Eva Gärtner, trans. Gütersloh/Berlin: Bertelsmann Fachverlag Reinhard Mohn.

Lee, John A. N. 1995. *International biographical dictionary of computer pioneers*. New York: Taylor & Francis.

Leroy, Charles-François-Antoine. 1844. *Traité de stéréotomie, comprenant les applications de la géométrie descriptive…* Paris: Bachelier.
DEUTSCH: 1873. *Die darstellende Geometrie*. E. F. Kauffmann, Übers. Stuttgart: Bach und Kitzinger.

Lynn, Greg. 2000. *Folding in Architecture*. London: Wiley-Academy.

Mallgrave, Harry Francis. 2010. *The Architect's Brain: Neuroscience, Creativity, and Architecture*. New York: John Wiley and Sons.

Marguin, Jean. 1994. *Histoire des instruments et machines a calculer*. Paris: Hermann.

Mazerolle, Louis. ca. 1895. *Traité théorique et pratique de charpente*. Paris. Reprint: 2002. Paris: Éditions Vial.

Monduit, Louis. 1889. *Traité théorique et pratique de stéréotomie*. Paris: C. Juliot.

Monge, Gaspard. 1798. *Géométrie descriptive*. Paris: Baudouin. Reprint of the 1799 Edition: 1989. Paris: Éditions Jacques Gabay.
DEUTSCH: 1900. *Darstellende Geometrie*. [Ostwalds Klassiker der exakten Wissenschaften. Nr. 117.] Robert Haussner, Übers. und Hrsg. Leipzig: W. Engelmann.
ENGLISH: 1851. *An elementary treatise on descriptive geometry*. John Fry Heather, trans. and ed. London: John Weale.

Morrison-Low, Alison. 2007. *Making Scientific Instruments in the Industrial Revolution*. Aldershot, UK: Ashgate.

Murray, Daniel Alexander. 1898. *An elementary course in the integral calculus*. American Book Company.

Oxman, Rivka/Robert Oxman, eds. 2010, Juli. "The New Structuralism." *Architectural Design*. London: Wiley.

Piedmont-Palladino, Susan. 2007. *Tools of the Imagination*. New York: Princeton Architectural Press.

Potie, Philippe. 1996. *Philibert de l'Orme: Figures de la pensée constructive*. Paris: Éditions Parenthèses.

Prager, Frank D./Gustina Scaglia. 1970. *Brunelleschi: Studies of His Technology and Inventions*. London: Dover.

Protot, C. 1838. *Cours spécial d'architecture, ou Leçons particulières de géométrie descriptive, comprenant les éléments de géométrie, stéréotomie, etc.* Troyes: L.-C. Cardon.

Thomson, James. 1875/76. "On an Integrating Machine Having a New Kinematic Principle." *Proceedings of the Royal Society of London*. Vol. 24: 262–265.

Turner, Gerard L'Estrange. 1983. *Nineteenth-century Scientific Instruments*. Berkeley: University of California Press.

Stanley, William Ford. 1878. *A Descriptive Treatise on Mathematical Drawing Instruments*. London: Butler and Tanner.

Suardi, Giambattista. 1752. *Nuovi istromenti per la descrizione di diverse curve antiche e moderne e di molte altre*. Brescia: G. M. Rizzardi.

Van Maanen, Jan. 1992. "Seventeenth-century Drawing Instruments for Drawing Conic Sections." *The Mathemetical Gazette*. Vol. 76, No. 476: 222–230.

Whitaker, Robert J. 2001, February. "Harmonographs. II. Circular design." *American Journal of Physics* Vol. 69, No. 2: 174–183.

Whitehead, Alfred North. 1911. *An Introduction to Mathematics*. New York: Henry Holt.
DEUTSCH: 1958 [1948]. *Eine Einführung in die Mathematik*. B. Schenker, Übers. Bern u.a.: Francke.

Wood, Christopher. 2002. "Why Autonomy?" *Perspecta*. "Mining Autonomy." Vol. 33: 48–53.

Picture Credits

Page 7 Courtesy of *Architectural Design*. London: Wiley.

Pages 8 and 9 Courtesy of the Houghton Library, Harvard University, EC75. Ad177.791gc.

Page 10 Courtesy of the Houghton Library, Harvard University, FC7 B5222 Eg723s.

Pages 15–18 From Mazerolle 2002 [1895]. Courtesy Éditions Vial, Paris.

Pages 24 and 25 From Monduit 1889.

Pages 36–41 Drawings and Text: Andrew Witt.

Pages 43 and 45 Courtesy of the Harvard Collection of Historical Scientific Instruments.

Jimenez Lai

On Types of Seductive Robustness

This is a twelve-page storyline about unreasonable actions in the Context of Knowledge. Two detectives interrogate a man for making love to an unfamiliar and grotesque figure. The man is accused of having violated the Parameter of Conduct, which is punishable by law. The charge against the man is: *conspiracy to commit cynicism against the Context of Knowledge.* He attributes his mistake to a type of seduction that overpowered his objective reasoning, and is eventually pardoned. The act between man and figure is overlooked, while the seductive qualities of the grotesque figure are chronicled in the Archive of Intuition. What was once anomalous is now welcomed as part of ethos, syntax, and zeitgeist.

Jimenez Lai

Anmerkungen zu Typen verführerischer Robustheit

Dies ist ein zwölfseitiges Handlungsgerüst über unvernünftige Aktivitäten im Kontext des Wissens. Zwei Detektive verhören einen Mann, der mit einer unbekannten und grotesken Figur Intimverkehr gehabt hat. Der Mann wird beschuldigt, den Verhaltenskodex verletzt zu haben – laut Gesetz eine strafbare Handlung. Die Anklage lautet auf *Verschwörung, welche dem Zynismus gegenüber dem Kontext des Wissens Vorschub leistet.* Der Mann führt sein Vergehen auf eine bestimmte Art der Verführung zurück, die sein objektives Urteilsvermögen überwältigte, was schließlich seine Begnadigung begründet. Der Geschlechtsakt zwischen Mann und Figur wird übersehen, während die verführerischen Eigenschaften der grotesken Figur im Archiv der Intuition aufgezeichnet werden. Was einst als regelwidrig angesehen wurde, ist nun akzeptierter Teil von Ethos, Syntax und Zeitgeist.

this is our secret

and no one will find us

Jimenez Lai
Seductive Robustness

Candide No. 3, 12/2010
Fiction

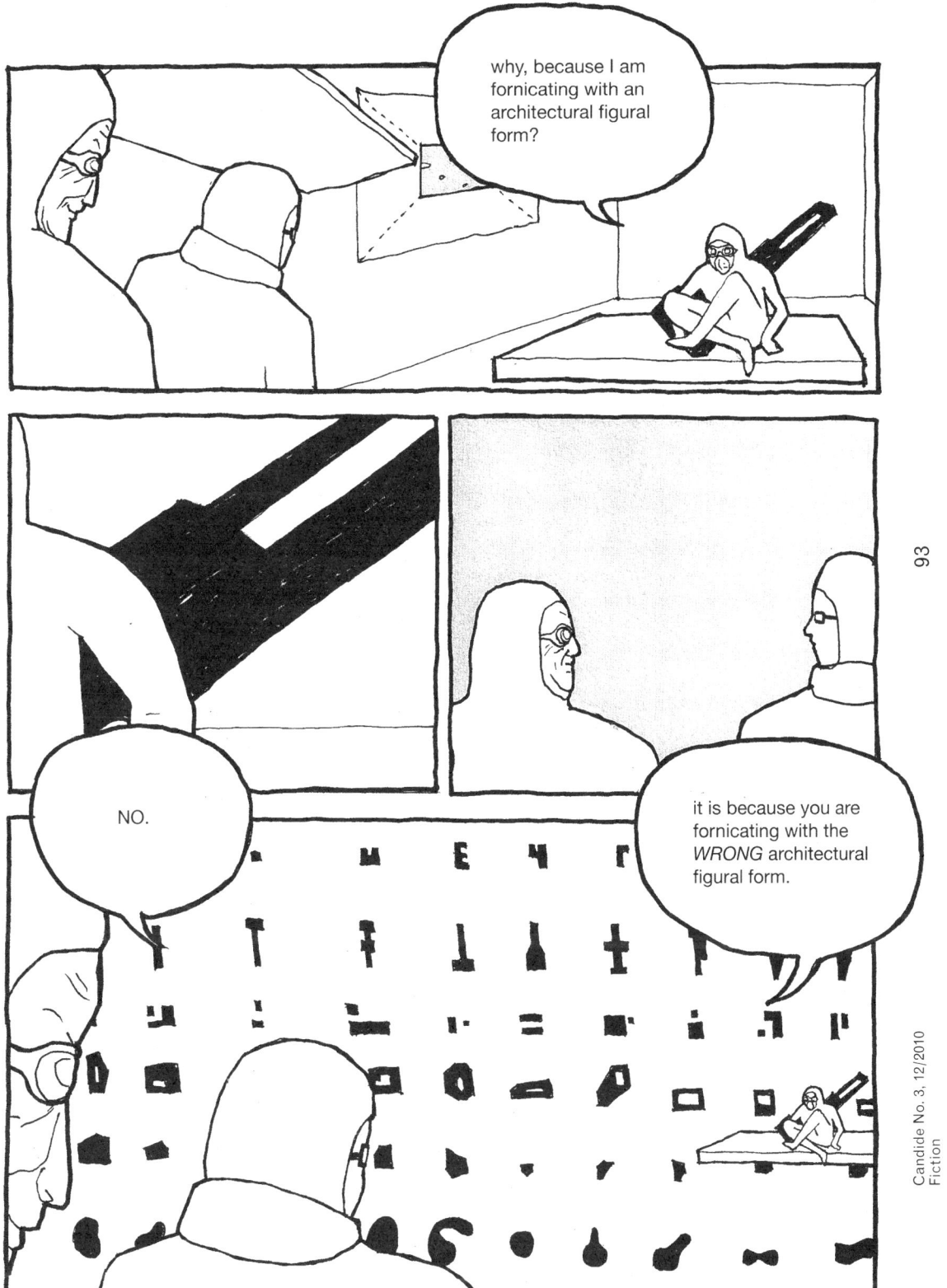

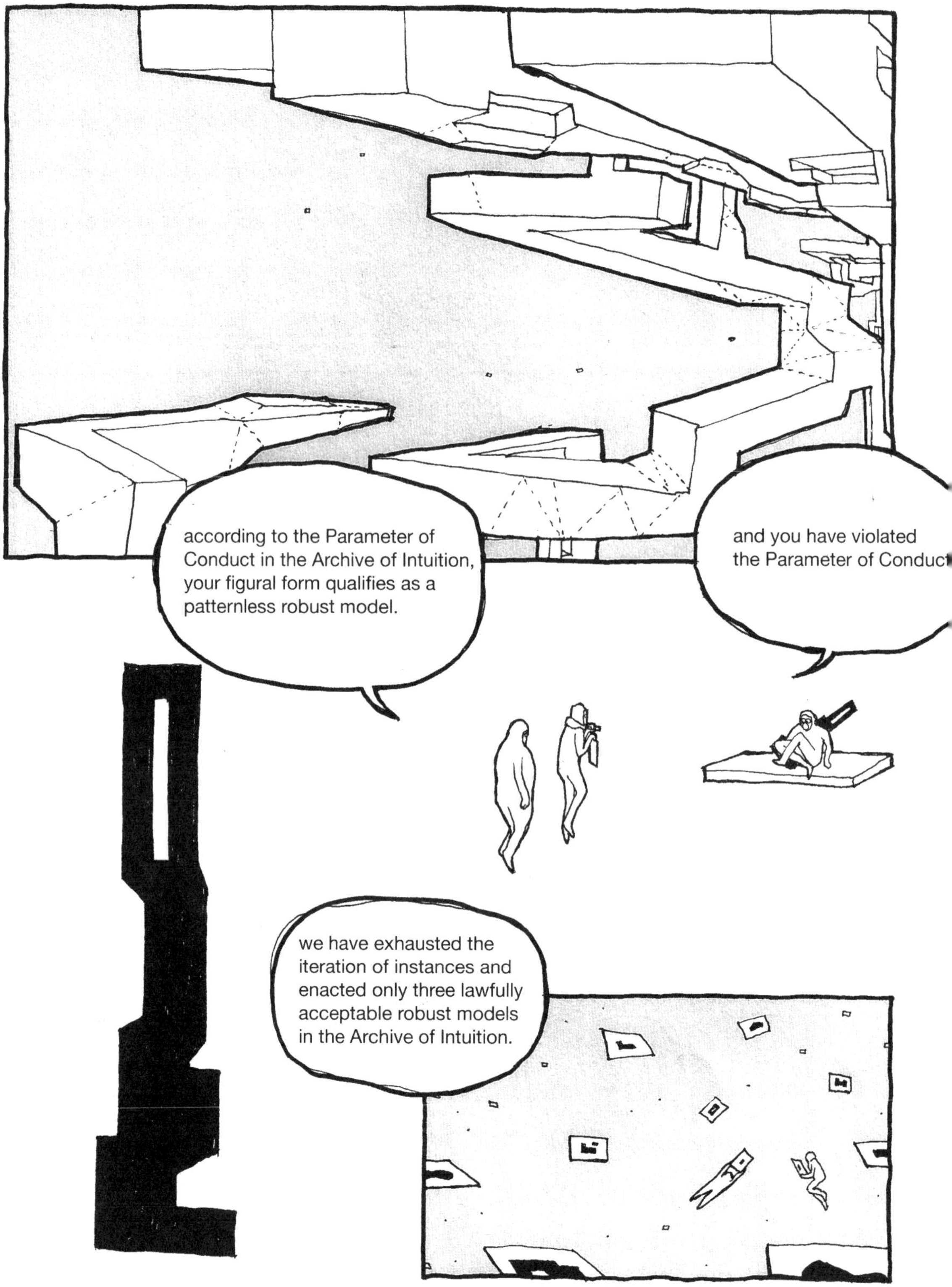
according to the Parameter of Conduct in the Archive of Intuition, your figural form qualifies as a patternless robust model.
and you have violated the Parameter of Conduct
we have exhausted the iteration of instances and enacted only three lawfully acceptable robust models in the Archive of Intuition.

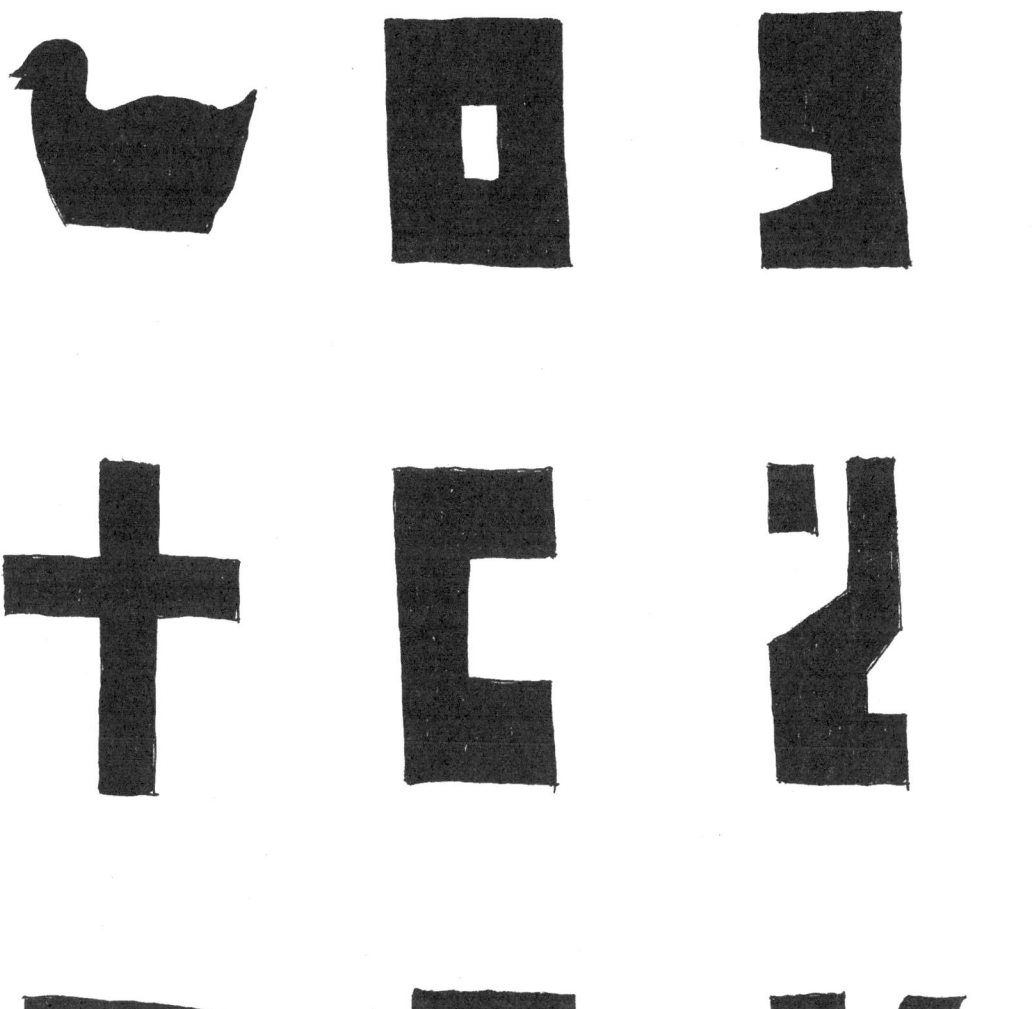

ROBUST MODEL 1: ICONOGRAPHY
A crude shape exempted from attention to detail to retain its legibility as ideogram.

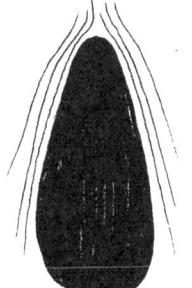

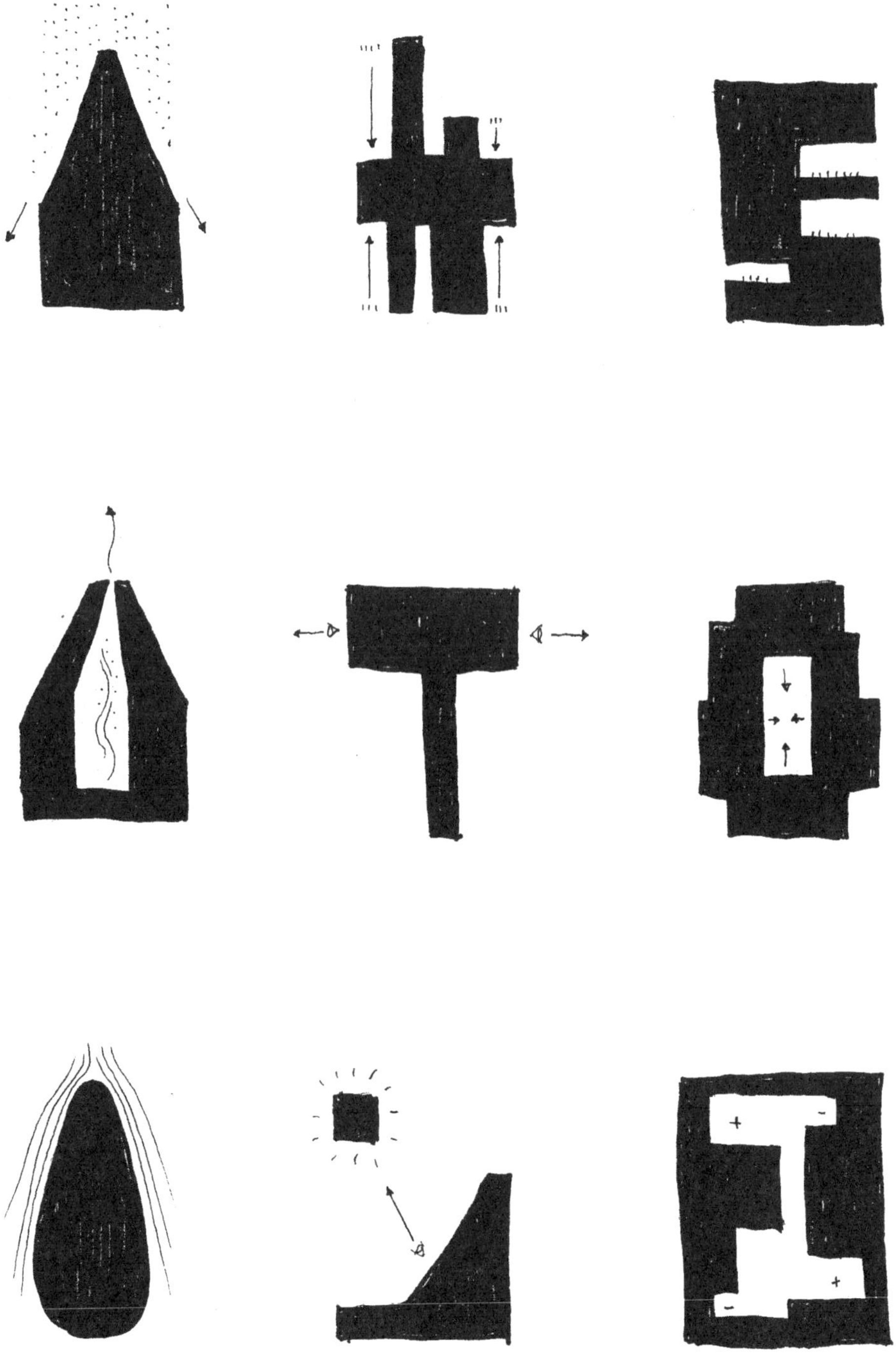

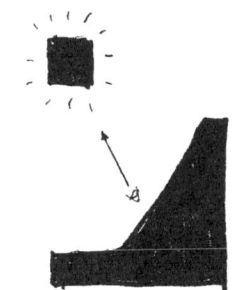

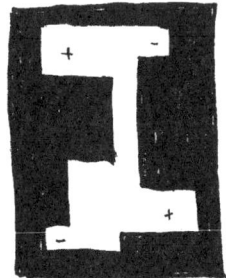

ROBUST MODEL 2: ECONOMY
A strong functionalism that allows the model to thrive in various contexts and conditions.

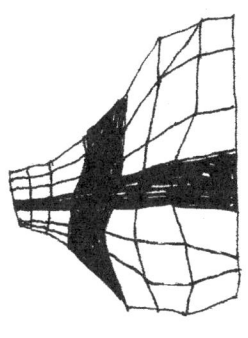
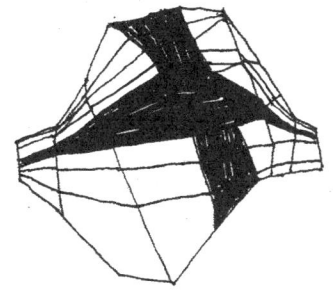
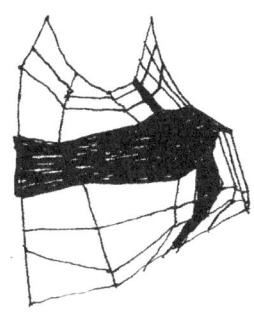

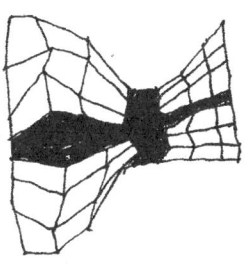
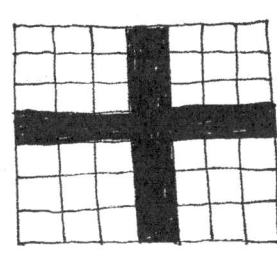
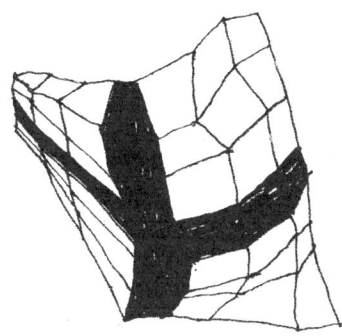

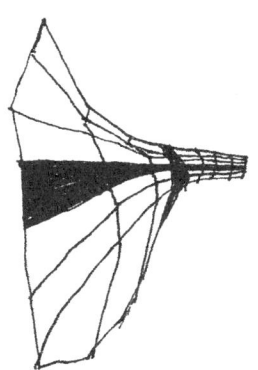
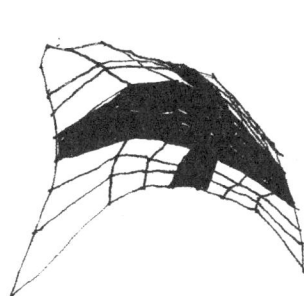

ROBUST MODEL 3: MORPHOLOGY
A resilient origin that responds to physical demands and result in transformations of the geometry.

This robust figure is not an icon, not economical and has no morphological basis.
It is simply grotesque in an ugly way.

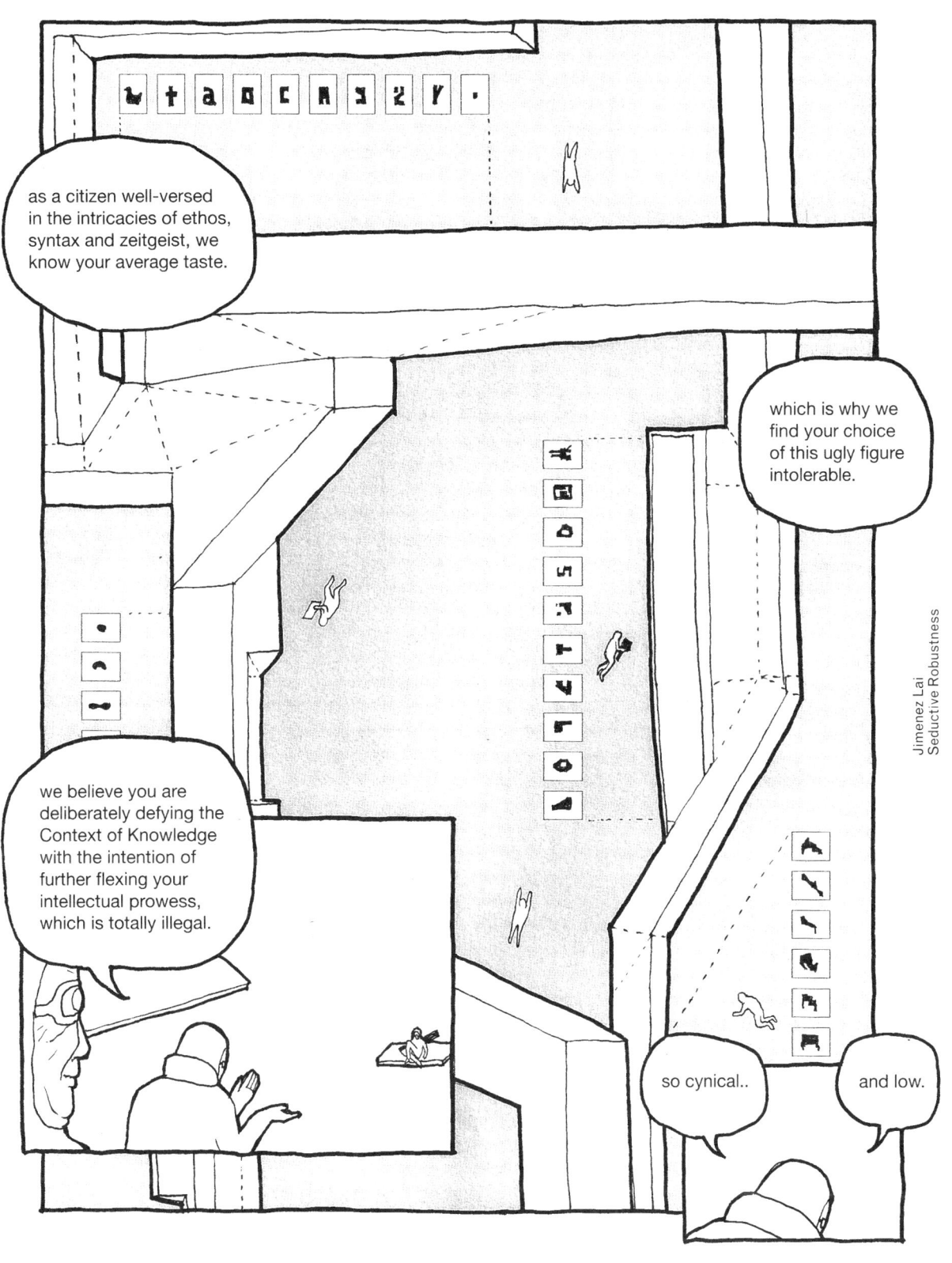

Jimenez Lai
Seductive Robustness

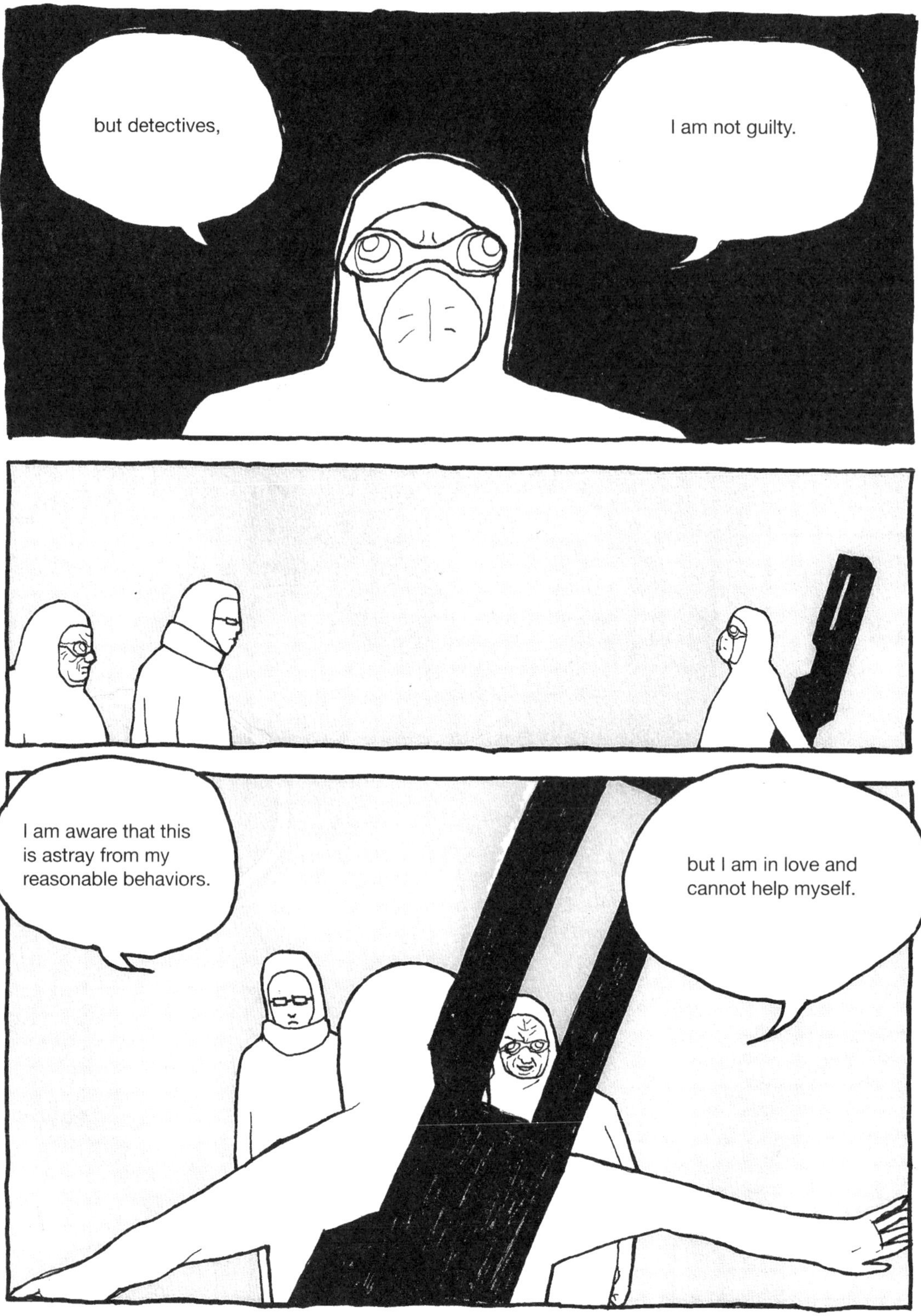

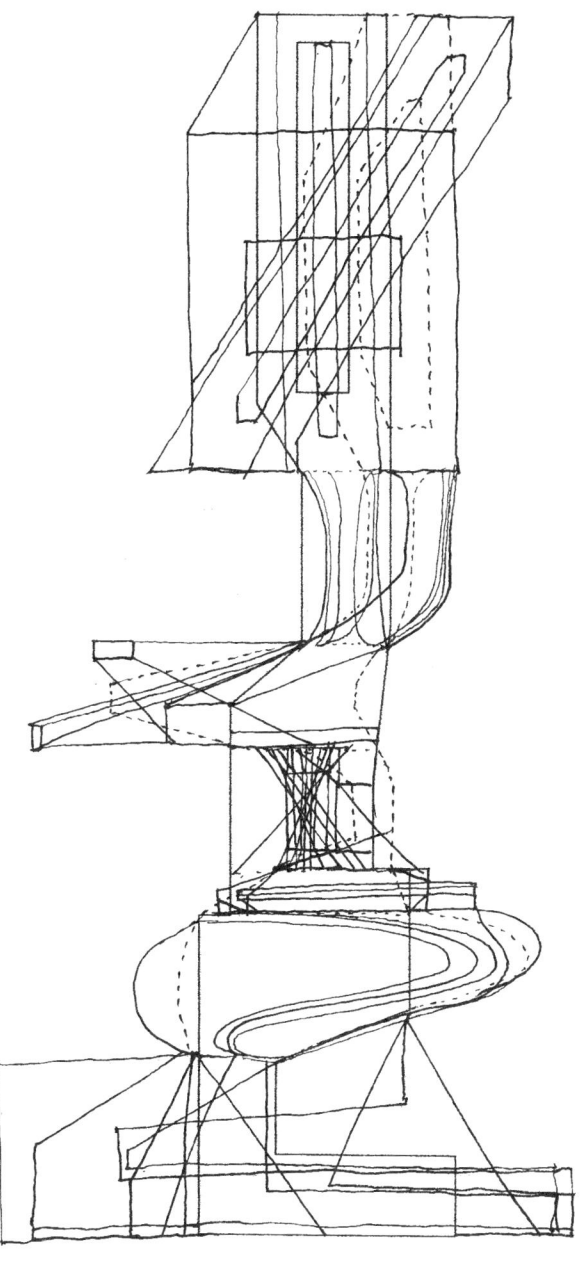

I have tried to objectively synthesize my perceptions. but I am overcome by a precious sort of seduction, enchanting me towards a terrible decision.

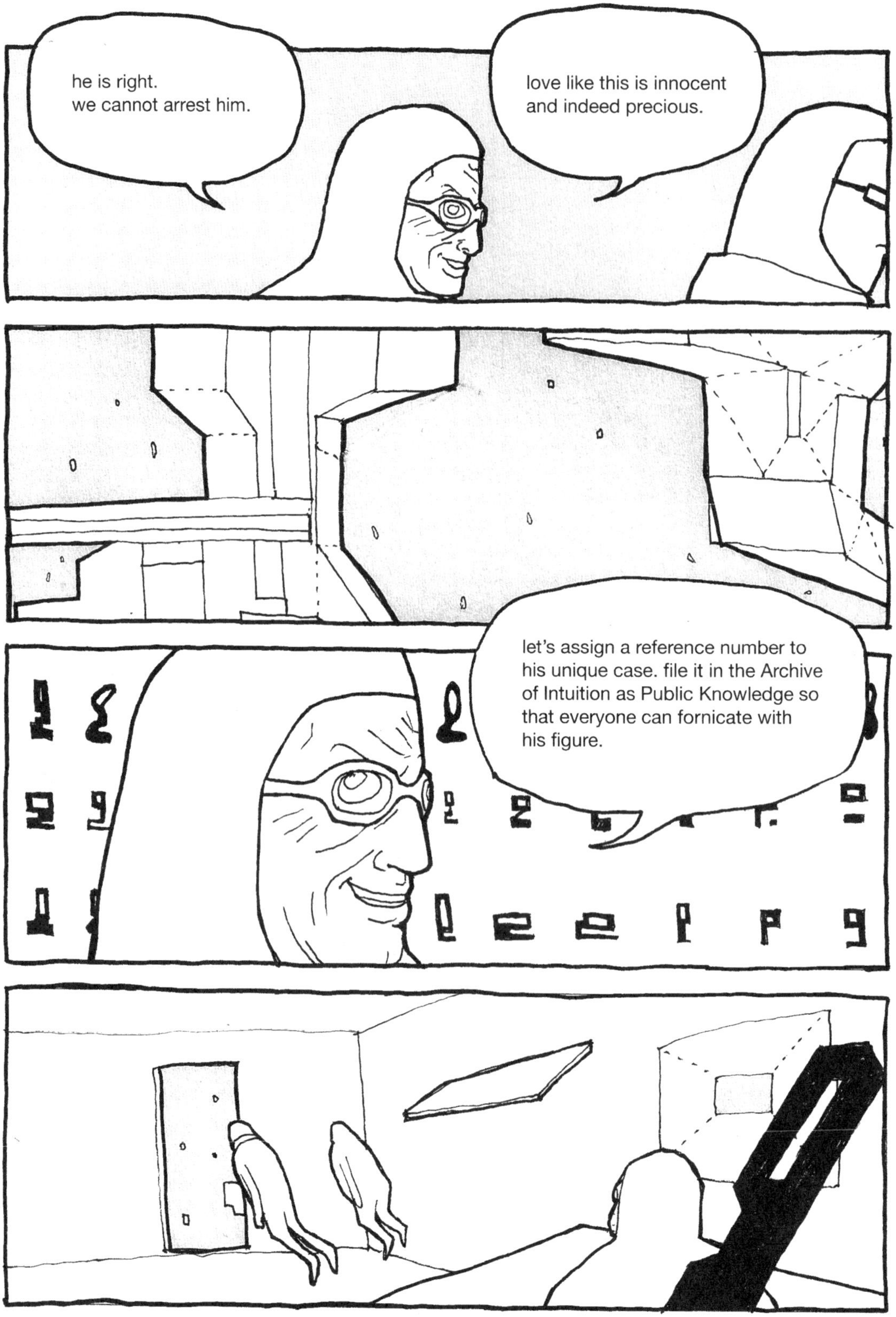

Jimenez Lai ist derzeit Clinical Assistant Professor an der University of Illinois in Chicago und leitet das Bureau Spectacular. Sein Studium an der University of Toronto schloss er mit einem Master of Architecture ab. Zuvor hatte Lai in der Wüste bei Taliesin (Arizona) und in einem Schiffscontainer des Ateliers Van Lieshout auf einem Hafenkai in Rotterdam gelebt und gearbeitet. Bei Wettbewerben in Japan, Europa und den USA erhielt Lai für seine Entwürfe lobende Erwähnungen. Als praktizierender Architekt war er Mitarbeiter der Architekturbüros MOS, AVL, RE X und OMA. Lais Installationen waren in Materials & Applications in Los Angeles und in der Extension Gallery in Chicago zu sehen. Er beteiligte sich außerdem an zahlreichen Gruppenausstellungen. Seine Zeichnungen sind vielfach publiziert worden, unter anderem in *archinect. com*, *306090*, *Conditions*, *Fresh Meat* und *Beyond*.

Deutsche Übersetzung:
Annette Wiethüchter.

Jimenez Lai is currently a Clinical Assistant Professor at University of Illinois at Chicago and Leader of Bureau Spectacular. He graduated with a Master of Architecture from the University of Toronto. Previously, Lai lived and worked in a desert shelter at Taliesin, Arizona, and resided in a shipping container at Atelier Van Lieshout on the piers of Rotterdam. Lai has received mentions in competitions in Japan, Europe, and the United States; and has worked with MOS, AVL, RE X, and OMA. Lai's installations have been featured at Materials & Applications in Los Angeles and at the Extension Gallery in Chicago; his work has also been part of numerous group exhibitions. His drawings have been widely published, including in *archinect.com*, *306090*, *Conditions*, *Fresh Meat*, *Pidgin* and *Beyond*.

Anmerkung des Verfassers:
Diese Geschichte ist eine Tragödie. Den Massen Kostbarkeiten zu verabreichen kommt dem Töten eines Einhorns gleich.

Verzerrung bedeutet die Veränderung einer ursprünglichen Form. Entgegen der Logik, die minutiöse Präzision erfordert, ist eine spontane, ungeplante Verzerrung in der Architektur mitunter wünschenswert. Die direkte Beziehung zwischen Fiktion und Verzerrung von Tatsachen ist das wirksamste Werkzeug für die Produktion von Kultur.

In meiner Arbeit setze ich Fiktion als kreative Strategie ein, um Gedanken über Architektur und die Verzerrung von Tatsachen zu verbreiten. Die Umsetzung von Kritik – gemischt mit Gesprächsinhalten – in mangaähnliche grafische Darstellungen als Teil des architektonischen Entwerfens ergibt einzigartige, aber lesbare Bilder. Die Kurzgeschichten ermöglichen eine neue Sicht der Dinge und weisen vielfach auf architektonische Probleme hin. Einige dieser Grafiken testen wir in Form von dreidimensionalen Installationen. Die Übertragung von der Attrappe in die Realität stellt einen fließenden Übergang von einer nicht messbaren Idee zu einem greifbaren Objekt dar.

Der Handlungsstrang des Raumschiffs innerhalb meiner Arbeit enthält in konzentrierter Form Gedanken zur Bedeutung von Maßstab, Projektion, Wahrnehmung, Präferenzen und Einzigartigkeit. Mein Phalansterium-Modul zum Beispiel ist ein Entwurf, der schon früh tatsächlich ausgeführt wurde – eine Studie zur Aufhebung der Schwerkraft, bei der alle orthografischen Zeichnungen Einfachprojektionen entsprachen. „Point Clouds" ist eine andere Geschichte, mit der ich die Grenzen der Parametrie ausgelotet und deren Bezug zu den Grenzen des menschlichen Körpers untersucht habe. Die Stärke der Fiktion liegt in ihrer Fähigkeit, bestimmte Themen sozusagen in einem luftleeren Raum zu isolieren. Sie erweitert die von uns akzeptierten Regeln und erhält im Austausch gegen die Verzerrung des Vertrauten eine Evolution der Formenvielfalt.

Author's note:
This story is a tragedy. The induction of preciousness into the masses is like killing a unicorn.

Distortion is the alteration of an original shape or form. Contrary to logic, which requires precision, unmanaged distortion is sometimes a desirable condition in the practice of architecture. The creation of a relationship between fiction and the distortion of facts is the most powerful tool in the fabrication of culture.

Fiction, in my practice, is deployed as a generative strategy to unpack thoughts on architecture and the distortion of facts. A manga-style graphic delivery compacts criticism with layers of conversations within the discipline into singular, legible images. My short stories offer a fresh point of view and reveal many architectural problems; some are tested as physical installations. The translation from the fake to the real presents a fluid transition from a non-measurable idea to a tangible object.

Specifically, the spaceship storyline within my work concentrates ideas about scale, projection, perception, preferences, and uniqueness. Phalanstery Module, for example, was an early built project that tested the lack of gravity, and rendered all orthographic drawings as single-projections. "Point Clouds" is another story that studies the limits of parametricism and its relationship to the limits of the human body. That it can isolate issues in a vacuum is one of fiction's greatest powers. It expands the rules we accept, and distorts conventions in the evolution of form making.

Oliver Schetter

"How come there's a window in our wall?"
The Construction of Knowledge in Mozambican Vernacular

Post-colonial development in Mozambique has led to a diminished interface between the general knowledge and the technical knowledge required to maintain a society that functions along the lines of modern statehood. This interface conditions society as a whole, but also impacts the applicability of specific knowledge, such as that of architecture. As the profession's tools regarding the management of resources often fail to correlate with cultural patterns regarding the organization of space, architects must engage with processes that seemingly contradict the terms of their work. By looking at vernacular architecture in post-colonial Mozambique, the author describes a process whereby formal and informal modes of production influence each other, resulting not only in a panoply of formal options, but also in a mode of knowledge production that is leading to a renewed rapprochement of general and technical knowledge.

Oliver Schetter

„Wieso haben wir ein Fenster in unserer Wand?"
Die Herstellung von Wissen in der vernakulären
Architektur * Mosambiks

Im Lauf der postkolonialen Entwicklung Mosambiks
hat sich die Schere zwischen dem für ein funktio-
nierendes modernes Staats- und Gesellschaftswesen
nötigen allgemeinen und technischen Wissen
weit geöffnet. Dies beeinflusst nicht nur die Gesellschaft als Ganzes, sondern auch die Anwendbarkeit
von spezifischem Fachwissen – wie dem Wissen
der Architektur. Da die Arbeitsmittel von Architekten im Hinblick auf das Management von
Ressourcen nicht den lokalen kulturellen, bei der
Raumorganisation greifenden Verhaltensmustern
entsprechen, müssen sich Architekten mit Prozessen
befassen, die scheinbar im Widerspruch zu den
Grundlagen ihres Berufs stehen. Am Beispiel der
vernakulären, postkolonialen Architektur Mosambiks
beschäftigt sich der Autor mit einem gesellschaftlichen Entwicklungsprozess, bei dem sich formelle
und informelle Produktionsweisen gegenseitig
beeinflussen. Daraus ergibt sich nicht nur eine Fülle
unterschiedlicher formaler Lösungen, sondern
auch eine Form der Wissensherstellung, die zu einer
neu gestalteten Annäherung zwischen Allgemeinwissen und Fachwissen führt.

---

* Der Begriff „vernakuläre Architektur" wirkt im Gegensatz zu dem im Englischen etablierten *vernacular
architecture* im Deutschen bisweilen etwas holprig. Dennoch haben wir uns für ihn entschieden, da
Übersetzungen wie „volkstümliche Architektur", „landestypische Bauweisen" oder „traditionelle
Architektur" der Offenheit von „vernakulär" im Hinblick auf Ursprung und Stil der beschriebenen
Architektur nicht entsprechen. Viele dieser deutschen Bedeutungsvarianten scheiden auch schon
deswegen aus, weil der vorliegende Text sich mit der formal und konstruktiv modernen vernakulären
Architektur und ihrer Beziehung zur formellen Architektur beschäftigt. Die Benutzung der oben
genannten Begriffe würde hier grundlegende Definitionswidersprüche schaffen.

2 I employ the term *general knowledge* to mean knowledge circulating in society, not exclusive to any particular act of production. General knowledge is what encompasses the values and core beliefs of a culture and constitutes the platform that brings culture as a tangible stratum into everyday life. Furthermore, general knowledge informs how technical knowledge is absorbed: I use the term *technical knowledge* to describe a domain that allows for the performance of specific tasks of production. Finally, I employ the term *architecture* as a specific subset of both technical and general knowledge to designate a product that combines structure, usability, and aesthetics, and draws on a set of techniques regarding both planning and implementation.

Introduction

I currently live and work—somewhat on the sidelines of my profession of architecture and regional planning—in the town of Inhambane in Mozambique, a country that, after nearly three decades of struggle for independence and civil war, is now one of the world's poorest. Employed by a German development agency, I have found that even after several years, most of my professional architectural knowledge is of limited applicability here. This circumstance still puzzles me, and in this essay I hope to expand on some explanations I have found, based both on the observation of this south-east African country's cultural habits as well as the particularities of its vernacular architecture. Drawing on Henri Lefebvre, I subscribe to the notion that knowledge relates both to the forces and the social relations of production.[1] Since no category of knowledge is universally applicable, knowledge cannot be ideologically neutral, and is subject to debate as a fundamental yet flexible link in the relationship between culture and modes of production [→ fig.1].

Architecture is the result of the application of knowledge that produces designs that may either be realized or remain ideas. It is important to understand the realization of designs as being dependent on limitations regarding capital, logistics, material, and services. In a peripheral location such as Mozambique, these very limitations contribute significantly toward the applicability of knowledge and are by themselves powerful reasons why knowledge may or may not be available. In fact, this holds true for the present paper: the arguments and definitions I work with are based largely on personal observation and are supported only in part by literature and information I have been able to obtain; libraries and other scholarly venues are, for the most part, inaccessible to me. From what I have gathered, many scholars who work in academia in Africa have to come to terms with at least some of these limita-

tions, as their work and the quality of their knowledge production is directly dependant upon them [→ fig. 2].

The essay is structured in two parts. In the first, I reflect on the relationship between general and technical knowledge and point to the challenge posed by relating new sets of knowledge to pre-existing cultural conditions and traditional bodies of knowledge.[2] I then touch upon the reciprocal influence of two modes of production—the formal and the informal—on the generation of physical space. In the second part, I explore Mozambique's vernacular architecture by looking in particular at how local knowledge building responds to a range of impulses from without and within, transforming both traditional and imported bodies of knowledge.

The Intricacies of Colonial and Post-colonial Knowledge

First, let us consider why the question of congruency between general and technical knowledge should at all be noteworthy. This question may seem redundant in many settings, but in any colonial or contemporary African post-colonial context it is paramount, as colonial projects bestowed and imposed knowledge alien to the existing cultural fabric on the subjects of their colonization. As the scholar Jean Boutrais sums up: "Like other forms of knowledge, local knowledge is something that undergoes construction and transformation. [...] In Africa, the early colonial era crystallized breaks and confrontations between different forms of knowledge. The colonizers developed entities with only scarce relevance to local reality, interpreting or inventing organizations to

Einführung

Zur Zeit lebe und arbeite ich an der Peripherie meines eigentlichen Berufs als Architekt
und Regionalplaner in der Stadt Inhambane
in Mosambik. Nach fast drei Jahrzehnten
Unabhängigkeitskampf und Bürgerkrieg gehört das Land heute zu den ärmsten der
Welt. Während meiner Tätigkeit für eine
deutsche Entwicklungsorganisation habe ich
festgestellt, dass auch nach mehreren Jahren
der Großteil meiner architektonischen
Fachkenntnisse nur begrenzt anwendbar ist,
und dieser Umstand verunsichert mich nach
wie vor. Mit diesem Essay versuche ich
einige mögliche Erklärungen dafür anzubie-
ten, wobei ich mich sowohl auf meine
Beobachtungen der kulturellen Sitten und
Gebräuche in diesem südostafrikanischen
Land beziehe, als auch auf die Besonderhei-
ten seiner vernakulären Architektur. Wie
Henri Lefebvre vertrete ich die Auffassung,
dass Wissen sich sowohl auf die Produktions-
kräfte wie auch auf die gesellschaftlichen
Beziehungen von Produktion bezieht.[1] Da
keine Wissenskategorie universell anwendbar
ist, kann Wissen nicht ideologisch neutral
sein und ist als grundlegendes, wiewohl
flexibles Bindeglied zwischen Kultur und
Produktionsweisen zu diskutieren [→ Abb. 1].

Architektur ist Ergebnis der Anwendung von Wissen, welches Entwürfe generiert, die entweder Gestalt annehmen oder
Absicht bleiben. Die Ausführung eines
Entwurfs steht dabei in direkter Abhängigkeit zu vorhandenem Kapital, Logistik,
Materialien und Dienstleistungen. An einem
peripheren Ort wie Mosambik wird die
Anwendbarkeit von Wissen in erheblichem
Maße von der eingeschränkten Verfügbarkeit
der Mittel bestimmt, und diese sind auch
für sich selbst genommen ein wesentlicher
Faktor für die Verfügbarkeit oder Nichtver-
fügbarkeit von Wissen. Das gilt ebenso
für diesen Text: Meine Definitionen und
Folgerungen basieren weitgehend auf persönlichen Beobachtungen und werden nur
teilweise durch Publikationen und andere

Informationsquellen gestützt. Zu Bibliotheken oder anderen Bildungsinstitutionen habe
ich kaum Zugang. Soweit ich weiß, müssen
sich viele Angehörige des akademischen Mili-
eus in Afrika zumindest teilweise mit diesen
Einschränkungen arrangieren, da ihre Arbeit
und die Qualität ihrer Wissensproduktion
direkt hiervon abhängen [→ Abb. 2].

Im ersten Abschnitt befasse ich mich
mit der Beziehung zwischen Allgemeinwissen
und Fachwissen und weise auf die Herausforderung hin, neue Wissensgebiete mit lokal
gültigen kulturellen Bedingungen und einem
traditionellen Wissenskorpus in Einklang
zu bringen.[2] Dabei untersuche ich auch den
gegenseitigen Einfluss zweier Produktionsweisen – der formellen und der informellen
– bei der Erzeugung von physischem Raum.
Im zweiten Teil untersuche ich die vernakuläre Architektur Mosambiks und beschäfti-
ge mich insbesondere mit der Frage, wie
die Herstellung von lokalem Wissen auf eine
Reihe von äußeren und inneren Anstößen
reagiert und dadurch sowohl einen traditionellen wie importierten Wissenskorpus verändert.

Komplexitäten des kolonialen und postkolonialen Wissens

Eingangs möchte ich untersuchen, warum
die Frage nach der Kongruenz von Allgemeinwissen und technischem Wissen überhaupt beachtenswert sein sollte. In vielen
Zusammenhängen erscheint diese Frage
vielleicht überflüssig, sie ist aber in jedem
kolonialen Umfeld und im gegenwärtigen
postkolonialen Kontext Afrikas von größter
Bedeutung, da die Kolonialmächte ihren

---

1 Lefebvre 2000: 8f.
2 Mit dem Begriff *Allgemeinwissen* bezeichne ich das in
einer Gesellschaft kursierende Gesamtwissen, das nicht
mit einer spezifischen Produktionshandlung verbunden
ist. Es umfasst die Werte und den Kernglauben
einer Kultur und stellt die Plattform dar, auf der diese
Kultur als Grundlage des täglichen Lebens greifbar
wird. Außerdem gibt das Allgemeinwissen Auskunft
darüber, wie *technisches Wissen* erworben wird. Mit
diesem zweiten Begriff beschreibe ich Wissensgebiete,
welche die Erfüllung bestimmter Produktionsaufträge
ermöglichen. Schließlich verwende ich den Begriff
Architektur im Sinne eines spezifischen Teilwissens
im Bereich des technischen Wissens wie auch des
Allgemeinwissens, um ein „Produkt" zu bezeichnen,
das Konstruktion, Zweckmäßigkeit und Ästhetik vereint und dabei auf verschiedene Planungs- und Ausfüh-
rungstechniken zurückgreift.

meet requirements of conquest and domination."[3] [→ fig. 4]

This mechanism of imposing a new order with limited relevance to local realities touches upon the whole range of knowledge, from simple knowledge of the "when the whistle blows, you have to hurry" sort, described by Joseph Conrad in his novel *Heart of Darkness*, to the understanding of complex relationships. Conrad's novel was written at the moment of nearly complete territorial domination of Africa by European powers, where "progress," for all that it is worth as well as the storyline are advanced by the maneuvers of a technical device, a riverboat on the Congo.[4] The boat—the imported object—determines the relationship of the colonizers to the indigenous population more than any protagonist's individual action could. Without devices like the boat and the technical knowledge they stand for, and, by consequence, the general knowledge required to make use of them, the story of colonization as played out in Africa would not have been feasible.

In the colonial setting, the paradigm of modernization did not emerge from among the social forces operating within a society. The resulting dichotomy between traditional and modernizing forces therefore is not the result of local historical development—rather, it was externally stimulated by the imposition of elements of novel general and technical knowledge. To the colonizers, it was essential to convey a more general side of knowledge, to promote categories in accordance with their standards of production, such as time management, diligence, thoroughness, obedience, and so forth. This type of general knowledge could not be imposed without significantly altering and ultimately even rupturing existing cultural codes, but it was generally the prerequisite to make a colonized people receptive to imported forms of technical knowledge.[5] This general knowledge is therefore the layer where the differences between cultures are most deeply felt—even though the results of the application of such knowledge may not be as visible as those regarding other forms of knowledge—as nothing is directly produced from it. However, things are produced by way of it.

3   Boutrais 1999: 490.
4   Cf. Conrad 1899.
5   The underlying knowledge-based transformation of a colony's society and culture was possible only by altering existing power relations and codes of conduct and allegiance. In African colonies, where colonial agents were available only in limited numbers, European colonial powers often used existing forms of chiefdom or replaced traditional rulers with competing classes and groups in order to exert power over indigenous populations by way of substitute rule. Cf. Gellar 1995. An example of this in Mozambique is the *assimilados*, Mozambicans who, in colonial times, adopted a Portuguese-dictated lifestyle and thereby gained access to certain rights and knowledge from which the majority were excluded. Sumich 2008: 324f.
6   Lefebvre 2000 [1974]: 190.

In the process of conveying new technical knowledge, locals were taught how to use tools and contribute to mechanisms formerly unbeknownst to them by executing specific tasks of production. These tasks may not have radically differed from what people already knew how to do, as African colonies in particular were geared toward agricultural production and the extraction of raw materials, both of which relied on intensive menial labor. In the most tangible sense, people may still have hacked, picked, carried, pulled, or pushed. Lefebvre points out that "in reality, whenever a society undergoes a transformation, the materials used in the process derive from another, historically (or developmentally) anterior social practice."[6] Yet the tools, the products, the scale, and the organization of intervention had changed, including their meaning, due to the extremely unfavorable terms that accompanied them.

By combining and managing both sets of knowledge, general and technical, colonial rule created what I refer to as a *landscape of knowledge on a subdued cultural topography*. The cultural topography describes the sum of habits existing in consonance with knowledge and representing the intellectual development of a social body. A landscape of knowledge involves everything that regards the application and applicability of knowledge on a given territory: people as bearers of knowledge, knowledge-disseminating institutions and mechanisms, and discernible knowledge contained in objects. Here, it is important to note that an object can only be part of a landscape of knowledge if the knowledge stored therein can be operated or

Untertanen ein den lokalen Gebräuchen fremdes Wissen aufzwangen. Jean Boutrais, französischer Geograf und Ethnologe, formuliert es so: „Wie andere Wissensarten auch ist jeder lokale Wissenskorpus dem Auf- und Weiterbau und Veränderungen unterworfen. [...] In Afrika förderte die frühe Kolonialzeit Brüche und Widersprüche zwischen unterschiedlichen Wissensformen zutage. Die Kolonialmächte etablierten Instanzen, die nur wenig Berührungspunkte mit der Realität vor Ort hatten, und interpretierten oder erfanden Organisationsstrukturen, um ihren Absichten von Eroberung und Vorherrschaft Genüge zu tun.“[3] [→ Abb. 4]

Der Mechanismus der Durchsetzung einer neuen Ordnung mit begrenzter Relevanz für örtliche Gegebenheiten betraf ein breites Wissensspektrum – von der simplen Erkenntnis, dass Eile geboten ist, wenn die Bootspfeife ertönt, wie von Joseph Conrad in *Herz der Finsternis* beschrieben, bis zum Verständnis komplexer Beziehungsgeflechte. Conrad veröffentlichte seinen Roman, als Afrika in seiner territorialen Ausdehnung fast vollständig von europäischen Staaten beherrscht wurde. Im Buch werden der „Fortschritt“(was immer das sein mag) und die Handlung von den Manövern eines technischen Apparats, und zwar eines Flussdampfers auf dem Kongo, vorangetrieben.[4] Das Schiff – das importierte Objekt – bestimmt die Beziehungen zwischen Europäern und Einheimischen mehr als jede individuelle Handlung der Protagonisten. Ohne technische Importe wie den Flussdampfer sowie das von ihnen verkörperte technische Wissen, und demzufolge ohne das für ihre Nutzung erforderliche Allgemeinwissen, wäre die Kolonialgeschichte, so wie sie in Afrika stattgefunden hat, nicht möglich gewesen.

Im kolonialen Zusammenhang ist das Paradigma der Modernisierung sozialen Kräften, die von außerhalb der Gesellschaft operieren, geschuldet; die Dichotomie zwischen Tradition und Moderne ergibt sich also nicht aus örtlichen Entwicklungen, sondern sie ist extern ausgelöst durch die Auferlegung neuer Elemente allgemeinen und technischen Wissens. Für die Kolonisatoren war es unerlässlich, lokalen Bevölkerungen zuvorderst eine allgemeine Seite von Wissen zu vermitteln, um Verhaltensweisen zu schaffen, die sich im Einklang mit ihren Produktionsstandards befanden, wie zum Beispiel Zeiteinteilung, Fleiß, Gründlichkeit, Gehorsam, usw. Diese Art Allgemeinwissen ließ sich nicht durchsetzen, ohne bestehende kulturelle Codes erheblich zu verändern und letztlich aufzubrechen, aber generell war dies die Voraussetzung dafür, kolonialisierte Bevölkerungen für importiertes technisches Wissen aufnahmebereit zu machen.[5] Das Allgemeinwissen bildet somit die Wissensschicht, in der sich kulturelle Unterschiede am stärksten bemerkbar machen – obwohl die daraus folgenden Wissensanwendungen vielleicht nicht so deutlich ins Auge springen wie im Fall anderer Wissensformen, da sie ja nicht selber unmittelbar greifbare Produkte hervorbringen. Dinge werden jedoch über sie, d.h. auf ihnen aufbauend, produziert.

Im Zuge der Vermittlung neuen Fachwissens lernten einheimische Bevölkerungen klar definierte Aufgaben zu erfüllen, indem sie mit Werkzeugen umgingen und Beiträge zu Produktionsprozessen leisteten, die ihnen vormals unbekannt waren. Die Aufgaben an sich unterschieden sich unter Umständen nicht grundlegend von denen, die ihnen bereits vertraut waren, denn insbesondere die afrikanischen Kolonien bauten auf einem System landwirtschaftlicher Produktion und dem Abbau von Bodenschätzen auf, das auf den intensiven Einsatz manueller Arbeitskraft zurückgriff. Im greifbarsten Sinne waren die Menschen daher immer noch mit

---

3 Boutrais 1999: 490 [Dt. Übers.: Annette Wiethüchter].
4 Vgl. Conrad 2006 [1899].
5 Die auf Wissen basierende Transformation der Gesellschaft und Kultur einer Kolonie war nur möglich, indem die bestehenden Machtverhältnisse, Verhaltensnormen und menschlichen Bindungen verändert wurden. In den afrikanischen Kolonien, wo es nur eine begrenzte Anzahl von Kolonialbeamten gab, nutzten die europäischen Kolonialmächte häufig bestehende Formen der Stammesherrschaft oder ersetzten traditionelle Häuptlinge durch andere Klassen oder Gruppen, um Kontrolle über einheimische Bevölkerungen durch eine Form von Ersatzherrschaft zu erhalten. Vgl. Gellar 1995. Ein Beispiel hierfür sind in Mosambik die sogenannten *assimilados*, Mosambikaner, die während der portugiesischen Kolonialzeit den Lebensstil der Portugiesen übernahmen und so bestimmte Privilegien und Kenntnisse erhielten, von denen die Mehrheit ausgeschlossen war. Sumich 2008: 324f.

unlocked by users. The knowledge contained in most objects is not readily available. Just as particular machinery can be seen as capital in circulation, it can also be understood as knowledge in circulation. Machinery that no longer functions, therefore, can be considered capital forfeited, in the sense that it no longer produces surplus value. By analogy, the nonfunctional machinery is no longer a part of the landscape of knowledge if no one has knowledge of how to operate or repair it. Conrad's riverboat, therefore, can be said to have been temporarily stranded, no longer a part of the landscape of knowledge of the Congo basin after the death of its Danish captain and prior to the arrival of his successor, the novel's protagonist, Charles Marlow. In a sense, however, the fact that the boat did circulate at a given time and that locals retain memory of its working (the whistle blowing, for instance), the carcass of the boat continues to play a part in the landscape of knowledge, albeit one lacking its intended functional dimension [→ fig. 3].

Conrad's boat had a certain range of action and influence by which it perpetrated a dynamic that turned dominant for a specific territory. In the colony and, from 1951 on, in the Portuguese Province of Mozambique, the dominant dynamic also implied a certain distinction between areas of Portuguese and areas of Mozambican values. Portuguese values dominated when relating to the colonial market, with its administrative, religious, transportational, agricultural, and agro-industrial infrastructures. However, the cultural topography also included values that were decidedly the result of an amalgamation of both Portuguese and Mozambican influence—in the case of language, for instance, local languages clearly influenced Portuguese speech patterns and grammar.[7]

The Mozambican landscape of knowledge changed significantly after independence was achieved in 1975, as the Portuguese exodus caused an immediate drought of technical knowledge in all sectors related to the colony's modernizing project. The departure of the colonizers led to the occupation of technical positions by Mozambicans who were ill-prepared for them: "The worst

7   Cf. Lopes/Sitoe/Nhamuende 2002: iiif.
8   Forjaz 2004 [Engl. trans.: Oliver Schetter].

legacy of colonialism lies […] at the level of education and the development of human resources. At the time of independence, the country had an illiteracy rate of more than ninety-five percent and an indigenous population without the capacity to perform anything other than non-specialized or semi-specialized jobs. Graduates of technical schools or universities were counted at the most in the dozens and, in some professions, even today they are counted on the fingers of a hand, as are, for instance, architects and regional planners."[8] The vast majority of Mozambicans neither possessed the necessary technical knowledge nor the experience to guarantee its application, causing diminishing efficiency and shrinking performance of bureaucracy, services, agricultural production, and agro-industries in the decades following independence.

After independence, many Mozambicans thus saw their position in society rearranged. The population was suddenly faced with the challenge of a bundled knowledge transfer in learning how to deal with objects they frequently did not know how to use, and whose functioning meant little to them since the requirements to operate many objects such as vehicles, machinery, or buildings contrasted with their behavioral patterns. Referring to Mozambicans occupying formerly Portuguese homes that had been nationalized upon independence, the country's first president, Samora Moisés Machel, described the difficulties arising from that particular contact between man and artifact in the following way:

A person used to live in a hut with a fireplace inside, without a window, with a straw door so low you have to bow or get on your knees to enter. We conquered the city; we conquered the buildings. Now he lives on the twelfth floor. The building has a sidewalk, an entrance, an elevator; it has windows with panes, blinds, doors inside the dwelling; it has electricity, it has closets along the wall, it has parquet, it has

Hacken, Pflücken, Tragen, Ziehen oder Schieben befasst. Laut Lefebvre leiten sich, „wenn sich eine Gesellschaft im Wandel befindet, die bei diesem Prozess verwendeten Mittel aus einer anderen, historischen (oder entwicklungsgeschichtlichen) vorausgegangenen gesellschaftlichen Praxis" ab.[6] Aber die Werkzeuge, die Produkte, der Maßstab und die Organisationsstrukturen veränderten sich ebenso wie die Bedeutungszusammenhänge angesichts von extrem ungünstigen Bedingungen für einheimische Bevölkerungen.

Durch Kombination und Steuerung beider Wissensformen – allgemeines und technisches Wissen – schufen Kolonialmächte das, was ich als eine *Wissenslandschaft auf einer unterdrückten kulturellen Topografie* bezeichne. Mit kultureller Topografie meine ich die Summe bestehender Sitten und Gebräuche, die im Einklang mit dem in der Gesellschaft vorhandenen Wissen den intellektuellen, gesellschaftlichen Entwicklungsstand darstellen. Die Wissenslandschaft umfasst alle Anwendungsarten und -möglichkeiten von Wissen auf einem bestimmten Territorium: Menschen als Wissensträger, wissensvermittelnde Institutionen und Mechanismen sowie erkennbares, in Gegenständen materialisiertes Wissen. Dabei ist zu beachten, dass ein Gegenstand nur dann Teil einer Wissenslandschaft sein kann, wenn das in ihm gespeicherte Wissen von Nutzern auch erschlossen und angewandt werden kann. In den wenigsten Fällen ist gespeichertes Wissen jedoch direkt vom Gegenstand ablesbar. Eine Maschine kann zum Beispiel sowohl als Kapital im Umlauf wie auch als Wissen im Umlauf angesehen werden. Daraus folgt, dass eine Maschine, die nicht länger funktioniert, als verwirktes Kapital gelten kann, weil sie keinen Mehrwert mehr produzieren kann. In Analogie dazu gehört eine Maschine auch nicht länger zur Wissenslandschaft, wenn niemand mehr das Wissen um ihren Betrieb und ihre Wartung besitzt. Conrads gestrandeter Flussdampfer kann also in der Zeit zwischen dem Tod des dänischen Kapitäns bis zur erneuten Inbetriebnahme durch dessen Nachfolger Charles Marlow, der Hauptfigur des Romans, als nicht zur Wissenslandschaft des Kongobeckens gehörend bezeichnet

werden. Unter der Maßgabe, dass das Schiff jedoch über bestimmte Zeiträume den Kongo befuhr und die Menschen am Fluss sich daran erinnern (etwa an den schrillen Ton der Bootspfeife), spielt das Wrack des Flussbootes jedoch auch interimsweise eine Rolle in der Wissenslandschaft, allerdings gemindert um seine ursprüngliche funktionale Dimension [→ Abb. 3].

Conrads Dampfer verfügte über einen bestimmten Aktionsradius und Einfluss im Gebiet des Kongobeckens, das er mit seiner Dynamik bewegte und beherrschte – wenngleich im Dialog mit der lokalen Kultur. In der Kolonie (und ab 1951 portugiesischen Überseeprovinz) Mosambik schuf die Dynamik der kolonialen Macht auch eine gewisse Abgrenzung zwischen den von portugiesischen und den von mosambikanischen Werten geprägten Bereichen. Die portugiesischen Werte herrschten im direkten Umfeld der Kolonialwirtschaft mit ihren administrativen, religiösen, logistischen, landwirtschaftlichen und agrarindustriellen Infrastrukturen vor. Zur kulturellen Topografie gehörten aber auch Werte, die eindeutig ein Amalgam aus beiden Kulturen darstellten. Ein Beispiel ist die Sprache: einheimische mosambikanische Sprachen haben in den Sprachmustern und der Grammatik des hiesigen Portugiesisch deutliche Spuren hinterlassen.[7]

Die Wissenslandschaft Mosambiks hat sich seit der Unabhängigkeit im Jahr 1975 erheblich verändert, da der Exodus der Überseeportugiesen in kürzester Zeit ein großes Loch in den vorhandenen Korpus an technischem Wissen gerissen hat. Die einst von Portugiesen eingenommenen technischen Führungspositionen wurden nun von Mosambikanern besetzt, die unzulänglich auf ihre neuen Aufgaben vorbereitet waren. „Die schlimmste Hinterlassenschaft des Kolonialismus besteht [...] in der mangelnden Ausbildung und Entwicklung menschlicher Ressourcen. Zur Zeit der Unabhängigkeit gab es 95% Analphabeten im Land und eine einheimische Bevölkerung, die lediglich

---

6 Lefebvre 2000: 190 [Dt. Übers.: Annette Wiethüchter].
7 Vgl. Lopes/Sitoe/Nhamuende 2002: iiif.

sanitary installations, has tubing, has septic tanks. This person was used to using the pestle and mortar for pounding food in his yard. We started a big campaign so that they wouldn't be brought into the houses. A building is calculated to support a certain weight. Some buildings today have loose parquet, holes in the cement [floor], cracked walls, broken windows and toilets because of the pounding of the mortar and the vibrations it creates.[9]

The example illustrates how, following independence, traditional knowledge re-conquered some modern spaces that were formerly off-limits. Even though the colonial push-effect on society—the external forces that had deformed the cultural topography—was partly replaced by a post-colonial pull-effect—the processes of modernization that are part of economic globalization—the post-colonial landscape of knowledge increasingly separated from the cultural topography. That is: despite Mozambicans being susceptible to the consumption of products, lifestyles, and privileges from which they were formerly excluded, they did not—or were not able to—embrace the habits or foster the general knowledge required to sustain the technical knowledge and modes of production that render such consumption possible.[10]

Former racial segregation has given way to a class structure that perpetuates what was originally a largely colonial division between country and town, marking a deep rift in most African societies. Additionally, Mozambique's civil war and economic hardship has resulted in a large migration into the cities. This transition from rural to urban contexts is frequently tantamount to a rupture of tradition and the adaptation to a modern lifestyle. Cities are, however, not the only places of change, as rural areas too are subject to rapid transformation;[11] urban life itself varies widely from a city's center to its periphery. The general underlying cultural conflict between traditional and modern ways of life, and their underlying bodies of knowledge, is very much alive and reproduces itself across all loci of Mozambican society.

9   Partido Frelimo 1983: 42 [Engl. trans.: Oliver Schetter].
10 The immediate concern of educating citizens was central to government campaigns in the early years after independence. Since then, people living in modern architecture in cities—Maputo, Beira, Nampula, and even small towns like Inhambane—have adapted to urban life. It also ceased to be a central public concern when the government started to privatize the formerly nationalized houses and apartments in the 1990s.
11 Cf. Robertson 1995.
12 Cf. Bruschi/Lage 2005.
13 Cf. Trindade/Do Valle/Bruschi 2003: 1.

A look at the development patterns of Mozambique's relatively young urban agglomerations illustrates the contrast between modern and traditional cultural habits, or formal and informal spatial processes. The cities' colonial centers are generally of a regular array, as they are the result of civil engineering and town planning regulations implemented by the colonial administration; they are also based on clear zoning.[12] Since independence, these formal parts of towns, the cidades de cementos (cement towns), have mostly remained frozen whereas the bairros de caniço or cidades de caniço (reed neighborhoods or reed cities) have proliferated.[13] Such settlements—originally consisting mainly of dwellings made of organic material—describe patterns of growth in stark contrast to the centers, although some of them have benefited from the partial implementation of plans. In the city centers, this contrast can also be noted in the architecture. Formally constructed buildings, overwhelmingly dating back to colonial times, have in many cases been altered by additions to their fronts, sides, or backs, the subdivision of functional units, or by the fragmentation and mixture of uses; public spaces are occupied by makeshift kiosks. This transformation of modern elements by traditional processes constitutes a phenomenon that has conquered all aspects of Mozambican society, spatially and metaphorically [→ fig. 7].

Technical knowledge as applied by the bureaucratic apparatus does play a role, as urban development does not occur entirely independently of state intervention. However, due to a lack of capacity for implementation and control, these dynamic processes outpace the cumbersome technical procedures

nicht spezialisierte oder gering spezialisierte Tätigkeiten ausführen konnte. Einheimische Absolventen von technischen Schulen oder Hochschulen zählte man bestenfalls in Dutzenden, und auch heute noch kann man sie in einigen Berufsfeldern – zum Beispiel in der Architektur und Regionalplanung – an den Fingern einer Hand abzählen."[8] Die allermeisten Mosambikaner verfügten weder über das notwendige technische Wissen noch über die Erfahrung, um es korrekt anzuwenden, was die Effizienz und den Leistungsumfang der nationalen Bürokratie, Dienstleistungen, landwirtschaftlichen Produktion und Agrarindustrie in den Jahrzehnten seit der Unabhängigkeit stark reduzierte.

Nach der Unabhängigkeit fanden sich viele Mosambikaner demnach in einer ganz anderen gesellschaftlichen Position wieder. Sie standen plötzlich vor der schwierigen Aufgabe, sich in kürzester Zeit das Wissen anzueignen, das für den Betrieb der von den Portugiesen hinterlassenen technischen Einrichtungen erforderlich war. Dabei handelte es sich unter anderem um Fahrzeuge, Instrumente, Maschinen und Gebäude, die sie vorher nicht vollständig selbst betreiben mussten oder durften und deren Funktion ihnen wenig bedeutete, da deren Nutzung nicht den eigenen Verhaltensmustern entsprach. Mit Bezug auf die mosambikanischen Bewohner vormals portugiesischer Häuser, die nach der Unabhängigkeit in Staatseigentum übergegangen waren, erklärte Mosambiks erster Präsident Samora Moisés Machel die Schwierigkeiten, die sich aus dem Kontakt zwischen Mensch und Artefakt ergaben, folgendermaßen:

„Ein Mensch lebte früher in einer fensterlosen Hütte mit einer Feuerstelle in der Mitte und einer Tür aus Stroh, die so niedrig war, dass man sich bücken oder auf die Knie gehen musste, um hineinzugelangen. Wir eroberten die Stadt. Wir eroberten die Gebäude. Nun wohnt der Mensch im 12. Stock. Das Gebäude hat einen Bürgersteig, einen Eingang, einen Aufzug, Glasfenster, Jalousien, Innentüren, Stromanschluss, Wandschränke, Parkettböden, sanitäre

Installationen, Leitungsrohre und Abwassergruben. Der Mensch war es gewohnt, hinter seiner Hütte Nahrungsmittel mit einem großen Stößel in einem Mörser zu zerstampfen. Wir führten eine große Kampagne durch, um ihn daran zu hindern, den Mörser in die [modernen] Häuser mitzunehmen. Ein Gebäude ist so bemessen, dass es nur eine bestimmte Last tragen kann. Einige Gebäude haben heute aufgrund der durch das Stampfen im Mörser verursachten Vibrationen lose Parkettstäbe, Löcher im Zement[fußboden], Risse in den Wänden, kaputte Fenster und Toiletten."[9]

Dieses Zitat zeigt beispielhaft, wie traditionelles, einheimisches Wissen nach der Unabhängigkeit moderne Räume (zurück-)eroberte, von denen die Mosambikaner zuvor aus-geschlossen waren. Die Stoßwirkung des kolonialen Projekts, welches die kulturelle Topografie der mosambikanischen Gesellschaft verformt hatte, wurde teilweise durch die Sogwirkung des postkolonialen Modernisierungsprozesses der wirtschaftlichen Globalisierung ersetzt. Dennoch klaffte die Schere zwischen der postkolonialen Wissenslandschaft und der kulturellen Topografie immer weiter auseinander. Die Mosambikaner wurden zwar empfänglich für den Konsum von Produkten, Lebensstilen und Privilegien, von denen sie vormals ausgeschlossen waren, übernahmen aber nicht in gleichem Maße die Gewohnheiten oder das erforderliche Allgemeinwissen (oder konnten es nicht übernehmen), welches das technische Wissen und die Produktionsweisen unterfütterte, die solchen Konsum überhaupt erst ermöglichen.[10]

8 Vgl. Forjaz 2004 [Dt. Übers.: Annette Wiethüchter].
9 Partido Frelimo 1983: 42 [Dt. Übers.: Annette Wiethüchter].
10 In den ersten Jahren nach der Unabhängigkeit waren Aufklärungskampagnen zur Volkserziehung ein vorrangiges Instrument des Staates. Seitdem haben sich die Einwohner von Städten wie Maputo, Beira, Nampula und selbst von Kleinstädten wie Inhambane an das moderne Stadtleben gewöhnt. Durch die Privatisierung der staatlichen Liegenschaften – u.a. Häuser und Apartments – ab den 1990er Jahren verlor die normierte Nutzung des privaten Wohnraums an öffentlicher Bedeutung.

of public administrations still operating with standards introduced by the Portuguese administration. These are generally too high for the limited social and economic resources, leading to their frequent noncompliance. In addition, technicians and bureaucrats, although they defend the necessity of standards within their specific domains, will likely not comply as readily with others, as these are not sustained by their cultural habits.[14]

Other negative developmental factors need to be taken into account when analyzing Mozambique's landscape of knowledge: the 1977–1992 civil war played an important part in the decline of a functioning state and national economy and accelerated the loss of knowledge. From the late 1970s on, the Mozambican government lost control of large portions of the national territory, and in parts of the country rule was effectively limited to urban agglomerations. The destruction of the physical infrastructure led to the isolation and rudimentary functioning of productive areas and sectors spread over the territory that previously functioned in conjunction. The destruction or reduced performance of transport infrastructures, especially, conditioned the demise of markets, and is a problem that persists to this day [→ figs. 5 and 6].

Furthermore, the knowledge-generating infrastructure of schools and universities was severely impacted. Teaching institutions that used to disseminate technical knowledge lost relevance as the content of their teaching could no longer be put into practice either by students or teachers, and subsequent generations of teachers, in turn, have less and less practical knowledge to pass on. Therefore, places of knowledge dissemination, despite their numbers having greatly increased since independence, confer less knowledge than before. As Mozambican society does not provide the necessary education to enable its members to effectively acquire, digest, and apply technical knowledge, it remains abstract and insignificant. Architects, once having completed their professional education, have limited possibilities to acquire practical knowledge in the absence of a creative architectural milieu outside the school of architecture. Like tech-

14 This dual behavior is not exclusively a Mozambican dilemma. Ekeh has suggested a model that can be also used as an explanation for this asymmetry regarding post-colonial Nigeria after independence in 1960 by introducing the concept of two publics, one civic and amoral and one primordial and morally binding. Whereas modern Western society is based on functional relations, and behavioral patterns of social kinship generally have a negative connotation, African societies tend to be based on the primacy of owing allegiance to kinship and it is morally accepted and even expected that the fulfillment of primordial relations conditions and influences functional relations among the civic public. Ekeh 1975: 106ff.

15 Cf. Bruschi/Carrilho/Lage 2005: 28.

nicians in other areas, they tend either to insist on the normative textbook dimensions of the technical knowledge they defend, or, in the worst of circumstances, they merely defend a role model of what being an architect signals socially and hierarchically, despite lacking the qualifications that should sustain the exercise of the profession [→ fig. 8].

The Intricacies of Traditional and Modern Vernacular

Much can be learned about the evolution of knowledge in Mozambique by looking at its vernacular architecture. Traditional vernacular architecture, that is, popular architecture built without the involvement of architects, is rooted in agrarian society; formal architecture, that is, architecture resulting from planning by architects according to laws and regulations, was imported with the goal of creating central places in the functional array of the colony. Despite this distinction, vernacular and formal architecture have reciprocally influenced each other since colonial times, adapting and incorporating products and spatial solutions from each other as circumstances allow or require.[15] Analyzing the related processes reveals which techniques, materials, solutions, elements, or programs are absorbed or adapted from the other realm, and helps to reflect what types of knowledge are applicable in a society with limited knowledge resources [→ fig. 9].

As almost every rural inhabitant and many residents of suburban neighborhoods build their own dwellings as a matter of course, informal or vernacular architecture vastly outnumbers formal architectural production.

Die frühere Rassentrennung ist einer Klassengesellschaft gewichen, welche die ursprüngliche, weitgehend während der Kolonialzeit geschaffene Kluft zwischen Stadt und Land in den meisten afrikanischen Ländern beibehalten und so tiefe gesellschaftliche Gräben gezogen hat. In Mosambik haben der Bürgerkrieg und wirtschaftliche Schwierigkeiten außerdem zu einer Zuwanderung der Menschen in die Städte geführt. Die Übersiedlung vom Land in die Stadt kommt häufig dem Bruch mit der Tradition und der Übernahme eines modernen Lebensstils gleich. Die Städte sind allerdings nicht die einzigen Orte, die sich wandeln, auch ländliche Gegenden erleben rapide Veränderungen,[11] und selbst in den Städten gibt es zwischen Zentrum und Peripherie erhebliche Unterschiede, was die Lebensweise der Einwohner angeht. Der diesem Phänomen zugrunde liegende kulturelle Konflikt zwischen dem traditionellen und dem modernen Leben mit den jeweils dazugehörigen Formen des Wissens macht sich in allen gesellschaftlichen Schichten des Landes bemerkbar.

Der Blick auf die Stadtentwicklungsmuster von Mosambiks meist relativ jungen städtischen Ballungsräumen illustriert den Kontrast zwischen modernen und traditionellen Sitten und Gebräuchen beziehungsweise zwischen formellen und informellen Prozessen der Raumentwicklung. Die meisten Kernstädte weisen ein regelmäßiges Planraster auf, da sie von der Kolonialverwaltung nach Baugesetzen und städtebaulichen Regeln angelegt wurden; sie fußen auch auf eindeutigen Flächennutzungsplänen.[12] Seit der Unabhängigkeit hat sich in diesen formellen Stadtgebieten, die *cidades de cementos* (Zementstädte) genannt werden, insgesamt wenig verändert, während die Anzahl der *bairros de caniço* oder *cidades de caniço* (Stadtviertel oder Städte aus Ried) im Gegensatz dazu stark zugenommen hat.[13] Ursprünglich bestanden die Wohnhäuser im Weichbild der Städte vor allem aus organischen Materialien, und die Viertel wuchsen im Kontrast zu den geordneten Stadtzentren; obwohl einige von ihnen unter anderem durch die teilweise Implementierung von Planwerken entstanden. In den Stadtzentren finden sich zudem

ähnliche Kontraste im Rahmen einzelner Gebäude. Die meisten formalen Architekturen stammen noch aus der Kolonialzeit; sie sind jedoch seither vielfach durch (vordere, seitliche oder rückseitige) Anbauten, durch Unterteilung von funktionalen Einheiten oder durch Fragmentierung von Nutzungen verändert worden. Öffentliche Räume werden zum Teil von Verkaufsständen besetzt. Das Phänomen dieser Anverwandlung moderner Elemente an einheimische Traditionen durchzieht – räumlich wie metaphorisch – die gesamte mosambikanische Gesellschaft [→ Abb. 7].

Das von der Bürokratie angewandte technische Wissen spielt dabei eine Rolle, da Stadtentwicklung sich nicht völlig frei von staatlichen Eingriffen vollzieht. Aufgrund fehlender Kapazitäten bei Durchführung und Kontrolle überholt jedoch die Eigendynamik des Wachstumsprozesses die langwierigen Verfahren öffentlicher Planungsbehörden, die immer noch im Wesentlichen nach den Normen der portugiesischen Kolonialmacht vorgehen. Diese Standards sind angesichts der begrenzten sozialen und ökonomischen Ressourcen des Landes im Allgemeinen zu hoch angesetzt, was häufig zu ihrer Nichtbeachtung und zu stagnierenden Prozessen führt. Außerdem verteidigen Technokraten und Bürokraten zwar die Notwendigkeit der Einhaltung von technischen Standards in ihrem Fachgebiet, sind aber möglicherweise nicht gewillt, mit dem gleichen Eifer die für andere als ihre eigenen Zuständigkeitsbereiche geltenden Normen einzuhalten, da diese eben nicht den eigenen kulturellen Gepflogenheiten entsprechen.[14 (S. 126)]

Bei der Analyse der mosambikanischen Wissenslandschaft gilt es noch andere negative Entwicklungen zu berücksichtigen. Der langjährige Bürgerkrieg (1977–92) trug in erheblichem Maße zum Niedergang eines funktionierenden Staatswesens und einer Nationalökonomie bei und beschleunigte den Verlust von Bildung und Wissen.

11 Vgl. Robertson 1995.
12 Vgl. Bruschi/Lage 2005.
13 Vgl. Trindade/Do Valle/Bruschi 2003: 1.

Falls nicht anders vermerkt, stammen alle Fotografien vom Verfasser.

Unless otherwise noted, all photographs are by the author.

1

1 Modell eines traditionellen vernakulären Wohnhauses im Fenster eines modernen Kolonialhauses, Provinzhauptstadt Inhambane.
2 Gesamtkatalog der Nationalbibliothek in Maputo.
3 Wandgemälde an der Fassade eines öffentlichen Gebäudes, Landkreis Inharrime, Provinz Inhambane.
4 Wandgemälde einer traditionellen, vernakulären Familieneinheit neben dem Kühlschrank einer Gaststätte, Landkreis Morrumbene, Provinz Inhambane.

1 Model of a traditional vernacular dwelling on display on the window ledge of a modern colonial house, Inhambane, Inhambane Province.
2 Complete catalog of the national library in Maputo.
3 Mural on the façade of a public facility, Inharrime District, Inhambane Province.
4 Mural of a traditional vernacular family unit next to a restaurant's refrigerator, Morrumbene District, Inhambane Province.

3

4

5

6

5 Teilweise zerstörte Ladenzeile an der Fernverkehrsstraße, Zandamela, Landkreis Zavala, an der Grenze zwischen den Provinzen Inhambane und Gaza.

6 Plastik einer Flüchtlingsgruppe im Stil der sogenannten Psikelekedana-Volkskunst, aus Maputo.

7 Ehemaliges Grand Hotel, heute das Zuhause von mehreren Tausend Obdachlosen, mit behelfsmäßigen Verkaufsständen vor der Zufahrt, Beira, Provinz Sofala.

8 Stelltafel vor der abgenutzten Wandtafel eines Grundschulklassenzimmers, Provinz Inhambane.

5 Row of partially destroyed shops along the national highway, Zandamela, Zavala District, on the border between Inhambane and Gaza Provinces.

6 Carving of a group of refugees made in a craft style known as Psikelekedana, origin Maputo.

7 Former Grand Hotel, home to several thousand squatters, with makeshift sales kiosks in front of the driveway, Beira, Sofala Province.

8 Mobile chalkboard in front of a worn-out wall-mounted chalkboard in a primary-school classroom, Inhambane Province.

8

7

9

9 Ladengebäude aus der Kolonialzeit neben einem zeitgenössischen Ver- kaufsstand, Provinz Inhambane.
10 Swahili-Haus mit Walmdach und lehmbeworfenen Flechtwerkwänden, Mossuril, Provinz Nampula. Foto: Margarita Gomez Salas de Schetter.
11 Teilansicht einer Gruppe von traditio- nellen vernakulären Wohnhäusern, Hinterland der Provinz Inhambane.

9 Colonial shop next to a contemporary sales kiosk, Inhambane Province.
10 Swahili house with hipped roof and wattle-and-daub walls, Mossuril, Nampula Province. Photo: Margarita Gomez Salas de Schetter.
11 Partial view of a group of traditional vernacular dwellings, interior of Inhambane Province.

11

10

12

12 Detail eines auf den Wänden einer traditionellen Hütte aufgesetzten Dachs, Hinterland der Provinz Inhambane.

13 Reihe typischer Swahili-Häuser aus Zementsteinen mit Walmdächern aus lokalen Materialien, Ilha de Mozambique, Provinz Nampula.
Foto: Margarita Gomez Salas de Schetter.

14 Ein modern-vernakuläres Wohnhaus aus industriellen Baustoffen, Landkreis Morrumbene, Provinz Inhambane.

12 Detail of roof structure resting on the walls of a traditional hut, interior of Inhambane Province.

13 Row of Swahili houses combining cement blocks with hipped roofs made of local materials, Ilha de Mozambique, Nampula Province.
Photo: Margarita Gomez Salas de Schetter.

14 A modern vernacular dwelling built of industrial materials, Morrumbene District, Inhambane Province.

13

14

15

15 Von mehreren Baustilen geprägtes
   vernakuläres Haus mit rechteckigem
   Grundriss, Flechtwerkwänden,
   aufgemalten Fenstern, Hinterland der
   Provinz Inhambane
16 Fenster, die in die ersten Konstruk-
   tionselemente eines modern-vernakulären Hauses eingehängt wurden
   (vgl. 18), Landkreis Massinga,
   Küstengebiet der Provinz Inhambane.
17 Vernakulärer Verkaufsstand, der
   traditionelle und moderne Einflüsse
   verbindet, Provinz Inhambane.

15 Vernacular dwelling of multiple
   influences with wattle-and-daub,
   rectangular layout and false windows,
   interior of Inhambane Province.
16 Windows hung into the first elements
   of the frame of a modern vernacular
   dwelling (compare to 18), Massinga
   District, coastal zone of Inhambane
   Province.
17 Vernacular sales kiosk combining
   modern and traditional influences,
   Inhambane Province.

16

17

19

18 Ein modern-vernakuläres Haus aus Wellblech, Landkreis Massinga, Küstengebiet der Provinz Inhambane.
19 Verfallene Krankenstation aus der Kolonialzeit, die den traditionellen Rundhütten nachempfunden wurde, Zandamela, Provinz Inhambane.
20 Vernakuläres Badezimmer in der Nähe des Tofo-Strands, Provinz Inhambane.
21 Teilansicht eines Hauses, das eine einfache koloniale Siedler-Einheit mit modern-vernakulären Elementen verbindet, Vorstadt von Inhambane.

18 Modern vernacular dwelling clad in corrugated sheet iron, Massinga District, coastal zone of Inhambane Province.
19 Decayed colonial health post referencing traditional round huts, Zandamela, Inhambane Province.
20 Vernacular bathroom near Tofo beach, Inhambane Province.
21 Partial view of a house combining a simple colonial rural settler unit with modern vernacular elements, suburbs of Inhambane.

21

20

23

22

22 Grundschule mit einem Freiluftklas-
senzimmer unter Bäumen und einem
Klassenzimmer aus organischen
Baustoffen, Provinz Inhambane.
23 Statisch stark beeinträchtigtes Haus
aus der Kolonialzeit, dessen Veranda-
dach notdürftig mit Baumstämmen
abgestützt wurde, Landkreis Massinga,
Provinz Inhambane.
24 Ein modern-vernakuläres Haus aus
lokalen und industriellen Baumaterialien, Landkreis Massinga, Küstengebiet der Provinz Inhambane.
25 Vernakuläres Wohnhaus mit unterschiedlichen Einflüssen, auf rechteckigem Grundriss, aus Materialien von
Kokospalmen gebaut, Landkreis Jangamo, Küstengebiet der Provinz Inhambane.

22 Primary school with an open-air
classroom under trees and a classroom built of organic materials,
Inhambane Province.
23 Structurally severely affected colonial
house with improvised load-bearing
solution made of tree trunks supporting the verandah roof, Massinga
District, Inhambane Province.
24 Modern vernacular dwelling combining
local and industrial materials, Massinga District, coastal zone of Inhambane Province.
25 Vernacular dwelling of multiple influences, based on a rectangular layout,
built of products obtained from the
coconut palm, Jangamo District,
coastal zone of Inhambane Province.

Oliver Schetter
Mozambican Vernacular

24

25

26

27

26 Zeitgenössischer Verkaufsstand vor
einem leerstehenden Kolonialgebäude,
Landkreis Massinga, Küstengebiet
der Prov. Inhambane.

27 Ländliches Wohnhaus zusammengesetzt aus unterschiedlichen modern-
vernakulären Typen, Landkreis
Massinga, Küstengebiet der Provinz
Inhambane.

28 Frau in der Türöffnung ihres Hauses
ihres modern-vernakulären Hauses,
Landkreis Funhalouro, Provinz
Inhambane.

29 Ehemaliges Bedienstetenzimmer des
Smiling Lion-Apartmenthauses in
Maputo, Architekt: Pancho Guedes.
Foto: Annett Bourquin, aus dem
Foto-Essay „Smiling Lions, Dragons,
and Other Revolutions – Pancho
Guedes in Mozambique".

26 Contemporary sales kiosk in front of
abandoned colonial building, Massinga
District, coastal zone of Inhambane
Province.

27 Rural home made up of several
modern vernacular types, Massinga
District, coastal zone of Inhambane
Province.

28 Woman in the doorway of her modern
vernacular home, Funhalouro District,
Inhambane Province.

29 Former staff room in the Smiling Lion
apartment building, architect: Pancho
Guedes.
Photo: Annett Bourquin, from the
photo-essay "Smiling Lions, Dragons,
and Other Revolutions—Pancho
Guedes in Mozambique."

28

29

If the formal references for modern vernacular nowadays are still largely based on modern architecture from colonial times, it is simply because there has been so little new formal architecture in Mozambique since 1975. Despite the reciprocal influence between formal and vernacular architecture, the divide between, on the one hand, deliberate planning and application of precise construction standards, and, on the other, reproduction of cultural patterns drawing on what is immediately available, is wide, as their foundations of knowledge are simply so different. This divide is, however, not insurmountable; as evidenced by projects in which architects have reconciled traditional vernacular architecture with criteria of formal architectural production, as is the case in Amâncio d'Alpoim Miranda ("Pancho") Guedes's Clandestine School of Reeds from 1968.[16] Guedes achieved an interesting synthesis by employing traditional vernacular building materials, construction techniques, and morphologies within the framework of a modern program and in conjunction with a functional overall site layout and individual building plan layouts. The result is architecture with distinct qualities, not so much because of the individual buildings but because of the effect produced by the ensemble. This was possible because the architect accepted the contemporary and immediately available vernacular as the proper solution to a hands-on problem of having to build a school on a very short schedule [→ fig. 29].

Academic discussions of vernacular architecture frequently lead to the question of what constitutes an original architectural type. According to Bruschi, Lage, and Carrilho, the search for an authentic autochthonous traditional architecture is futile, as tradition is alive and in constant transition.[17] Indeed, the perception of what constitutes traditional architecture itself is subject to change. To illustrate this: the traditional Mozambican house is made up of a number of circular dwellings enclosing single interior spaces arranged on a plot of land; the house is considered to be the sum of its exterior and interior spaces, with most of the private social life occurring in its exterior portion.[18]

16 Guedes 2009: 173.
17 Bruschi/Lage/Carrilho 2005 [2003a]: 43.
18 Carrilho 2004: 5.
19 Cf. Bruschi/Lage/Carrilho 2005 [2003b]: 29.
20 Cf. Bruschi 2004.

However, in northern Mozambique the Swahili house, rectangular in plan, predominates. This type has spread across large parts of the territory in the course of the last two hundred years and in many areas has replaced the round huts.[19] An explanation for this has to do with its technical adaptability and its functional versatility; it is receptive to both traditional and modern lifestyles.[20] The Swahili house, once an import, has become tantamount to a traditional house [→ figs. 10 and 11].

Analyzing the knowledge pertaining to specific elements of construction, such as the roof, can help to elucidate why certain architectural solutions gain acceptance. In the traditional Mozambican house the roof is the dominant feature, and its constructive logic determines the shape and size of the house. Staves acting as rafters are interconnected at a single point at the crest of the roof, resulting in a stable cone by way of circumferential rings and a reinforced eaves ring. If the roof structure is small enough, it can be assembled independently of the walls and mounted in its entirety. The traditional Swahili house, on the other hand, is crowned with a relatively complex hipped roof whose gable ends are folded slightly underneath the main roof surfaces in order to prevent infiltration from rain. This spatial and constructive complexity did not hinder the successful dissemination of the model throughout northern Mozambique. A powerful explanation lies in the fact that the material and dimensions employed for roof cladding and rafters are comparable, as are the details of how the construction is assembled. Even if, formally, both types of roofs appear to be quite different, they resort to the same traditional knowledge regarding techniques and materials [→ figs. 12 and 13].

The assimilation of modern architectural elements poses a greater challenge: it presumes different technical knowledge. In addition, industrial materials such as

Seit Ende der 1970er Jahre verlor die Regierung Mosambiks die Kontrolle über weite Teile des Landes, und ihre Macht beschränkte sich in einigen Landesteilen de facto auf die städtischen Siedlungsräume. Infolge der Zerstörung infrastruktureller Anlagen wurden weit auseinander liegende, aber einst miteinander vernetzte produktive Standorte voneinander abgeschnitten und konnten – so isoliert – nur mühsam und ineffektiv weiterarbeiten. Vor allem die Zerstörung oder reduzierte Kapazität der Transportinfrastruktur führte zum bis heute nachwirkenden Niedergang von Märkten und Wirtschaftszweigen [→ Abb. 5 und 6].

Hinzu kommt, dass die wissenschaffende Infrastruktur der Bildungseinrichtungen (Schulen und Universitäten) stark beeinträchtigt wurde. Lehrstätten für technisches Wissen verloren an Bedeutung, weil die an ihnen vermittelte Lehre weder von Studenten noch von Lehrern länger in die Praxis umgesetzt werden konnte. Der Lehrernachwuchs der nachfolgenden Generation kann wiederum immer weniger praktisches Wissen weitergeben. Aus diesem Grund wird in diesen Institutionen weniger qualifiziertes Wissen vermittelt als früher, obwohl ihre Anzahl seit der Unabhängigkeit erheblich zugenommen hat. Da die mosambikanische Gesellschaft nicht die nötige Bildung vermitteln kann, die es ihren Bürgern ermöglichte, technisches Wissen zu erwerben, zu verinnerlichen und effektiv anzuwenden, bleiben die vermittelten Kenntnisse in den verschiedenen technischen Fächern abstrakt und für die Praxis wenig bedeutend. Durch das Fehlen einer kreativen Architekturszene haben Absolventen eines Architekturstudiums nur begrenzte Möglichkeiten, außerhalb der Universität nennenswertes praktisches Wissen zu erwerben. Wie Techniker anderer Fachgebiete neigen auch sie dazu, starr auf erlernten Normen und akademischen Lehren zu beharren oder ungünstigstenfalls einfach das gesellschaftliche und hierarchische Rollenbild des Architekten zu transportieren, ohne über die erforderliche Qualifizierung zur Ausübung des Berufs zu verfügen [→ Abb. 8].

Die traditionelle und moderne vernakuläre Architektur im Detail

Die Betrachtung der vernakulären mosambikanischen Architektur gibt einigen Aufschluss über die Herstellung von Wissen in Mosambik. Historisch gesehen wurzelt die vernakuläre Architektur, d.h. populäre Architektur, die ohne Architekten entsteht, in der Agrargesellschaft; die formale Architektur hingegen, d.h. Architektur, die unter Einbeziehung von Architekten und unter Berücksichtigung von Planungsprozessen und Genehmigungsverfahren entsteht, wurde mit dem Ziel importiert, zentrale Orte für das funktionale Gefüge der Kolonialverwaltung zu schaffen. Trotz dieses Unterschieds haben sich beide Architekturformen seit der Kolonialzeit wechselseitig beeinflusst, Bauprodukte oder räumliche Lösungen voneinander übernommen und den jeweiligen Situationen und Erfordernissen angepasst.[15] Die Analyse der damit einhergehenden Prozesse offenbart, welche Techniken, Materialien, Entwurfslösungen, Elemente oder Raumprogramme übernommen und abgewandelt wurden, und hilft bei der Bestimmung, welche Arten von Wissen in einem Land mit begrenzten Bildungsmöglichkeiten anwendbar sind [→ Abb. 9].

Da fast alle Landbewohner und viele Bewohner städtischer Randgebiete mit größter Selbstverständlichkeit ihre eigenen Behausungen bauen, ist die informelle, vernakuläre gegenüber der formellen Architekturproduktion weit in der Überzahl. Wenn die formalen Bezüge für gegenwärtige,

14 Dieses zwiespältige Verhalten ist kein ausschließlich mosambikanisches Dilemma. Ekeh hat ein Modell vorgeschlagen, das auch als Erklärung für diese Asymmetrie im postkolonialen Nigeria (nach der Unabhängigkeit im Jahr 1960) dienen kann. Er spricht von zwei Öffentlichkeiten, einer staatsbürgerlich-amoralischen und einer ursprünglichen, moralisch-verbindlichen. Während sich moderne westliche Gesellschaften auf „funktionale Beziehungen" gründen und in ihnen Verhaltensmuster, die Verwandtschaftsbeziehungen in den Vordergrund stellen, gemeinhin einen negativen Beigeschmack haben, gilt in afrikanischen Gesellschaften hingegen zuvorderst die der Verwandtschaft geschuldete Loyalität. Es ist ethisch akzeptabel, und es wird sogar erwartet, dass die Berücksichtigung der Verpflichtung gegenüber Familien- und Sippenangehörigen die funktionalen Beziehungen im Bereich der Civitas konditionieren und beeinflussen. Ekeh 1975: 106ff.

15 Bruschi/Carrilho/Lage 2005: 28.

corrugated sheet iron, profiled timber, cement, and iron bars require significantly greater monetary resources. However, roofs made of these materials tend to be simpler in terms of geometry, technically less elaborate, and work with a minimum amount of materials. Rafters usually span flat between two walls to make a lean-to roof. If the roof is to have a more pronounced slope, one of the two walls supporting the rafters is simply raised more; girders are inexistent in modern vernacular housing typologies, from what I have seen to date. If the intended effect is that of a solid, flat, concrete roof, eaves made of reinforced cement hide a simple corrugated sheet iron surface. By employing these techniques and materials, the resulting buildings frequently contrast sharply from traditional vernacular [→ fig. 14].

Another revealing element in the discussion of the reciprocal influence of formal and informal architecture in Mozambique is the window: it shows how building elements can be re-appropriated and change the concept of what a house is. The window was introduced by Arabic and Portuguese settlers, who erected dwellings based on an orthogonal layout that were internally subdivided into several rooms. In Xitsua, one of Mozambique's local languages spoken in Inhambane Province, *livati* is the term for "door"; the term *nijanela*, denoting "window," is borrowed from the Portuguese *janela*, as the traditional society did not know the window. The window has, however, been widely adopted. Even in vernacular dwellings, interior spaces are now being subdivided into several rooms and this subdivision is accompanied by the appearance of the window. But the adaptation also produces different ramifications: the window may appear as a false or painted-on element on the façades of vernacular houses made from traditional materials. Employing building elements in ways that do not correspond to their original function stems from a redefinition of architecture by crossing formal and constructive aspects of different cultural origin [→ figs. 15, 16, and 17].

Both the transition of modern elements into vernacular building and the adaptation

21 Bruschi/Sondeia 2003: 63.
22 Cf. César 2000: 20ff.
23 Lage 2004: 78.

of traditional architectural elements into formal architecture have to do with economically, politically, or aesthetically generated processes of imitation. Architects in colonial times, for instance, diversified their repertoire by imitating traditional types, looking for an aesthetic and environmental benefits better adapted to local conditions.[21] Yet, they also may have searched for legitimization by building on the local languages. Builders of vernacular architecture, on the other hand, often imitate aspects of formal architecture without attaining the functional qualities of the original; the aspect of owning a desired object often seems to be more important than the actual usability of that object. Therefore, the false window assimilates only the formal qualities of its model.

Many Mozambicans, just like people anywhere, desire a modern house for reasons of status; the willingness to adopt the cultural habits embedded in an architectural type, however, is not a given.[22] Therefore, the modern vernacular house made of concrete blocks is frequently surrounded by complementary traditional architectures. The modern house, almost always the central piece on a plot of land, can seem like an exhibition piece, as many aspects of family life—cooking, hygiene, getting together—continue to take place outside. Even houses that include bathrooms and kitchens frequently have additional cooking areas, washing corners, and toilets outside. Reasons for this are multiple: installations might not cater to the actual functioning of the family, their use may by restricted to the head of a household or for specific occasions, and they may very well be of symbolic use[23] [→ figs. 18, 19, 20, and 21].

An important dimension to consider regarding vernacular architecture is the role of scarcity. Scarcity is an integral part of Mozambican and many other African cultures. Possibilities of surplus production are limited, and the availability of products is dependant on circumstance. Given the generally low life expectancy of the population,

moderne vernakuläre Architektur immer noch weitgehend auf die moderne Kolonialarchitektur verweisen, dann einfach deshalb, weil seit 1975 nur wenige von Architekten geplante Gebäude in Mosambik entstanden sind. Trotz der wechselseitigen Beeinflussung von formeller und vernakulärer Architektur besteht eine tiefe Kluft zwischen vorsätzlicher Planung unter Anwendung präziser Baustandards auf der einen und der Reproduktion kultureller Vorbilder auf der Basis lokal vorhandener Ressourcen auf der anderen Seite. Denn das beiden zugrunde liegende Wissen ist einfach zu unterschiedlich. Diese Kluft ist allerdings nicht unüberbrückbar, wie aus Projekten ersichtlich wird, bei denen Architekten traditionelle einheimische Bauweisen mit den Standards der modernen Architekturplanung in Einklang gebracht haben, so etwa Amâncio d'Alpoim Miranda („Pancho") Guedes' 1968 erbaute Geheime Riedschule.[16] Guedes gelang eine interessante Synthese, indem er traditionelle einheimische Baustoffe, Bautechniken und Bauformen im Rahmen eines modernen Raumprogramms, eines funktionalen Gelände- und Lageplans sowie individueller Gebäudegrundrisse vereinte. Das Ergebnis war eine Architektur von eigenständiger Qualität, nicht so sehr aufgrund der einzelnen Gebäude, sondern wegen der Gesamtwirkung des Gebäudeensembles. Diese wurde möglich, weil der Architekt eine zwar formal modernisierte, doch ortstypische Bauweise als beste Lösung für die Aufgabe ansah, fast buchstäblich über Nacht einen Schulkomplex zu errichten [→ Abb. 29].

Akademische Diskussionen über vernakuläre Architektur münden vielfach in die Frage, was eigentlich einen ursprünglich-volkstümlichen Bautyp ausmacht. Für Bruschi, Lage und Carrilho ist die Suche nach einer authentischen, autochthonen, traditionellen Architektur hinfällig, weil Traditionen lebendig sind und stetem Wandel unterliegen.[17] Selbst die Auffassung von traditioneller Architektur wandelt sich ständig. Ich zitiere ein Beispiel: Das traditionelle mosambikanische Haus besteht aus einer Reihe kreisrunder Ein-Raum-Hutten, die auf einem Grundstück angeordnet sind. „Haus" bedeu-

tet dabei die Summe der Außen- und Innenräume des Ensembles, wobei das private und soziale Leben sich überwiegend im Außenraum abspielt.[18] Die im Norden des Landes vorherrschenden Swahili-Häuser basieren dagegen auf einem orthogonalen Grundriss. Im Verlauf der letzten 200 Jahre fand dieser Bautyp weite Verbreitung und hat in vielen Gegenden die Rundhütten verdrängt.[19] Ein Grund hierfür ist die technische Anpassungsfähigkeit und funktionale Vielseitigkeit dieses Typs, in dem sowohl traditionelle als auch moderne Lebensweisen möglich sind.[20] Das Swahili-Haus – einst ein Import – ist inzwischen dem traditionellen Haus gleichgesetzt [→ Abb. 10 und 11].

Die Untersuchung des Fachwissens zur Konstruktion einzelner Bauelemente (etwa des Dachs) kann Aufschluss darüber geben, warum bestimmte architektonische Lösungen sich durchsetzen. Das beherrschende Element der traditionellen mosambikanischen Behausung ist das Dach, dessen konstruktive Logik deren Form und Größe bestimmt. Holzstöcke dienen als Sparren. Sie werden im Gipfelpunkt des Runddaches miteinander verbunden und ergeben zusammen mit umlaufenden Pfettenringen und einem verstärkten Traufring eine stabile Kegelform. Wenn die Dachkonstruktion klein genug ist, lässt sie sich auf dem Boden fertigen und dann als Ganzes auf die runde Hauswand setzen. Das traditionelle Swahili-Haus hingegen wird mit einem in der Konstruktion relativ komplexen Walmdach gedeckt, dessen Giebelwände etwas unter die Hauptdachflächen geschoben werden, um es besser und einfacher gegen eindringenden Regen zu schützen. Trotz seiner räumlichen und konstruktiven Komplexität hat sich dieses Modell jedoch im ganzen Norden Mosambiks durchgesetzt. Eine mögliche Erklärung liegt in der Tatsache, dass beide Dächer mit ähnlichen Materialien gebaut werden und auch die Dimensionen der Sparren- und Deckmaterialien ebenso wie die Montagetechniken

16 Guedes 2009: 173.
17 Bruschi/Lage/Carrilho 2005 [2003a]: 43.
18 Carrilho 2004: 5.
19 Vgl. Bruschi/Lage/Carrilho 2005 [2003b]: 29.
20 Vgl. Bruschi 2004.

planning, in the private realm, does not have the same standing as it does in other cultures. Traditional vernacular has little need of planning, as well-established models and morphologies dictate the size and shape of a dwelling. A modern vernacular building is more malleable, as it is ultimately the result of an open time frame regarding the availability of materials and the contracting of services. Add to this the limitations imposed by logistics and scarce capital and materials, and it becomes clear why building processes frequently stagnate. Builders phase their houses and collect construction materials until a critical mass is obtained. Circumstance allowing, construction begins. Building shells become inhabitable as soon as the roof is on. The question of whether a building is finished leads nowhere, as even ruins can be used as a habitat. Obviously, a plastered home provides more comfort than one without plaster, and a home that has painted walls is more comfortable still than a plastered one. Yet each state has its reason and justification. Furthermore, elements are added not only in accordance with the economic situation, but also according to a generally rapidly fluctuating family size [→ figs. 22 and 23].

While knowledge of traditional and modern provenance comes together in the contemporary Mozambican house, the amalgamation also results in a loss or misunderstanding of existing knowledge. Populations in urban settlements partially lose their knowledge regarding traditional construction techniques at the rate with which they move out of traditional society. Conversely, materials originating in the formal construction sector are used by builders in the informal sector without the necessary quality control. Not understanding the relevance of modern building techniques, builders resort to traditional techniques that are not applicable to formal construction. Concrete, for instance, is frequently watered down, irrespective of its setting process—it is used like clay thereby forfeiting its structural qualities. Corrugated sheet iron is generally set at too small a grade and with insufficient overlap, resulting in leaking roofs. There are frequently too few

rafters set too far apart, and their dimensions are wrong or the material properties are not sufficient for the load being borne, making the roof bend. Therefore, the outcome is frequently of poor structural quality and buildings are inaugurated with inherent pathologies that burden their performance and life cycle.

The transformation of the Mozambican house and the knowledge that generates it has therefore also, quite simply, been the result of how builders have been able to use and respond to available construction materials. In the coastal areas of Inhambane Province the Portuguese cultivated coconut palm groves on a large scale beginning in the nineteenth century. As the sandy soil provides scarce building resources, the palm trees have turned into the main source of construction material for what is referred to as *construção precária* (precarious construction), buildings made mainly of organic material. Here, part of the structural frame, the cladding of the walls, and the thatching of the hipped roofs are made from the wood and the woven fronds of the coconut palm. While the material realization of the buildings would not be conceivable without the remnants of the colonial economy, the palm plantations, the house morphology too has changed. The huts are rectangular in plan, not round, as with the traditional vernacular in the rest of the province, because the materials presuppose a rectangular house design. The rigid spine of the coconut palm frond serves well as thatching for a rectangular roof surface; it makes it unsuitable for the thatching of conical roofs. In addition, while the wattle and daub of traditional houses is assembled from sticks in profiles and sizes basically as found in nature, the trunks of the coconut palm have to be processed by sawing, resulting in rectangular wooden profiles, again pointing toward a rectangular solution. The technique of assembly, on the other hand, can lean either toward the traditional, by tying the elements with organic ropes; or toward the partially modern (more often employed), by resorting to nails and metal wire. Further variation is possible: the roof can be substituted by a lean-to roof

vergleichbar sind. Selbst wenn beide Dach-
typen in formaler Hinsicht ganz unterschiedlich erscheinen, basieren sie auf denselben
traditionellen Kenntnissen handwerklicher
Bautechniken und einheimischer Materialien [→ Abb. 12 und 13].

Die Assimilation moderner Bauelemente
stellt dagegen eine größere Herausforderung
dar, weil ihre Anwendung ein anderes technisches Wissen voraussetzt. Noch dazu erfordern industriell hergestellte Baustoffe wie
Wellblech, Holzprofile, Zement und Armie-
rungseisen weitaus größere finanzielle Mittel.
Dächer aus diesen Materialien sind daher
meist einfacher gestaltet, technisch weniger
ausgearbeitet und lassen sich mit wenig
Material konstruieren. Die Sparren werden
meist gerade auf zwei verschieden hohe
Mauerkronen gelegt – als Grundlage für ein
Pultdach. Wenn dieses steiler sein soll, wird
der Höhenunterschied zwischen den Auf-
lagern vergrößert. Nach meinen bisherigen
Beobachtungen gibt es bei den modernen
vernakulären Wohnhäusern daher keine
Dachstühle. Wenn das Haus solider aussehen
soll, so als hätte es ein Betonflachdach,
verkleiden massive Traufkanten aus armier-
tem Zement, welche innenliegende Regenrin-
nen bilden, die mit Wellblech gedeckten
Dachflächen. Durch die Anwendung solcher
Bautechniken und Materialien unterscheiden
sich diese Bauten daher vielfach deutlich
von den in traditioneller Bauweise errichte-
ten Häusern [→ Abb. 14].

Ein weiteres aufschlussreiches Element,
das bei der wechselseitigen Beeinflussung der
geplanten und der ungeplanten Architektur
Mosambiks eine Rolle gespielt hat, ist das
Fenster. Es zeigt, wie Bauteile immer wieder
auf andere Art und Weise angeeignet werden
können und die Vorstellung dessen verändern, was ein Haus zu einem Haus macht.
Zusammen mit ihren Häusern auf rechtwink-
ligem Grundriss und mit mehreren Zimmern
brachten arabische und portugiesische Siedler
auch das Fenster nach Mosambik. In der
Bantusprache Xitsua, die auch in der Provinz
Inhambane gesprochen wird, heißt Tür
livati und Fenster *nijanela* nach dem portugiesischen *janela*, weil die mosambikanischen
Hütten keine Fenster hatten und es deshalb

auch kein Wort dafür gab. Inzwischen sind
Fenster jedoch weit verbreitet. Auch verna-
kuläre Häuser weisen Grundrisse auf, die aus
mehreren Räumen bestehen, und in diesem
funktionalen Zusammenhang kommen
entsprechend auch Fenster zur Anwendung.
Es gibt weitere Formen der Adaption des
Fensters: Es erscheint zum Beispiel auch
schon einmal als auf die Fassade aufgemaltes
Element einer (fensterlosen) Hütte aus
lokalen Baustoffen. Die Verwendung von
Bauteilen, die von ihrer ursprünglichen
Funktion abweicht, ergibt sich dabei aus der
Neudefinition von Architektur durch die
Kreuzung ästhetischer und konstruktiver
Details aus verschiedenen Kulturkreisen
[→ Abb. 15, 16 und 17].

Dass moderne Elemente in die vernakuläre Architektur und traditionelle in die
formelle Architektur Mosambiks Eingang
gefunden haben, hat mit den wirtschaftlich,
politisch oder ästhetisch motivierten Prozessen der Imitation zu tun. Die Architekten
der Kolonialzeit erweiterten zum Beispiel ihr
architektonisches Repertoire, indem sie traditionelle Typologien imitierten, um ihre
Bauten ästhetisch wie klimatisch den Verhältnissen im Land anzupassen.[21] Vielleicht
bemühten sie sich auch um Legitimation,
indem sie auf dem vorgefundenen Formenvokabular aufbauten. Die mosambikanischen
Baumeister ihrerseits imitieren häufig
bestimmte Elemente der importierten Architektur, ohne deren funktionale Qualität zu
erreichen. Der Anschein, ein begehrtes Ding
zu besitzen, ist dabei offenbar wichtiger als
die Gebrauchsfähigkeit des Gegenstands. Das
aufgemalte Fenster assimiliert daher nur die
formalen Eigenschaften seines Vorbilds.

Wie anderswo auch wünschen sich viele
Menschen in Mosambik aus Statusgründen
ein modernes Haus westlicher Prägung, sind
aber nicht bereit, die von dessen Architektur
vorgegebene Kultur und Lebensweise zu
übernehmen.[22] Daher ist das moderne vernakuläre Einfamilienhaus aus Betonsteinen
vielfach von traditionellen Bauten umgeben.
Meist nimmt das moderne Haus die zentrale

21 Bruschi/Sondeia 2003: 63.
22 Vgl. César 2000: 20ff.

covered with corrugated sheet iron, and the walls can be executed in concrete blocks. The hut can be a simple rectangular building, or a building of composite volumes with several lean-to roofs pointing in different directions. Ultimately, therefore, from a very simple vernacular solution, a number of typologies and morphologies have derived that, one way or another, are ubiquitous in the coastal areas of the province where the palm tree is available [→ figs. 24 and 25].

Conclusion

The forces shaping the landscape of knowledge in Mozambique, as I have sketched them in this essay, could easily be interpreted by the outside observer as detrimental to the development of knowledge. From a Mozambican perspective, however, the setting could equally and rightfully be defined as a process of coming to terms with the available technical knowledge and adapting it to the context in which it operates, ensuring its applicability. Such technical knowledge is dependant on its being embedded in the broader knowledge context in which it operates. It responds and adapts to the prevalent cultural patterns, and the cultural environment assimilates certain aspects of imported products, which technical knowledge helps to generate. The result is not only a loss, but a transformation of knowledge, allowing it to be understood by society at large. In the process of post-colonial nation building, technical knowledge is in fact being consolidated to constitute a more slender body, and general knowledge, as I would describe it today, reflects a post-colonial society of many facets [→ fig. 26].

We are today, therefore, at a curious moment in the process of transformation of both architecture and the underlying cultural habits in Mozambique. A people that have been shaken by massive social and cultural change have learned how to negotiate several parallel codes, and their architecture is responsive to this. Mozambique's builders are generating a broad variety of solutions from an extremely limited number of typologies, materials, and techniques. The variety results from the immediacy and interchangeability of materials employed in construction, not from

the application of a predominant, established logic. We are in the middle of a transitional period of confluence between traditional and modern architectural systems.

As a consequence, Mozambican homes are round and square, inhabited on the outside and on the inside, made of traditional materials, of improvised, and of formal materials, covered with straw and with corrugated sheet iron; houses can be intact or in ruins, in use or abandoned, finished or under construction. These characteristics coexist without apparent contradictions, as the definitions of use and users' intentions adapt to circumstance and circumstantial knowledge. Most of the formal architecture in Mozambique is, for the time being, technically limited compared to what was achieved in previous moments.[24] But the language and technology of the modern vernacular architecture that is being realized as a spin-off of formal architecture is evolving toward an expression more in tune with local conditions [→ fig. 27].

Today, many Mozambicans look out at the world through a window; others do so through a door. In all likelihood, the observer's livelihood and his personal level of knowledge correspond to the type of element framing his or her view. Whether that element is of traditional, colonial or post-colonial, formal or vernacular making, it is part of a landscape of knowledge that, taken in its entirety, will not attain in any conceivable future the minimum thresholds of knowledge dictated by Western capitalist societies. Mozambicans today are in the midst of a process in which the parameters of knowledge and production—be they local or external, traditional or modern—mingle to construe a society in transition. In the process, the landscape of knowledge and the cultural topography on which it resides are again moving closer together, not predominantly through the imposition of readily recognizable external force, but through the visible and invisible forces that propel today's globalizing societies from without and within [→ fig. 28].

Position auf dem Grundstück ein und kommt einem Ausstellungsobjekt nahe, da sich das Familienleben – Kochen, Wäschewaschen, Körperhygiene und Beisammensein – weiterhin überwiegend im Freien abspielt. Selbst Häuser mit Badezimmern und Küchen haben vielfach noch Kochstellen, Waschecken und Toiletten außerhalb des Hauses. Hierfür gibt es viele Gründe. Die Installationen bedienen gegebenenfalls nicht die wirklichen Bedürfnisse der Hausbewohner, sie sind vielleicht dem Haushaltsvorstand oder für besondere Anlässe vorbehalten oder lediglich von symbolischer Bedeutung für ihre Besitzer[23] [→ Abb. 18, 19, 20 und 21].

Ein weiterer wichtiger Faktor bei der Betrachtung der vernakulären Architektur ist der Mangel. Versorgungslücken sind ein integraler Bestandteil des Lebens in Mosambik und vielen anderen afrikanischen Ländern. Die Möglichkeiten der Überschussproduktion sind begrenzt, und die Verfügbarkeit von Produkten hängt von den Umständen ab. Angesichts der allgemein niedrigen Lebenserwartung der Bevölkerung wird leicht begreiflich, warum Planung bei privaten Bauvorhaben nicht die gleiche Bedeutung hat wie in anderen Kulturkreisen. Traditionelle vernakuläre Bauten erfordern nicht viel Vorausplanung, da bewährte Modelle und Morphologien die Form und Größe eines Hauses diktieren. Der Bau eines modernen vernakulären Hauses erfolgt auf flexiblere Weise, da immer erst dann weitergebaut wird, wenn die nötigen Baustoffe und/oder Handwerker verfügbar sind. Wenn noch die Einschränkungen, denen ein Bauprojekt durch mangelhafte Logistik, fehlendes Kapital und Produktverfügbarkeit unterworfen ist, hinzugenommen werden, ist leicht verständlich, warum Bauprozesse häufig stagnieren. Selbstbauer und Bauunternehmer errichten ihre Häuser deshalb phasenweise und sammeln Baumaterialien, bis sie eine kritische Menge beisammen haben, um weiterzubauen, wenn es die Umstände erlauben. Sobald der Rohbau ein Dach hat, ist er bezugsfähig. Die Frage, ob ein Haus fertig ist, führt dabei nicht weiter, denn selbst Ruinen können bewohnt werden. Natürlich bietet ein fertig verputztes Haus mehr Komfort als ein Roh-

bau, und ein Haus mit gemalerten Wänden bietet noch mehr Komfort als ein nur verputztes. Für jeden Bauzustand gibt es aber berechtigte Gründe. Außerdem sind spätere Anbauten nicht nur der wirtschaftlichen Situation einer Familie geschuldet, sondern vielfach auch der wachsenden Anzahl ihrer Mitglieder [→ Abb. 22 und 23].

Das zeitgenössische mosambikanische Haus vereint traditionelles und modernes architektonisches Wissen. Diese Fusion geht allerdings auch einher mit dem Verlust oder der Fehlinterpretation des zuvor vorhandenen Fachwissens. Städtische Bevölkerungen verlieren Teile ihres Wissens um traditionelle Bautechniken in dem Maße, in dem sie sich von traditionellen Lebensbedingungen und Sinnzusammenhängen entfernen. Baustoffe aus dem formalen Bausektor werden ohne Qualitätskontrolle von Baumeistern und Eigenheimbauern verwendet, die nicht über die nötigen Fachkenntnisse und Fertigkeiten verfügen. In Unkenntnis der Relevanz moderner Bautechniken verlassen sie sich auf traditionelle Bautechniken und Methoden, die für normgerechte moderne Konstruktionen ungeeignet sind. Beton wird zum Beispiel oft ohne Beachtung des Abbindungsprozesses wiederholt mit Wasser verdünnt, weil er wie Lehm behandelt wird. So verliert er seine Trageigenschaft. Wellblechdächer werden meist mit zu geringer Neigung gebaut. Das Ergebnis sind undichte Dächer. Sparren werden häufig in zu großen Abständen montiert, sind zu dünn oder ohne ausreichende Trageigenschaften für die Dachlast, so dass sich die Dachflächen durchbiegen. Die Häuser sind daher oft von schlechter konstruktiver Qualität und Schäden sind vorprogrammiert, die ihre Funktionalität und Lebensdauer beschneiden.

Der Wandel des mosambikanischen Hauses und der Wandel des zugrunde liegenden Wissens ist daher schlichtweg auch das Ergebnis der Fähigkeit, verfügbare Materialien zu nutzen und auf diese einzugehen. In den Küstengebieten der Provinz Inhambane zum Beispiel haben die Portugiesen großräumige Kokospalmenplantagen angelegt, die auf

23 Lage 2004: 78.

das 19. Jahrhundert zurückgehen. Da der sandige Boden kaum Baustoffe hergibt, bilden Palmholz und -blätter die Hauptmaterialien für Gebäude aus organischen Baustoffen, die als *construção precária* (prekäre Konstruktion) bezeichnet werden. Teile der Rahmenkonstruktion sowie die Wandverkleidungen werden aus Palmenholz errichtet und die Walmdächer mit Flechtmatten aus Palmblättern gedeckt. Ohne die Überbleibsel der Kolonialwirtschaft in Form der Kokosplantagen wären die hiesigen materiellen Hausformen so nicht denk- und machbar. Die Morphologie der Gebäude hat sich dadurch ebenfalls gewandelt. Früher waren vernakuläre Wohngebäude überall in der Provinz rund. Heute sind sie rechteckig, weil die Baustoffe diese Form vorgeben. Die starren Mittelrippen der Palmwedel eignen sich als Deckmaterial für rechteckige Dachflächen, nicht aber für die Deckung von Kegeldächern. Während traditionelle lehmbeworfene Flechtwerk-Hauswände aus nahezu unbearbeiteten Holzstöcken, wie sie in der Natur auffindbar sind, gefertigt werden können, müssen die Stämme der Kokospalme erst zu Kanthölzern und Latten verarbeitet werden, wodurch ebenfalls orthogonale Lösungen impliziert sind. Für die Montage können entweder traditionelle Techniken angewandt werden (Verbund von Bauteilen mit Hilfe von Pflanzenfasern) oder auch, was häufiger vorkommt, teilweise moderne Techniken unter Nutzung von Nägeln und Metalldraht. Dabei sind auch weitere Abwandlungen möglich, zum Beispiel durch die Kombination mit Pultdächern aus Wellblech oder Mauern aus Betonsteinen. Das Gebäude kann eine einfache kastenförmige Hütte sein oder ein zusammengesetztes Volumen, bestehend aus mehreren miteinander quasi verbundenen Hütten mit Pultdächern, die in verschiedene Richtungen weisen. Letztlich hat sich so aus einer ganz einfachen vernakulären Lösung eine ganze Reihe von Haustypen und Bauformen entwickelt, die in den Küstenstrichen der Provinz, in denen Kokospalmen wachsen, allgegenwärtig sind [→ Abb. 24 und 25].

Fazit

Aufgrund meiner obigen Ausführungen könnte ein Außenstehender auf den Gedanken kommen, dass sich die Kräfte, welche die Wissenslandschaft Mosambiks gestalten und bestimmen, negativ auf die Wissensbildung auswirken. Aus mosambikanischer Perspektive könnte die Situation jedoch ebenso und berechtigterweise als ein Prozess des sich Arrangierens und der Adaption des verfügbaren Fachwissens an die lokalen Gegebenheiten definiert werden, der dessen Anwendbarkeit sicherstellt. Denn dieses technische Wissen ist nicht zu trennen von dem umfassenderen Wissenskontext, in dem es angewandt wird. Technische Kenntnisse reagieren auf und passen sich an vorherrschende kulturelle Muster an, und das kulturelle Umfeld assimiliert bestimmte Elemente importierter Produkte, die mit Hilfe von technischem Wissen erzeugt werden. Das verursacht nicht nur einen Verlust an Wissen, sondern auch eine Veränderung des Wissens, damit es von der Allgemeinheit verstanden und angenommen werden kann. Im Zuge der postkolonialen Staatsbildung wird technisches Wissen generell konsolidiert und dabei sozusagen verschlankt, und das Allgemeinwissen entspricht nach meinem Dafürhalten dem Bild einer facettenreichen postkolonialen Gesellschaft [→ Abb. 26].

Derzeit befinden wir uns also an einem merkwürdigen Punkt in einem Umwandlungsprozess, der sowohl die Architektur als auch die ihr zugrunde liegenden kulturellen Gewohnheiten Mosambiks betrifft. Ein Volk, das massive soziale und kulturelle Veränderungen verkraften musste, hat gelernt, mit mehreren parallelen Codes umzugehen – und seine Architektur bietet ein Spiegelbild dieser Entwicklung. Die Baumeister des Landes schaffen mit einer extrem begrenzten Anzahl von Typologien, Materialien und Bautechniken eine Fülle unterschiedlicher Lösungen. Diese Vielfalt beruht nicht auf der Anwendung einer etablierten vorherrschenden Entwurfslogik, sondern ist das Ergebnis der unmittelbaren Verfügbarkeit und Auswechselbarkeit der verwendeten Baustoffe. Wir befinden uns hier mitten in dem Prozess der

Verschmelzung von traditionellen und modernen Architekturen.

Demzufolge sind mosambikanische Häuser rund oder auch rechteckig, im Außenbereich und im Innern bewohnt, bestehen aus traditionellen oder zufällig gefundenen oder auch aus industriellen Baumaterialien, und sind mit Kokospalmblättern, Ried oder Wellblech gedeckt. Mosambikanische Häuser sind fertig oder auch Ruinen, bewohnt oder verlassen, fertiggestellt oder gerade im Bau befindlich. Das alles koexistiert offenbar konfliktfrei, da die Definition von Nutzung und Nutzerintention stets den Umständen und dem vorhandenen Wissensstand angepasst wird. Verglichen mit den Errungenschaften vergangener Zeiten sind die meisten gegenwärtigen formellen, d.h. von Architekten geplanten Gebäude in Mosambik technisch recht begrenzt.[24] Aber das Formenvokabular und die Bautechniken der modernen vernakulären Architektur, die sozusagen Nebenprodukte der formalen Architektur westlicher Prägung darstellen, entwickeln architektonische Ausdrucksformen, die besser zu den lokalen Verhältnissen passen [→ Abb. 27].

Heute sehen viele Mosambikaner die Außenwelt durch ein Fenster, andere hingegen durch eine Tür. Aller Wahrscheinlichkeit nach entsprechen die Lebensgrundlagen und der Bildungsgrad des Betrachters der Art der Wandöffnung, die seine Aussicht einrahmt. Egal ob das Fenster oder die Tür traditionellen, kolonialen oder postkolonialen, modernen oder vernakulären Ursprungs ist, die Öffnung ist in jedem Fall Teil einer Wissenslandschaft, die in ihrer Gesamtheit in absehbarer Zukunft nicht den minimalen Grad an Bildung erreichen wird, wie er von westlich-kapitalistischen Ländern diktiert wird. Die Mosambikaner befinden sich heute mitten in einem Entwicklungsprozess, dessen Wissens- und Produktionsparameter, ob lokal oder extern, traditionell oder modern, sich vermischen und eine transformierte Gesellschaft bilden. Dabei findet wieder eine Annäherung zwischen Wissenslandschaft und unterfütternder kultureller Topografie statt, nicht in erster Linie auf Druck einer leicht

erkennbaren externen Macht, sondern durch die sichtbaren und unsichtbaren Kräfte, die heute globalisierende Gesellschaften von außen und von innen prägen [→ Abb. 28].

24 Vgl. Ferreira 2008.

134

Oliver Schetter, geboren 1968, Architekturdiplom an der Universität der Künste Berlin, Gaststudien an Architekturfakultäten in São Paulo und Porto. Master of Professional Studies in International Development am Institute for Food, Agriculture and Development der Cornell University in Ithaca, NY. Tätigkeit als wissenschaftlicher Mitarbeiter für Entwerfen und Städtebau an der Johann Gottfried Leibniz Universität in Hannover, wo er 2004 zusammen mit Jens Giesecke G+S Architects gründete. Das Büro hat u.a. das Ferry Porsche Congress Center in Zell am See, Österreich, entworfen. Seit 2006 lebt Schetter in Inhambane, Mosambik, wo er als Architekt in der Entwicklungszusammenarbeit tätig ist.

Deutsche Übersetzung:
Annette Wiethüchter.

Oliver Schetter born in 1968, holds a degree in architecture from the Berlin University of the Arts, having pursued part of his studies at the Universities of São Paulo and Porto. He received a Master of Professional Studies in International Development at the International Institute for Food, Agriculture and Development at Cornell University. Schetter worked as a research assistant and lecturer in Urban Planning at the Department of Architecture at Leibniz University in Hanover, a city where he subsequently was one of the founding partners of G+S Architects. The practice's projects include the Ferry Porsche Congress Center in Zell am See, Austria. Since 2006 he has lived in Inhambane, Mozambique, working in development aid and architecture.

References

Boutrais, Jean. 1999. "Herdsmen in the South, Herdsmen in the North—and the Others." In Holtedahl, Lisbet/Siri Gerrard/Martin Z. Njeuma/Jean Boutrais, eds. *The Power of Knowledge: From the Arctic to the Tropics.* Paris: Editions Karthala.

Bruschi, Sandro. 2001. [Original title not available.] In *Um Olhar para o Habitat Informal Moçambicano: De Lichinga a Maputo.* ENGLISH: 2004. "The Survival of Mozambican, Pre-colonial Architecture." In Carrilho/Bruschi/Menezes/Lage 2004.

Bruschi, Sandro/Benjamin Alfredo Sondeia, coordinators. 2003. *Inhambane: Elementos de história urbana.* Maputo: FAPF.

Bruschi, Sandro/Luís Lage/Júlio Carrilho. 2003a, 9. Dezember. "Arquitectura tradicional, arquitectura pobre…ou, mais simplesmente, arquitectura: Notícias." In Bruschi/Carrilho/Lage 2005.

———. 2003b, 23. Dezember. "A palhota cilíndrica, a casa Swahili e a hitória complicada das suas transformações: Notícias." In Bruschi/Carrilho/Lage 2005.

Bruschi, Sandro/Luís Lage. 2005. *O desenho das cidades: Moçambique até ao séc. XXI.* Maputo: FAPF.

Bruschi, Sandro/Júlio Carrilho/Luís Lage. 2005. *Era uma vez uma palhota: História da casa moçambicana.* Maputo: UEM Faculdade de Arquitectura e Planeamento Físico.

Carrilho, Júlio. 2001. [Original title not available.] In *Um Olhar para o Habitat Informal Moçambicano: de Lichinga a Maputo.* ENGLISH: 2004. *Life in the Peripheral Districts of Lichanga.* In Carrilho/Bruschi/Menezes/Lage 2004.

Carrilho, Júlio/Sandro Bruschi/Carlos Menezes/Luís Lage. 2004. *Traditional Informal Settlements in Mozambique: From Lichinga to Maputo.* Carola Cuoco, trans. Maputo: Faculdade de Arquitectura e Planeamento Físico.

César Santos, Miguel. 2000. "Tradição, modernidade, habitação e habitat (ou tradição versus modernidade)." In Carlos Serra, director. *Conflito E Mestiçagem.* Maputo: Livraria Universitária, Universidade Eduardo Mondlane.

Conrad, Joseph. 1899. *Heart of Darkness.* Edinburgh, London. DEUTSCH: 2006 [1979]. *Herz der Finsternis.* Elli Berger, Übers. Köln: Anaconda.

Ekeh, P.P. 1975, January. "Colonialism and the Two Publics in Africa: A Theoretical Statement." *Comparative Studies in Society and History,* 17 (1), 91–112.

Ferreira, André Faria. 2008. *Obras Publicas em Moçambique: Inventário da produção arquitectónica executada entre 1933 e 1961.* Lisboa: Edições Universitárias Lusófonas.

First, Ruth, director of investigation. 1998. *O Mineiro Moçambicano: Um estudo sobre a exportação de mão-de-obra em Inhambane.* Maputo: Centro de Estudos Africanos, Universidade Eduardo Mondlane.

Forjaz, José. 2004. "A planificação física em Moçambique independente." (http://www.joseforjazarquitectos.com/textos/planmocind.html). Accessed 29 September 2010.

Gellar, Sheldon. 1995. "The Colonial Era." In Martin/O'Meara.

Guedes, Pancho, ed. 2009. *Pancho Guedes. Vitruvius Mozambicanus.* Lisbon: Museo Colecção Berardo.

Lage, Luís. 2001. [Original title not available.] In *Um Olhar para o Habitat Informal Moçambicano: de Lichinga a Maputo.* ENGLISH: 2004. *The Building of Informal Dwellings: Case Study of Maputo.* In Carrilho/Bruschi/Menezes/Lage 2004.

Lefebvre, Henri. 1974. *Production de l'espace.* Editions Antrophos. ENGLISH: 2000 [1991]. *The Production of Space.* Donald Nicholson-Smith, trans. Oxford, Malden: Blackwell.

Lopes, Armando Jorge/Salvador Júlio Stioe/Paulino José Nahmuende. 2002. *Moçambicanismos: Para um Léxico de Usos do Português Moçambicano.* Maputo: Livraria Universitária UEM.

Martin, Phyllis M./Patrick O'Meara. 1995. *Africa.* Bloomington: Indiana University Press.

Partido Frelimo. 1983. *Defender a pátria, eliminar a fome: tarefa de todos os moçambicanos: Colecção IV Congresso.* Maputo: Instituto Nacional do Livro e do Disco.

Robertson, Claire. 1995. *Social Change in Contemporary Africa.* In Martin/O'Meara 1995.

Sumich, Jason. 2008. *Construir uma Nação: Ideologias de Modernidade da Elite Moçambicana. Análise Social.* XLIII (2°), 319–345. (www.scielo.oces.mctes.pt/pdf/aso/n187/n187a06.pdf). Accessed: 12 September 2010.

Trindade, Carlos T.G./Karyin B. Do Valle/Sandro Bruschi. 2003. *Informal Settlement Upgrading in Manica City.* Manuscript for the 4th International Symposium Remote Sensing of Urban Areas, 27–29 June, 2003. Regensburg, Germany.

Amy Catania Kulper

Encountering the List
Georges Perec and the Archive as
Spatial Paradigm

Archives, lists, and taxonomies are central to the
narrative structure of French writer and filmmaker
Georges Perec's writing. Transcending the impetus
to impose spatial order, for Perec they are the
locus of literary invention. Through an analysis of
the spatial narratives of Perec's texts and, in particular, the transition from taxonomy to archive
embodied in his works *Species of Spaces* (1974) and
Life: A User's Manual (1978), Kulper describes
three strategies that the discipline of architecture
can learn from Perec's approach. Through Perec's
example, architects can tap into the generative
capacity of classification by activating the situation
of the category (both its locus and the practices
it engenders), by recognizing the creative potential
inherent in the act of naming, and by allowing the
multitude of empirical observations to yield to the
figures that emerge from them.

Amy Catania Kulper

Begegnung mit der Liste
Georges Perec und das Archiv als Raumparadigma

Archive, Listen und Taxonomien sind zentrale
Elemente der Erzählstruktur in den Schriften des
französischen Schriftstellers und Filmemachers
Georges Perec. Für ihn, der den Drang nach
Errichtung einer räumlichen Ordnung überwindet,
sind sie der Ort literarischer Erfindung. Durch
die Analyse von Perecs Raumerzählungen und insbesondere den Übergang von Taxonomie zu Archiv,
der seinen Werken *Träume von Räumen* (1974) und
Das Leben. Gebrauchsanweisung (1978) innewohnt,
umreißt Kulper drei Strategien, welche Architekten
von Perecs Herangehensweise lernen können.
Sie können erstens lernen, wie man die schöpferische
Kraft der Klassifikation einsetzt, um Kategorien
zu verorten. Zweitens können sie das Potenzial
erschließen, das dem Akt der Namensgebung innewohnt und drittens können sie von Perec lernen,
wie man aus der empirischen Beobachtung den Stoff
für Figuren gewinnt.

1 van Eck 1994: 216. This citation is from a chapter in which van Eck discusses the various manifestations of scientific organicism, and it is significant that in an effort to eschew art-historical categorization, Gottfried Semper turns to scientific taxonomic models in which the familial relationships are functional rather than visible. In another article I discuss the exchange of taxonomical schemas between Georges Buffon and Joachim Winckelmann; see Kulper 2006.

2 van Eck 1994: 228. Van Eck describes Semper's project as a problem of meaning and interpretation. How can we access the art of the past without mindlessly imitating it? And this is where Semper locates the idea of invention. Van Eck writes: "The rest of his career … was devoted to these problems, which could be described as, in the first place, a search for a scheme of interpretation of the visual arts; secondly, a concern with articulating the nonliteral meanings of visual art; and in the third place, a search for the systematic laws that regulate the development of artistic tradition." van Eck 1994: 229. This third ambition, the search for systematic laws, leads to the identification of invariant characters that eschew traditional art historical categories.

In the summer of 1830, a historic debate between two renowned biologists, Baron Georges Cuvier and Etienne Geoffroy Saint-Hilaire, took place. What was at stake in this debate? "Put briefly, the issue that caused the debate was the question whether the forms of organisms are determined by their function—the position defended by Cuvier—or whether all organic forms can be deduced from one basic type, regardless of their function—the view held by Geoffroy."[1] Prior to this debate, form was the primary filter for the categorization of natural organisms. Cuvier's contribution to modern biological thinking was to classify according to function rather than form. What relevance does this debate have for the discipline of architecture?

In an 1853 lecture entitled "Entwurf eines Systems der vergleichenden Stillehre" (Sketch of a comparative theory of style), Gottfried Semper described his many visits to the Jardin des Plantes in Paris, where he was a student from 1826 until 1830. Whenever he visited the gardens, he was inexorably drawn to the displays of fossils and skeletons arranged by Cuvier; in particular he was fascinated by nature's efficacy in producing such unity within diversity. As if struck by the potentially confining nature of this kind of typological thinking in architectural discourse, Semper draws an analogy between taxonomic species and artistic styles, and speculates that Cuvier's system might imbue architecture with new methods of stylistic invention: "It could be important to designate some of these fundamental types of artistic forms and to follow their gradual progress…. Such a method, similar to the one followed by Baron Cuvier, when applied to art and especially to architecture, would at least help to gain a clear survey of the whole field and perhaps even the basis of a theory of style and a kind of *Topica* or method of invention, which could lead to some knowledge of the natural process of invention."[2]

What is most notable about Semper's speculation is his conclusion that importing taxonomies from natural history might spawn "natural processes of invention" in architecture. More precisely, any analogy between the classification of living species and man-made artifact requires an appropriate level of comparison. Semper identified groups of artifacts by a set of invariants. These invariants do not rely on art-historical categories, but on the logic inherent to both matter and fabrication. Thus artifacts belonging to one specific group can stem from different epochs; Semper conceives of families of textile, tectonic, ceramic, and stereotomic arts. Using Semperian theory as a source for invention would mean thinking about new objects as necessarily being part of existing groups of artifacts. Creativity would therefore be enhanced by the identification of invariant characters common to all items belonging to a specific group, no matter whether they were old or new.

It is against this background that I would like to consider the spatial narratives of Georges Perec, and in particular, the transition from taxonomy to archive embodied in his texts *Species of Spaces* (1974) and *Life: A User's Manual* (1978). Different from Semper's approach, Perec's methods do not, at first glance, resort to general theories and available systems of classification. His lists and inventories seem to be empirically obtained through meticulous observations and the description of material settings,

Im Sommer 1830 gab es eine historische Debatte zwischen zwei berühmten Biologen, Baron Georges Cuvier und Étienne Geoffroy Saint-Hilaire. Worum ging es dabei? „Kurz gesagt war die Frage, die diese Debatte auslöste, ob die Formen von Organismen von deren Funktion bestimmt werden – die Meinung von Cuvier – oder ob alle organischen Formen aus einem Grundtypus hergeleitet werden können, unabhängig von deren Funktion – die Meinung von Geoffroy."[1] Vor dieser Debatte war die Form das Hauptbestimmungselement bei der Kategorisierung von Organismen der Natur. Cuviers Beitrag zum modernen Denken in der Biologie bestand darin, nach Funktion und nicht nach Form zu kategorisieren. Welche Bedeutung hat diese Debatte für die Architekturdisziplin?

In einer Vorlesung mit dem Titel „Entwurf eines Systems der vergleichenden Stillehre" im Jahr 1853 erzählte Gottfried Semper von seinen vielen Besuchen im Jardin des Plantes in Paris, wo er von 1826 bis 1830 studierte. Immer wenn er den botanischen Garten besuchte, fühlte er sich magisch von der Sammlung von Fossilien und Skeletten, die Cuvier aufgebaut hatte, angezogen, und besonders war er fasziniert davon, wie effizient die Natur eine solche Einheit innerhalb der Vielfalt produzieren konnte. Tief beeindruckt von den möglichen Eingrenzungen, die diese Art typologischen Denkens für den Architekturdiskurs bieten könnte, zieht Semper eine Analogie zwischen taxonomischen Gattungen und Kunststilen und wagt die These, dass Cuviers System neue Methoden der Erfindung im Bereich der Stile für die Architektur bieten könnte: „Es dürfte von Wichtigkeit sein, einige dieser Grundtypen der künstlerischen Formen zu bezeichnen und sie in ihrem stufenweisen Fortschritte…zu verfolgen. Eine solche Methode, ähnlich derjenigen, welche Baron Cuvier befolgte, auf die Kunst und speziell auf die Architektur angewandt, würde zum mindesten dazu beitragen, einen

klaren Überblick über deren ganzen Bereich zu gewinnen und vielleicht sogar die Basis einer Lehre vom Stile und einer Art von Topik oder Erfindungsmethode, welche zur Erkenntnis des natürlichen Prozesses des Erfindens führen könnte."[2]

Bemerkenswert an Sempers Überlegungen ist seine Schlussfolgerung, wonach das Übernehmen von Taxonomien aus der Naturkunde „natürliche Prozesse der Erfindung" in der Architektur hervorbringen könnten. Genauer gesagt, für jede Analogie zwischen der Klassifikation von Lebewesen und vom Menschen geschaffenen Artefakten bedarf es einer angemessenen Vergleichsebene. Semper identifizierte Gruppen von Artefakten durch eine definierte Reihe unveränderlicher Merkmale. Diese Invarianten haben keinen Bezug zu kunsthistorischen Kategorien, sondern zu der Logik, die mit der Materie und der Fertigung zusammenhängt. Damit können Artefakte, die zu einer bestimmten Gruppe gehören, aus unterschiedlichen Epochen stammen; für Semper gab es die Familien der textilen Kunst, der Tektonik, der Keramik und der Stereotomie. Wenn man Sempers Theorie als eine Quelle für Erfindungen nutzen würde, hieße das, dass neue Objekte zwangsläufig Teil

1 Zitiert in van Eck 1994: 216. Dieses Zitat stammt aus einem Kapitel, in dem van Eck die verschiedenen Manifestationen eines wissenschaftlichen Organizismus beschreibt. Es ist bedeutend, dass Gottfried Semper, auf den wir gleich zu sprechen kommen, in seinem Versuch, kunsthistorische Kategorisierungen zu vermeiden, sich wissenschaftlichen taxonomischen Modellen zuwendet, in denen die verwandtschaftlichen Beziehungen auf funktionaler und nicht auf sichtbarer Ebene bestehen. In einem anderen Artikel bespreche ich die Wechselwirkung taxonomischer Schemata von Georges Buffon und Joachim Winckelmann, siehe Kulper 2006.

2 Zitiert in van Eck: 2004: 228. Van Eck beschreibt Sempers Projekt als ein Problem von Bedeutung und Interpretation. Wie kann auf die Kunst der Vergangenheit zugegriffen werden, ohne sie gedankenlos zu imitieren? Genau hier verortet Semper die Idee der Erfindung. Van Eck schreibt: „Den Rest seiner Karriere widmete er sich diesen Problemen, die sich erstens als eine Suche nach einem Interpretationsschema der darstellenden Künste beschreiben ließen, zweitens als ein Ringen um Ausdruckselemente für die figurativen Bedeutungen der darstellenden Künste und drittens als eine Suche nach den Gesetzmäßigkeiten, die die Entwicklung der künstlerischen Tradition steuern." van Eck 1994: 229 [Dt. Übers.: SAW]. Dieser dritte Punkt, die Suche nach den Gesetzmäßigkeiten, führt zum Erkennen unveränderlicher Merkmale, die traditionelle kunsthistorische Kategorien vermeiden.

situations, and patterns of use found in everyday life. If Perec's spatial narratives can activate the list for the purpose of invention, can the discipline of architecture too see beyond the epistemological certainty of the list, the taxonomy, or the archive—methodological appropriations from scientific disciplines—to their inventive capacity?

Before proceeding with this question, a clarification of terminology and conceptual lineage is in order. This argument is predicated upon the relationship between lists, archives, and taxonomies in Perec's work and their potential applications to the practice of architecture. "Lists" refer to an ad hoc collection or inventory that is random, and that seeks to be exhaustive while always remaining open-ended. Similarly, an "archive" refers to the assimilation or collection of things; however, the question of access to archives imposes an order upon the randomness of a list—things must be stored in such a way that they can be easily retrieved, and typically this entails either the imposition of a chronology or a serialization of some sort. This ordering of the archive entails a prioritized sense of organization, a connotation of the term that is preserved in the verb "archive," alluding to the transfer of materials to a lower level in the hierarchy of memories. And while the list can be entirely subjective, and may thus fall squarely within the realm of privacy, the archive confers upon its contents the status of public records. "Taxonomy" represents the most rigid organization of the three terms, for it seeks familial or genealogical affiliations among things according to general laws or principles. Taxonomies are systematic worldviews, and the example of Cuvier illustrates that it is possible to shift the criteria of familial relations to such an extent that these affinities are no longer even visible.[3] Function, then, is accessed through this systematic understanding, emancipating taxonomies to the status of the universal, and creating a science of classification. Thus it is possible to consider the relationship of the list, the archive, and the taxonomy with respect to three different conceptual trajectories: their locus, their collective status as nouns and verbs, and their proximity to experience.

3 See Foucault 1970 [1966]: 288. Foucault writes: "From Cuvier onward, function, defined according to its non-perceptible form as an effect to be attained, is to serve as a constant middle term and to make it possible to relate together totalities of elements without the slightest visible identity." Tacit, I believe, in Foucault's argument is a potential logic for the shift from taxonomic to archival organization in Perec's narratives. At this moment when the logic of belonging together ceases to be visible, the common ground of the taxonomy is potentially lost to us, which is why his reference to Borges's Chinese encyclopedia is amusing and unsettling in equal measure.

From the vantage point of locus, the private nature of the list, the status of the archive as a housing of public documents, and the emancipated universality of the taxonomy are revealed. The combination and reciprocity of passive and active, reified and generative connotations of lists, archives, and taxonomies, the fact that each operates as both a noun and a verb, attests to their continuing stakes in both continuity and invention. And finally, with respect to the proximity to experience, the list is a product of immediacy, the archive mediates between immediacy and memory, and the taxonomy assumes a position of distance and omniscience, elevating the enterprise to a science of classification and its results to epistemological certainties.

Housing the Archive

It is not inconsequential that Perec locates his literary forays into the list—his spatial narratives laden with ubiquitous taxonomies and abundant archives—in domestic settings. *Species of Spaces*, a non-fictional narrative commissioned by a collaborator trained as an architect and written while Perec held a full-time job as an archivist in a scientific research laboratory, begins with an act of Semperian invention. The first space under consideration in this narrative is the space of the page, but again, not a generic page, rather a page upon which Perec's first words are "I write ..." Through this inscription, the author domesticates the page, filling it, habituating it with words that describe his own tendencies as a writer, words that territorialize the page as a spatial entity, words that simultaneously render him as both author and subject of the exercise. From the discrete space of the page, Perec extends his topological investigation incrementally, from page

einer bestehenden Gruppe von Artefakten sind. Kreativität gründet in der Bestimmung invarianter Merkmale, die allen Objekten einer Gruppe eigen sind, ganz unabhängig davon, ob sie alt oder neu sind.

Vor diesem Hintergrund sollen die Raumerzählungen von Georges Perec und insbesondere der Übergang von Taxonomie zu Archiv, wie er in seinen Texten *Träume von Räumen* (*Espèces d'espaces*, 1974, dt. Erstausgabe 1990) und *Das Leben. Gebrauchsanweisung* (*La vie mode d'emploi*, 1978, dt. Erstausgabe 1982) zum Ausdruck kommt, untersucht werden. Im Gegensatz zu Sempers Ansatz greifen Perecs Methoden auf den ersten Blick nicht auf allgemeine Theorien der Klassifikation und deren verfügbare Systeme zurück. Seine Listen und Inventare scheinen empirisch durch sorgfältige Beobachtungen und die Beschreibung tatsächlich vorhandener Szenarien, Situationen und Verwendungsmuster aus dem Alltag ermittelt zu sein. Wenn Perecs Raumerzählungen die Liste zum Zweck der Erfindung aktivieren können, kann dann auch die Architekturdisziplin hinter die epistemologische Gewissheit der Liste, der Taxonomie oder des Archivs – methodologische Aneignungen aus naturwissenschaftlichen Disziplinen – auf deren narratives Potenzial blicken?

Bevor näher auf diese Frage eingegangen werden soll, bedarf es einer Klärung der Terminologie und der Herleitung der Konzepte. Die Diskussion baut auf der Beziehung zwischen Listen, Archiven und Taxonomien in den Arbeiten von Perec und deren mögliche Anwendbarkeit auf die Praxis in der Architektur auf. „Liste" bedeutet eine ad-hoc-Sammlung oder ein Inventar, die ungeordnet und zufällig sind und versuchen, vollständig zu sein, jedoch immer offen bleiben. In ähnlicher Weise bezieht sich ein „Archiv" auf die Aneignung oder Sammlung von Dingen. Aber aufgrund der Forderung nach Zugänglichkeit zu den Archiven muss die Zufälligkeit einer Liste in eine Ordnung überführt werden – die Dinge müssen so aufbewahrt werden, dass sie leicht zurückverfolgt werden können. Daraus folgt in der Regel entweder die Einführung einer Chronologie oder einer anderen Form der Reihung. Für dieses Ordnen eines Archivs bedarf es primär einer Organisationsbereitschaft, und genau diese Bedeutung schwingt auch in dem Verb „archivieren" mit, das darauf anspielt, Material in eine tiefere Ebene in der Hierarchie der Erinnerungen zu verlagern. Und während die Liste absolut subjektiv und damit etwas ganz Privates, Persönliches sein kann, verleiht das Archiv seinen Inhalten den Status öffentlicher Aufzeichnungen. „Taxonomie" bezeichnet die strengste Organisationsform unter den drei Begriffen, denn sie sucht auf der Basis allgemeiner Gesetze oder Grundsätze nach verwandtschaftlichen beziehungsweise genealogischen Verbindungen zwischen den Dingen. In Taxonomien wird die Sicht auf die Welt systematisiert, und das Beispiel Cuviers zeigt, dass es möglich ist, die Kriterien verwandtschaftlicher Beziehungen in einem solchen Ausmaß zu verändern, dass diese Affinitäten gar nicht mehr sichtbar sind.[3] Den Zugang zur Funktion erhält man durch dieses systematische Verstehen, wodurch die Taxonomien den Status des Universellen erhalten und eine Wissenschaft der Klassifikation geschaffen wird.

Daher ist es möglich, die Beziehung von Liste, Archiv und Taxonomie anhand von drei unterschiedlichen konzeptionellen Überlegungen zu betrachten: ihrem Ort, ihrem Status als Substantive und Verben sowie ihrer Nähe zur Erfahrung. Hinsichtlich des Ortes werden die Privatheit der Liste, der Status des Archivs als Heimstatt öffentlicher Dokumente und die errungene Universalität der Taxonomie deutlich. Die Kombination und Reziprozität von passiv und

---

3 Siehe Foucault 1974 [1966]: 324. Foucault schreibt: „Seit Cuvier dient die in der nicht wahrnehmbaren Form der zu erreichenden Wirkung definierte Funktion als mittleres konstantes Glied und gestattet, Gesamtheiten aus Elementen, die der geringsten sichtbaren Identität ermangeln, aufeinander zu beziehen." Unausgesprochen, glaube ich, liegt in Foucaults Aussage eine mögliche Erklärung für den Wechsel von einer taxonomischen Ordnung hin zu einer Ordnung in Archiven in Perecs Erzählungen. In dem Moment, da die Logik, die alles zusammenhält, nicht mehr sichtbar ist, geht für den Leser oder Betrachter die gemeinsame Grundlage der Taxonomie unter Umständen verloren, und dies ist wohl auch der Grund, warum sein Bezug zu der chinesischen Enzyklopädie von Borges in gleichem Maße amüsant wie auch verunsichernd ist.

to bed, from bed to bedroom, from bedroom to apartment, from apartment to apartment building, from apartment building to street, from street to neighborhood, from neighborhood to town, from town to countryside, from countryside to country, from country to Europe, from Europe to the world, and from the world right back to space where his narrative began. This topological movement from the page to the world takes what is most familiar and known as its conceit, and proceeds to domesticate increasingly larger spatial territories through this lens. However, beginning with the most intimate topology—the page—Perec establishes this stable situation as the locus of invention as well. His exploitation of the spatiality of the page coupled with his inclination to subjectivize a purportedly "objective" classification of territories, constitute acts of invention that the seemingly benign act of taxonomizing appears to preclude.

The novel *Life: A User's Manual* also makes use of a domestic setting, in this case, a Parisian apartment building. Perec first toyed with the idea of the novel in the section of *Species of Spaces* devoted to the apartment building, in which he writes: "I imagine a Parisian apartment building whose façade has been removed ... so that all the rooms in front, from the ground floor up to the attics, are instantly and simultaneously visible. The novel, whose title is *Life: A User's Manual* restricts itself...to describing the rooms thus unveiled and the activities unfolding in them..."[4] Perec cites Saul Steinberg's 1952 cartoon *The Art of Living* [→ fig. 1] as a source of inspiration for the novel, and brainstorms, in the form of a list extending almost three pages, about the sorts of things to be found in such a place [→ fig. 2]. The ad hoc nature of this list, which details everything contained within the apartment building, from termites to toy trains, appears to carry over into the novel, whereas the table of contents reads like a haphazard inventory, placing occupants—"Two *Beaumont*"—in seamless adjacency with equipment—"Thirty-Eight *Lift Machinery*"—and locales within the building—"Sixty-Eight *On the Stairs*."

4   Perec 1997 [1974]: 40. The conventions of removing the façade or representing an inhabited section are not new to the discipline of architecture. See Periton 2004: 289–304. Unique to Steinberg's cartoon within this representational trajectory is that the drawing is not so much about the lifestyle of the inhabitants of the apartments as it is concerned with an inventory of their belongings as a demonstration of that lifestyle.
5   Perec 1997 [1974]: 41.
6   Vesely 2004: 368. In the context of Vesely's argument about the paradigmatic nature of dwelling, these examples are cited as evidence of the fact that early twentieth century projects for experimental houses, were not, in the end, very experimental. The stability of the domestic situation, in Vesely's sense, becomes the locus of continuity in the archive, which is a continuity of practice.

However, upon closer examination, Perec adheres to certain genealogical principles in the list in *Species of Spaces*; for example, he observes "ten adult individuals of the male sex" and then differentiates them based upon their activities, "...one is typing...one is having a shower...one is eating toast."[5] Embodied in this transition from *Species of Spaces* to *Life: A User's Manual* is a subtle shift in Perec's writing, in which the archive supplants the taxonomy as the paradigmatic source of spatial order. In the table of contents of *Life: A User's Manual*, the ordering of space according to species yields to space that is ordered according to local affinities and coincidental adjacencies, much like the archive. Perec's directive to make the content of the apartment building "instantly and simultaneously visible" privileges chance occurrences and instigates an ordering system predicated upon contingency and local inflection. Perec acknowledges Saul Steinberg's act of representational invention—the removal of the façade from the apartment building. The subsequent shift in his writing from taxonomy to archive attempts to tap into the creative potential and inventive possibilities of non-familial adjacency.

Perec's taxonomic and archival lists are located in domestic settings because the domestic represents the ultimate paradigmatic situation. Dalibor Vesely describes the role of the paradigmatic situation as organizing "individual events and elements of praxis" and conferring upon them "a higher and more universal meaning."[6] Vesely articulates the stability and continuity of the domestic setting when he writes: "The best

aktiv, verdinglichten und schöpferischen Konnotationen von Listen, Archiven und Taxonomien, die Tatsache, dass alle in gewisser Form sowohl Substantiv wie auch Verb sein können, ist ein Beweis für deren beständige Einsatzmöglichkeiten sowohl im Bereich der Kontinuität als auch der Erfindung. Und schließlich ist die Liste bezüglich ihrer Nähe zur Erfahrung ein Produkt der Unmittelbarkeit, das Archiv vermittelt zwischen Unmittelbarkeit und Erinnerung, und die Taxonomie nimmt eine Position von Distanz und Allwissenheit ein und erhebt das Unterfangen zu einer Wissenschaft der Klassifikation und deren Ergebnisse zu epistemologischen Gewissheiten.

Dem Archiv eine Heimstatt geben

Es folgt einer gewissen Logik, dass Perec seine literarischen Ausflüge in die Welt der Listen – seine Raumerzählungen voller allgegenwärtiger Taxonomien und üppiger Archive – in häuslichen Umgebungen ansiedelt. *Träume von Räumen*, eine sachliche Erzählung, die von einem Kollegen mit einer Architektenausbildung in Auftrag gegeben worden war und geschrieben wurde, als Perec in Vollzeit als Archivar bei einem wissenschaftlichen Forschungslabor arbeitete, beginnt mit einem Akt Semper'scher Erfindung. Der erste Raum, der in dieser Erzählung betrachtet wird, ist der Raum der Buchseite, aber nicht irgendeiner Seite, sondern einer Seite, auf der Perecs erste Worte „Ich schreibe..." stehen. Durch diese Beschriftung domestiziert der Autor die Seite – füllt sie, arbeitet auf ihr, gewöhnt sie an Wörter, die seine eigenen Neigungen als Schriftsteller beschreiben, Wörter, die sich auf der Seite als eine räumliche Einheit ihren Platz erobern, Wörter, die ihn gleichzeitig zum Autor und zum Subjekt der Übung machen. Vom diskreten Raum der Seite, dehnt Perec seine topologischen Erkundungen aus und lässt sie immer weitere Kreise ziehen, von der Seite zum Bett, vom Bett zum Schlafzimmer, vom Schlafzimmer zur Wohnung, von der Wohnung zum Wohnhaus, vom Wohnhaus zur Straße, von der Straße zum Stadtviertel, vom Stadtviertel zur Stadt, von der Stadt zum Kreis, vom Kreis zum Land, vom Land zu Europa, von Europa zur Welt und von der Welt direkt zurück zum Raum, in dem seine Erzählung begann. Seine topologische Bewegung von der Seite zur Welt beginnt mit dem Vertrauten und Wohlbekannten und domestiziert davon ausgehend immer größere Räume und Gebiete. Aber indem Perec mit der intimsten Topologie – der Buchseite – beginnt, baut er diese stabile Situation auch als den Ort der Erfindung auf. Er nutzt die Räumlichkeit der Seite und verbindet damit seine Neigung, eine angeblich „objektive" Klassifikation der Territorien zu subjektivieren; dies lässt Akte der Erfindung entstehen, die der scheinbar harmlose Akt des Taxonomierens auszuschließen scheint.

Der Roman *Das Leben. Gebrauchsanweisung* nutzt ebenfalls eine häusliche Szenerie, in diesem Fall ein Wohnhaus in Paris. Perec spielte zunächst mit der Idee des Romans in dem Teil von *Träume von Räumen*, der dem Mietshaus gewidmet ist und in dem er schreibt: „Ich stelle mir ein Pariser Mietshaus vor, dessen Fassade entfernt worden ist, so daß vom Erdgeschoß bis zu den Mansarden alle nach vorne liegenden Räume augenblicklich und gleichzeitig sichtbar sind. Der Roman – dessen Titel ,Das Leben, Gebrauchsanweisung' lautet – beschränkt sich darauf, die so enthüllten Räume sowie die sich darin abspielenden Tätigkeiten zu beschreiben".[4] Perec nennt den Cartoon *The Art of Living* aus dem Jahr 1952 [→ Abb. 1] von Saul Steinberg als eine wichtige Inspirationsquelle für seinen Roman und erarbeitet darüber hinaus Assoziationsketten in Form einer fast drei Seiten langen Liste der Dinge, die an einem solchen Ort zu finden sind [→ Abb. 2]. Das Spontane der Liste, in der alles, was in dem Wohngebäude zu finden ist, aufgeführt wird, von Termiten

---

4   Perec 1994 [1974]: 52. Die Konvention, die Fassade zu entfernen oder einen bewohnten Schnitt darzustellen, ist in der Architektur nichts Neues. Siehe Periton 2004: 289–304. Das Besondere an Steinbergs Cartoon in dieser Entwicklungslinie ist, dass die Zeichnung nicht so sehr vom Lebensstil der Bewohner der Wohnungen handelt, sondern sich mit einem Inventar der Dinge, die ihnen gehören, als eine Darstellung von eben diesem Lebensstil befasst.

DOUBLING UP

Abb. 1
Saul Steinberg, *Doubling Up*, 1946. Tinte auf Papier.
Diese Zeichnung wurde später als *The Art of Living* in einem
gleichnamigen Buch veröffentlicht.

Fig. 1
Saul Steinberg, *Doubling Up*, 1946. Ink on paper.
This drawing was later published as *The Art of Living* in a book
of the same title.

3 bathrooms. The one on the third floor is empty, in the one on the second, a woman is taking a bath; in the one on the ground floor, a man is having a shower.

3 fireplaces, varying greatly in size, but all on the one axis. None of them is working (no one has lit a fire in them, if you prefer). The ones on the first and second floors are equipped with fire-dogs; the one on the first floor is split into two by a partition which also divides the mouldings and the ceiling rose.

6 candelabra and one Calder-style mobile

5 telephones

1 upright piano with stool

10 adult individuals of the male sex, of whom

1 is having a drink

1 is typing

2 are reading the newspaper, one sitting in an armchair, the other stretched out on a divan

3 are asleep

1 is having a shower

1 is eating toast

1 is coming through the doorway into a room where there is a dog

10 adult individuals of the female sex, of whom

1 is doing her chores

1 is sitting down

1 is holding a baby in her arms

2 are reading, one, sitting down, the newspaper, the other, lying down, a novel

1 is doing the washing-up

1 is having a bath

1 is knitting

1 is eating toast

1 is sleeping

6 young children, 2 of whom are certainly little girls and 2 certainly little boys

2 dogs

2 cats

1 bear on wheels

1 small horse on wheels

1 toy train

1 doll in a pram

6 rats or mice

a fair number of termites (it's not certain they are termites; the sorts of animals in any case that live in floorboards and walls)

at least 38 pictures or framed engravings

1 negro mask

29 lights (over and above the candelabra)

10 beds

1 child's cot

3 divans, one of which serves uncomfortably as a bed

4 kitchens or rather kitchenettes

7 rooms with parquet flooring

1 carpet

2 bedside rugs or mats

9 rooms where the floor is no doubt covered with moquette

3 rooms with tiled floors

1 interior staircase

8 pedestal tables

5 coffee tables

5 small bookcases

1 shelf full of books

2 clocks

5 chests of drawers

2 tables

1 desk with drawers with blotting-pad and inkwell

2 pairs of shoes

1 bathroom stool

11 upright chairs

2 armchairs

1 leather briefcase

1 dressing gown

1 hanging cupboard

1 alarm clock

1 pair of bathroom scales

1 pedal bin

1 hat hanging on a peg

1 suit hanging on a hanger

1 jacket hanging on the back of a chair

washing drying

3 small bathroom cabinets

several bottles and flasks

numerous objects hard to identify (carriage clocks, ashtrays, spectacles, glasses, saucers full of peanuts, for example)

Abb. 2
Georges Perec, *Träume von Räumen*. Das Mietshaus: Beschreibung des Inhalts des Gebäudes, das in Saul Steinbergs *Doubling Up* dargestellt ist.

Fig. 2
Georges Perec, *Species of Spaces*. The Apartment Building: description of the contents of the building depicted in Saul Steinberg's *Doubling Up*.

place to start is the sphere of typical situations close to everyday existence. Because we always live somewhere, the situations most familiar to us are those related to the place of our dwelling. These have changed very little in comparison to situations related to other spheres of life—places of work and places of commercial and public life, such as schools, hospitals, theaters, and museums."[7] The persistence and constancy of the domestic setting, its paradigmatic nature, proffer the continuity against which taxonomic difference can appear.

Jacques Derrida, in his unpacking of the etymology of archive in the text *Archive Fever*, reveals another important connection between the archive and the domestic setting when he writes: "…the meaning of 'archive,' its only meaning, comes to it from the Greek *arkheion*: initially a house, a domicile, an address, the residence of the superior magistrates, the *archons*, those who commanded."[8] Here, Derrida designates the dwelling as the place where domestic and institutional practices meet: "At the intersection of the topological and the nomological, of the place and the law, of the substrate and the authority, a scene of domiciliation becomes at once visible and invisible."[9] What Derrida's observations about the archive make clear is that encountering the list is an act of domestication, both tacit and explicit. His use of the term "domiciliation" suggests that for Derrida the domestic is more than a locale; it is also a practice. In both *Species of Spaces* and *Life: A User's Manual* Perec is similarly acknowledging the role of the domestic setting in situating the list, both spatially and with respect to practice. In Perec's writing the domestic is a paradigmatic situation framed as both setting and event, which constitutes an interface between private and institutional practices. Perec's fascination with materialism is apparent in spatial narratives that feature the domestic as the locus of cultural commodification. The detritus of everyday life renders the denizens of the domestic as both collectors and curators of their own chosen lifestyles. Through the act of housing the archive, Perec embraces the situation of the list, rather than pursuing

7 Vesely 2004: 376.
8 Derrida 1995: 2.
9 Derrida 1995: 3. Derrida's evocation of domesticity that is both visible and invisible establishes the domestic as the reciprocity of setting and event, or of locus and practice. In Perec's fiction, the visible dimensions of domiciliation are the purview of the lists, archives, and taxonomies, whereas the invisible resides in the domestic practices of the narrative.

classification as a universal condition of abstraction. For the discipline of architecture, the intersection between the internal logic of the list, archive, or taxonomy and its spatial situation can potentially become the locus of invention.

Naming the Species
Before happening upon a single written word by Perec, the reader of *Species of Spaces* first encounters an image from Lewis Carroll's *Hunting of the Snark* entitled "Map of the Ocean" [→ fig. 3]. This image, or lack of image as the case may be, is revelatory with respect to Perec's taxonomic project. In naming the image "Map of the Ocean," Carroll evokes certain taxonomic conventions. He alludes to the ocean as something that we can name, map, and definitively know, and his deployment of the geometric frame gives visual expression to this epistemological certitude. Paradoxically, the absence of anything within that frame articulates the utter folly of taxonomic endeavors. The blankness of the image points simultaneously to the overwhelming extensity of the ocean and to the human inability to comprehend its scale or understand it in any meaningful way. For Perec, this image establishes the tone for all of his future taxonomic endeavors. In naming, Perec consistently evokes conventions, while cleverly subverting conventional expectations and counteracting the very logic of classification. In this sense, he is explicitly augmenting Semperian invention, paradoxically through the practice of naming—an act that tends to limit conceptual possibilities through the conceit of "knowing" something, rather than extemporaneously riffing on an idea to produce projective trajectories.

In his discussion of archives, Derrida references the "nomological principle"—

bis Spielzeugeisenbahnen, scheint in den Roman hineinzureichen, dessen Inhaltsverzeichnis sich wie eine willkürliche Zusammenstellung liest und in dem die Bewohner – „Zweites Kapitel: Beaumont" – übergangslos neben Gerätschaften – „Achtunddreißigstes Kapitel: Maschinenraum des Aufzugs" – und Schauplätzen innerhalb des Gebäudes – „Achtundsechzigstes Kapitel: Treppenhaus" stehen.

Bei näherer Betrachtung folgt Perec in der Liste in *Träume von Räumen* jedoch bestimmten genealogischen Grundsätzen. So beobachtet er beispielsweise „10 Erwachsene männlichen Geschlechts" und arbeitet dann Unterschiede anhand ihrer Aktivitäten heraus, „…1 schreibt Schreibmaschine… 1 duscht…1 isst Toastscheiben".[5] In diesem Übergang von *Träume von Räumen* zu *Das Leben. Gebrauchsanweisung* findet sich ein sachter Wandel in Perecs Schreibstil, bei dem das Archiv die Taxonomie als die paradigmatische Quelle räumlicher Ordnung ablöst. Im Inhaltsverzeichnis von *Das Leben. Gebrauchsanweisung* weicht das Ordnen von Raum gemäß bestimmter Gattungen einem Raum, der gemäß örtlicher Affinitäten und zufälliger Nachbarschaftsbeziehungen ganz ähnlich wie ein Archiv geordnet wird. Perecs Vorgabe, den Inhalt des Wohnhauses „augenblicklich und gleichzeitig sichtbar" zu machen, gibt zufälligen Begebenheiten den Vorzug und inspiriert zu einem Ordnungssystem, das auf Unvorhergesehenem und örtlichen Wendungen aufbaut. Perec erkennt Saul Steinbergs Akt darstellerischer Erfindung an – die Entfernung der Fassade von dem Wohngebäude. Die anschließende Wendung in seinem Werk von der Taxonomie zum Archiv versucht, das kreative Potenzial und die erfinderischen Möglichkeiten der nicht-verwandtschaftlichen Nachbarschaftsbeziehungen zu nutzen.

Perecs taxonomische Listen sowie seine Archivlisten sind in häuslichen Umgebungen verortet, weil das Häusliche die ultimative paradigmatische Situation darstellt. Dalibor Vesely beschreibt die Rolle der paradigmatischen Situation als das Organisieren „einzelner Ereignisse und Elemente der Praxis" und das Zuordnen „einer höheren und

universelleren Bedeutung".[6] Vesely beschreibt die Stabilität und Kontinuität der häuslichen Umgebung folgendermaßen: „Der beste Aus-gangsort ist der Bereich der typischen Situationen, die eng mit dem alltäglichen Leben zusammenhängen. Da wir immer irgendwo wohnen, sind die Verhältnisse, die uns am vertrautesten sind, diejenigen mit einem Bezug zu dem Ort, an dem wir wohnen, zu unserer Wohnung. Diese haben sich nur wenig verändert im Vergleich zu den Verhältnissen in anderen Bereichen unseres Lebens – Orte der Arbeit und Orte des Geschäfts- und öffentlichen Lebens, wie Schulen, Krankenhäuser, Theater und Museen."[7] Der Fortbestand und die Beständigkeit der häuslichen Umgebung, deren paradigmatisches Wesen, bilden die Kontinuität, vor der sich ein taxonomischer Unterschied abzeichnen kann.

Jacques Derrida analysiert die Etymologie des Archivs in dem Text *Dem Archiv verschrieben* und macht damit eine weitere wichtige Verbindung zwischen dem Archiv und der häuslichen Umgebung deutlich. Daher, so Derrida, „kommt der Sinn von ‚Archiv', dessen einziger Sinn von dem griechischen *archeîon*: zuerst ein Haus, ein Wohnsitz, eine Adresse, die Wohnung der Magistratsangehörigen, der *árchontes*, diejenigen, die geboten."[8] Hier beschreibt Derrida die Wohnung als den Ort, an dem häusliche und institutionelle Praktiken zusammentreffen: „In der Überkreuzung des Topologischen und Nomologischen, von Ort und Gesetz, Träger und Autorität, wird ein Schauplatz verbindlicher Ansiedlung sichtbar und unsichtbar zugleich."[9] (S. 150) Derridas Beobachtungen hinsichtlich der Archive machen deutlich, dass die Begegnung mit der Liste implizit und explizit ein Akt der

---

5 Perec 1994 [1974]: 53.

6 Vesely 2004: 268 [Dt. Übers.: SAW]. Innerhalb Veselys Argumentation hinsichtlich des paradigmatischen Wesens des Wohnens werden diese Beispiele als Beweis für die Tatsache genannt, dass experimentelle Hausprojekte zu Beginn des 20. Jahrhunderts letztlich gar nicht so sehr experimentell waren. Die Stabilität der häuslichen Situation im Sinne Veselys wird zum Ort der Kontinuität in dem Archiv, das heißt eine Kontinuität der Praxis.

7 Vesely 2004: 376 [Dt. Übers.: SAW].

8 Derrida 1997 [1995]: 11.

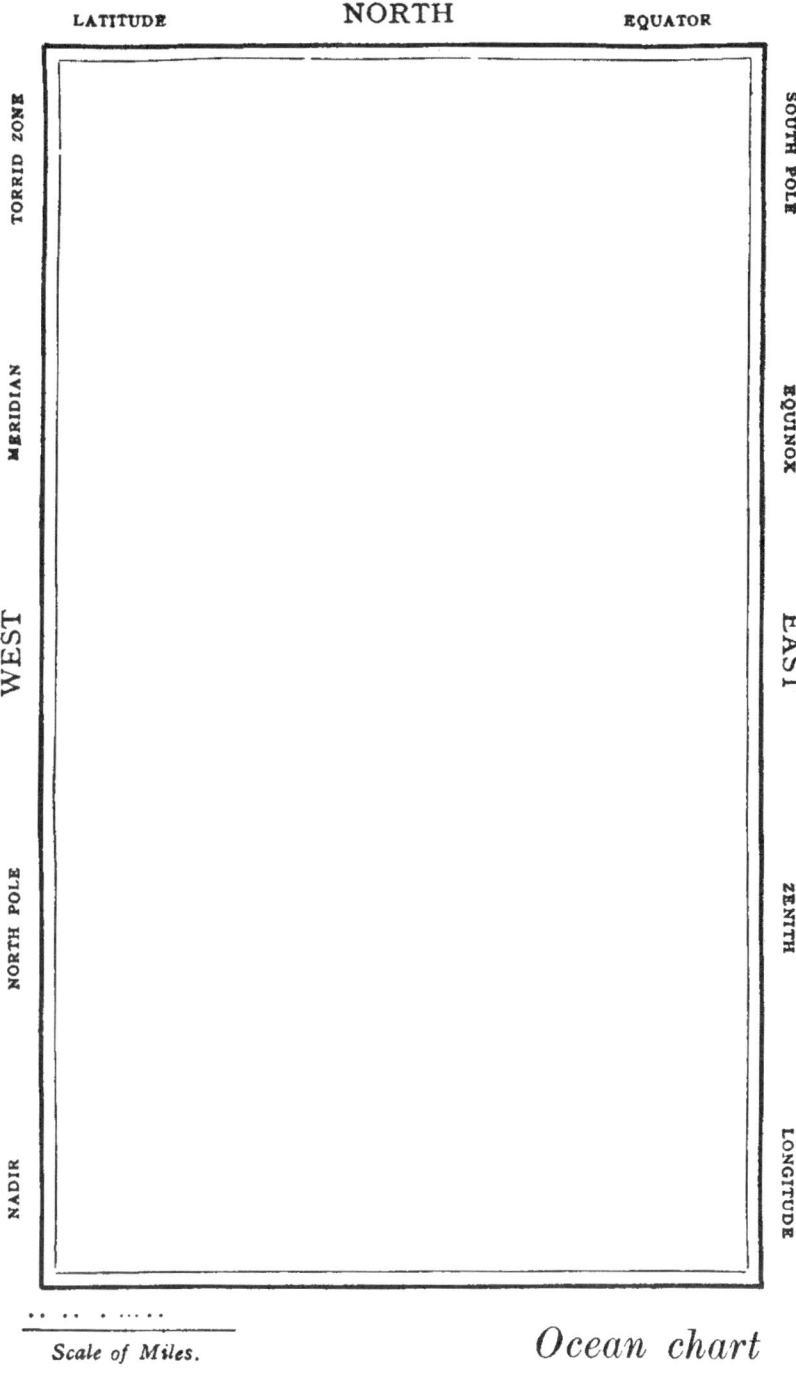

NORTH

EQUATOR

SOUTH POLE

TORRID ZONE

EQUINOX

MERIDIAN

WEST

EAST

NORTH POLE

ZENITH

NADIR

LONGITUDE

Scale of Miles.

Ocean chart

Abb. 3
Henry Holiday, *Seekarte*, aus Lewis Carrolls
Die Jagd nach dem Schnark, 1874.

Fig. 3
Henry Holiday, *Ocean Chart*, from Lewis Carroll's
Hunting of the Snark, 1874.

Domestizierung ist. Seine Verwendung des Begriffs „Domizilierung" [verbindliche Ansiedlung] lässt vermuten, dass für Derrida das Häusliche mehr als ein Schauplatz ist, es ist auch eine Praxis. Sowohl in *Träume von Räumen* als auch in *Das Leben. Gebrauchsanweisung* erkennt Perec in ähnlicher Weise die Rolle der häuslichen Umgebung beim Aufstellen der Liste sowohl räumlich als auch in Bezug auf die Praxis an. In Perecs Schriften ist das Häusliche eine paradigmatische Situation, die sich als Schauplatz wie auch als Ereignis darstellt und ein Bindeglied zwischen privaten und institutionellen Praktiken darstellt. Perec ist fasziniert vom Materialismus, und dies wird deutlich in den Raumerzählungen, in denen es um das Häusliche als Ort kultureller Kommodifizierung geht. Die Überbleibsel des Alltagslebens macht die Bewohner des Häuslichen sowohl zu Sammlern als auch zu Kuratoren ihres eigenen, so gewählten Lebensstils. Durch den Akt, dem Archiv eine Heimstatt zu geben, macht sich Perec die Situation der Liste zu eigen, statt nach der Klassifikation als universeller Abstraktionsbedingung zu streben. Für die Disziplin Architektur kann die Überkreuzung der inneren Logik der Liste, des Archivs oder der Taxonomie und deren räumliche Situation zum Ort der Erfindung werden.

Benennung der Gattungen

Bevor der Leser von *Träume von Räumen* auf ein einziges Wort von Perec trifft, findet er ein Bild aus Lewis Carrolls *Die Jagd nach dem Schnark* mit dem Titel „Seekarte" [→ Abb. 3]. Dieses Bild, oder eigentlich das Fehlen eines Bildes, sagt bereits sehr viel aus über Perecs taxonomisches Projekt. Indem Carroll dem Bild den Titel „Seekarte" gibt, erinnert er an bestimmte taxonomische Konventionen. Er spielt darauf an, dass die See etwas ist, was wir benennen und kartografieren können und ganz sicher kennen, und die Verwendung des geometrischen Bilderrahmens gibt dieser epistemologischen Gewissheit einen optisch sichtbaren Ausdruck. Paradoxerweise zeigt die Abwesenheit von etwas Dargestelltem innerhalb dieses Rahmens die absolute Verrücktheit taxonomi-

scher Bemühungen. Die Leere des Bildes hebt die überwältigende Weite des Meeres und zugleich die Unfähigkeit des Menschen hervor, dessen Ausmaße zu erfassen oder es in angemessener Weise zu verstehen. Für Perec ist dieses Bild bestimmend für alle seine zukünftigen taxonomischen Anstrengungen. Bei seinen Benennungen lässt Perec beständig Konventionen anklingen, aber unterwandert zugleich geschickt konventionelle Erwartungen und handelt so entgegen der eigentlichen Logik der Klassifikation. In diesem Sinne erweitert er die Semper'sche Erfindung paradoxerweise durch die Praxis des Benennens – einen Akt, der dazu neigt, die konzeptionellen Möglichkeiten dadurch einzuschränken, dass man sich einbildet, etwas zu „wissen", statt aus dem Stegreif virtuos großartige neue gedankliche Linien zu entwickeln.

Derrida bezieht sich in seiner Diskussion über Archive auf das „nomologische Prinzip" – ein Lehrsatz, der anerkennt, dass der Akt der Benennung zugleich auch ein Akt des Aufstellens und Interpretieren des Gesetzes (*nomos*) ist. Indem Derrida den „topo-nomologischen" Charakter des Archivs herausarbeitet, stellt er damit implizit die Frage, ob dieses Zusammenziehen von *topos* und *nomos*, Ort und Benennung (oder Gesetz), ein Kontinuum oder ein Auferlegen darstellt. Erwächst die Ordnung des Archivs aus einem kreativen topologischen Dialog oder stellt der Akt des Archivierens das Aufzwingen einer rationalen Ordnung auf die zufällige Welt der Dinge dar? In der ersten und vielleicht am wenigsten offensichtlichen Gattung von Raum, die Perec bespricht, – der Seite – stellt er übergangslos die quantitativen und höchst persönlichen Beschreibungen einer Einheit nebeneinander, von der angenommen wird, dass sie, sobald sie einmal benannt ist, dem Leser aufs Intimste bekannt

---

9 Derrida 1997 [1995]: 12. Indem Derrida die Häuslichkeit heraufbeschwört, die sowohl sichtbar als auch unsichtbar ist, führt er das Häusliche als die Wechselbeziehung von Szenerie und Ereignis beziehungsweise von Ort und Praxis ein. In Perecs Geschichten erscheinen die sichtbaren Dimensionen einer Domizilierung der Geltungsbereiche Liste, Archiv und Taxonomie; während das Unsichtbare den häuslichen Praktiken der Erzählung innewohnt.

a tenet that acknowledges that the act of naming is simultaneously an act of establishing and interpreting the law (*nomos*). When Derrida articulates the "topo-nomological" nature of archives, he implicitly raises the question of whether this elision of *topos* and *nomos*, place and name (or law), is a continuum or an imposition. Does the order of the archive emerge from a creative topological dialogue, or does the act of archiving represent the imposition of a rational order upon the haphazard world of things? In the first, and perhaps least obvious, species of space that Perec discusses—the page—he seamlessly pairs quantitative and highly personal descriptions of an entity that, once named, is assumed to be known intimately by his readers. It is precisely this assumption of knowledge that Perec targets in his taxonomic forays. He begins with this quantitative description of the page: "The space of a sheet of paper (regulation internal size, as used in Government departments, on sale at all stationers) measures 623.7 sq. cm."[10] In offering the standard measure of the page and assigning it to both institutional and commercial locales, Perec offers the reader precisely what he expects, what the name "page" evokes. He continues: "You have to write a little over sixteen pages to take up one square meter. Assuming the average format of a book to be 21 by 29.7 cm, you could, if you were to pull apart all the printed books kept in the Bibliothèque Nationale and spread the pages out one beside the other, cover the whole, either of the island of St. Helena or of Lake Trasimeno."[11] In this eccentric extension of quantitative logic, Perec nudges the reader beyond the realm of expectation and spatializes the page through the evocation of large territories. Perec trumps expectation, and utilizes the most banal, quantitative description of the page as a springboard for spatial invention.

In *Life: A User's Manual*, Perec continues to explore the possibility of naming as an inventive spatial practice. The apartments and their basements become the headings of various chapters, and since the basements are used for storage, they become the locale of the list, inventory, or collection, whereas

10 Perec 1997 [1974]: 16. Such descriptions in Perec's work also parody scientism, or the belief that science holds the answers to our most pressing cultural problems. To discuss the page in terms of its quantifiable attributes is anathema to most writers, and it poignantly demonstrates, in Perec's able hands, what such instrumental descriptions lack, without having to elaborate upon precisely where these deficits reside.
11 Perec 1997 [1974]: 16. Here, the expansion of Perec's initial quantification of the page serves both as a spatialization of the page and a cautionary tale about the potential vehicles through which scientism spreads and legitimizes itself.

the apartments themselves become the catalysts to more elaborate events and descriptions. A brief glance at the basements of the Altamonts and the Gratiolets gives the impression that Perec's exhaustive inventory is an end in itself, but upon closer examination it becomes apparent that these extensive lists are the staging area for subsequent character developments and plot twists—though they appear in the form of collections, the basements paradoxically establish context [→ figs. 4 and 5]. From these lists, we can surmise that the Altamonts are fastidious and organized, and are well-off gourmands who keep up appearances, whereas the Gratiolets are disorganized, eclectic, athletic, and are avid travelers. Perec's extensive inventories of basements and the relational structure that they establish with the apartments and their inhabitants forge a dialogue between the epistemologies and events of everyday life. His lists, inventories, and collections are not exclusively objective, nor are his description of the building's inhabitants lacking in facts or objectified data. This mutual approximation of the epistemological and the ontological—the situation of positively observed facts in the context of lived experience—advances praxis as the critical concern of spatial knowledge, while undermining empiricism's claim that naming is an epistemological end in itself. From Perec, architecture can learn the evocative potential of naming as a practice that reveals the possibilities for invention, in lieu of language's capacity to discursively overdetermine and therefore eschew discovery.

Letting the Figure Emerge
As stated earlier, the logic of the list in Perec's *Species of Spaces* is the logic of taxonomy

ist. Und genau auf die Annahme einer solchen Kenntnis zielt Perec in seinen Ausflügen in die Taxonomie. Er beginnt mit dieser quantitativen Beschreibung der Seite: „Der Raum eines Blatts Papier (Internationales Maß, bei allen Verwaltungen üblich, in allen Schreibwarengeschäften erhältlich, in Deutschland als DIN A4 bekannt) misst 623,7 cm^2."[10] Indem Perec mit dem Standardmaß der Seite arbeitet und es sowohl institutionellen als auch gewerblichen Schauplätzen zuordnet, bietet er dem Leser genau das an, was dieser erwartet, was das Wort „Seite" evoziert. Er fährt fort: „Um einen Quadratmeter auszufüllen, muß man etwas mehr als sechzehn Seiten schreiben. Gesetzt den Fall, das Durchschnittsformat eines Buches beträgt 21 x 29,7 cm, so könnte man, wenn man alle in der Pariser Nationalbibliothek aufbewahrten Druckwerke auseinandernimmt und die Seiten sorgfältig nebeneinander legt, damit entweder die Insel Helena oder den Trasimenischen See vollständig bedecken."[11] In dieser ausgefallenen Erweiterung quantitativer Logik führt Perec den Leser weit über dessen Erwartungen hinaus und verräumlicht die Seite, indem er große Territorien vor dem inneren Auge aufziehen lässt. Perec sticht die Erwartung aus und benutzt die sehr banale quantitative Beschreibung der Seite als Sprungbrett für räumliche Erfindung.

In *Das Leben. Gebrauchsanweisung* fährt Perec fort, die Möglichkeit der Benennung als eine erfinderische und schöpferische Raumpraxis zu erkunden. Die Wohnungen und deren Keller werden zu Überschriften verschiedener Kapitel, und da die Keller als Lagerräume dienen, werden sie zum Schauplatz von Liste, Inventar oder Sammlung, während die Wohnungen dagegen zu Katalysatoren für größere Ereignisse und Beschreibungen werden. Ein kurzer Blick auf die Keller der Altamonts und der Gratiolets vermittelt den Eindruck, dass Perecs umfassende Inventare Selbstzweck sind, aber bei genauerer Betrachtung wird deutlich, dass diese ausführlichen Listen die Bühne bilden, auf der sich die darauf folgenden Entwicklungen der Charaktere und gewundenen Handlungsstränge abspielen – auch wenn die Keller in Form von Sammlungen erscheinen,

bilden sie paradoxerweise doch einen Kontext [→ Abb. 4 und 5]. Aus diesen Listen lässt sich mutmaßen, dass die Altamonts übergenaue, wohl organisierte und reiche Schlemmer sind, die einen äußeren Schein wahren; dagegen sind die Gratiolets schlecht organisiert, eklektisch, athletisch und reisen gerne. Perecs ausführliche Inventare der Keller und der Beziehungsstruktur, die sie mit den Wohnungen und ihren Bewohnern schaffen, bauen einen Dialog zwischen den Epistemologien und den Ereignissen des Alltags auf. Seine Listen, Inventare und Sammlungen sind durchaus nicht rein objektiv, wie es seiner Beschreibung der Einwohner des Gebäudes auch nicht an Fakten und objektivierten Daten mangelt. Diese gegenseitige Annäherung des Epistemologischen und des Ontologischen – das Platzieren tatsächlich beobachteter Fakten im Kontext gelebter Erfahrung – bringt die Praxis als das entscheidende Anliegen des räumlichen Wissens voran und unterminiert zugleich den Anspruch der Empirie, dass Benennung epistemologischer Selbstzweck ist. Die Architektur kann von Perec das evokative Potenzial der Benennung lernen: eine Praxis, die die Möglichkeiten der Erfindung offenlegt und dabei eine Sprache vermeidet, die dazu neigt, weitschweifig über die Maßen zu bestimmen und damit Entdeckung zu vereiteln.

Die Figuren entstehen lassen

Wie bereits oben ausgeführt, ist die Logik der Liste in Perecs *Träume von Räumen* die Logik der Taxonomie mit einer Betonung der verwandtschaftlichen Eigenschaften (Gattungen)

---

10 Perec 1994 [1974]: 16. Solche Beschreibungen in Perecs Arbeiten sind eine Parodie auf den Szientismus beziehungsweise den Glauben daran, dass die Wissenschaft die Antworten auf unsere dringlichsten kulturellen Probleme besitzt. Die Diskussion über die Seite hinsichtlich ihrer quantifizierbaren Attribute ist ein Anathema für die meisten Schriftsteller, und durch seine begnadete Art kann Perec damit auf den Punkt bringen, was solchen Hilfsbeschreibungen fehlt, ohne dass er dabei genau herausarbeiten muss, wo genau diese Defizite liegen.

11 Perec 1994 [1974]: 16. Hier dient die Erweiterung von Perecs anfänglicher Quantifizierung der Seite sowohl als eine Verräumlichung der Seite als auch einer Lehrgeschichte über die möglichen Vehikel, mit deren Hilfe sich der Szientismus ausbreitet und legitimiert.

The Gratiolets' cellar. Here generations have heaped up rubbish unsorted and unordered by anyone. Three fathoms deep it lies, under the watchful eye of a fat ginger-striped cat crouching high up on the other side of the skylight, tracking through the wire netting the inaccessible but nonetheless just perceptible scuttling of a mouse.

The eye, becoming slowly accustomed to the dark, could end up making out beneath the layer of fine grey dust heteroclite remains coming from each of the Gratiolets: the base and posts of an Empire bed, hickorywood skis having lost their spring long ago, a pith helmet that was of purest white once upon a time, tennis racquets held in heavy trapezoidal presses, an old Underwood typewriter of the celebrated *Four Million* model, which was held to be, in its time, and owing to its automatic tabulator, one of the most sophisticated objects ever made, and on which François Gratiolet began to type his invoices when he decided he had to modernise his accounting systems; an old *Nouveau Petit Larousse Illustré* beginning with a half-page 71 – ASP *sbs* (Grk *aspis*). Colloquial for viper. *Fig. Asp-tongue* perpetrator of calumnies – and ending with page 1530: MAROLLES-LES-BRAULTS (Dept of Sarthe, Mamers County): pop. 2,000 (vill. 950); an old cast-iron coatstand still holding up a raw-wool cloak patched with pieces of different colours and even different materials: the overcoat worn by Pte Gratiolet, Olivier, taken prisoner at Arras on 20 May 1940, released as early as May 1942 thanks to the efforts of his uncle Marc (Marc, the son of Ferdinand, was not Olivier's uncle but his father Louis's second cousin, but Olivier called him "my uncle" just as he said "uncle" to his father's other cousin, François); an old cardboard globe, with quite a few holes; piles and piles of incomplete runs of papers: *L'Illustration, Point de Vue, Radar,* *Détective, Réalités, Images du Monde, Comédia;* on a cover of *Paris-Match*, Pierre Boulez, wearing a tuxedo, waves his baton at the première of *Wozzeck* at the Paris Opera; on a cover of *Historia* two adolescents can be seen, one in the uniform of a colonel in the Hussars – white kerseymere trousers, midnight-blue dolman with pearl-grey frogging, tasselled shako – and the other in a black cloak and lace cravat and cuffs, rushing into each other's arms, above the following legend: *Did Louis XVII secretly meet Napoleon II at Fiume on 8 August 1808? The most amazing mystery of French history finally solved!* A hatbox full of curling photographs, of yellowed or sepia-tinted snapshots you can never remember of what, or taken by whom: three men on a country lane; that dark man of graceful carriage, with curling black moustaches, wearing light-coloured check trousers, is surely Juste Gratiolet, Olivier's great-grandfather, the first proprietor of the block of flats, with friends of his, who might be the Bereaux, Jacques and Emile, whose sister Marie he married; and those other two, standing in front of the War Memorial in Beirut, both with empty right sleeves and rows of medals on their chests, are Bernard Lehameau, a cousin of Marthe, François's wife, and his old friend Colonel Augustus B. Clifford, for whom he worked as interpreter at Allied Forces General HQ at Péronne, where, like the colonel, he lost his right arm when the said GHQ was bombed by Richthofen, the "Red Baron", on 19 May 1917; and the other one, the obviously short-sighted man reading a book on a raked lectern, is Gérard, Olivier's grandfather.

Abb. 4
Georges Perec, *Das Leben. Gebrauchsanweisung.*
Beschreibung des Kellers der Gratiolets.

Fig. 4
Georges Perec, *Life: A User's Manual.*
Description of the Gratiolets' cellar.

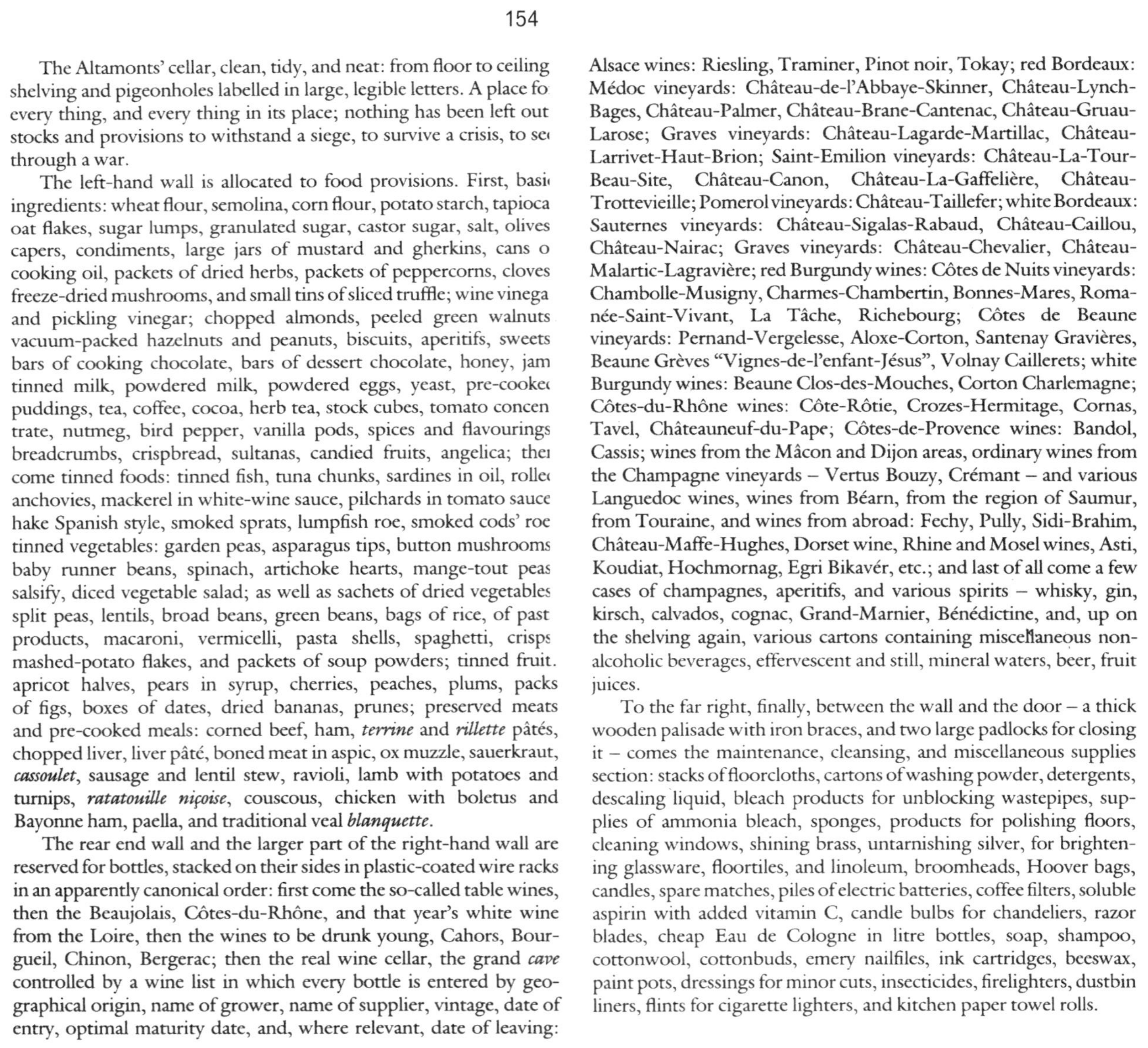

The Altamonts' cellar, clean, tidy, and neat: from floor to ceiling shelving and pigeonholes labelled in large, legible letters. A place fo[r] every thing, and every thing in its place; nothing has been left out stocks and provisions to withstand a siege, to survive a crisis, to se[e] through a war.

The left-hand wall is allocated to food provisions. First, basi[c] ingredients: wheat flour, semolina, corn flour, potato starch, tapioca oat flakes, sugar lumps, granulated sugar, castor sugar, salt, olives capers, condiments, large jars of mustard and gherkins, cans o[f] cooking oil, packets of dried herbs, packets of peppercorns, cloves freeze-dried mushrooms, and small tins of sliced truffle; wine vinega[r] and pickling vinegar; chopped almonds, peeled green walnuts vacuum-packed hazelnuts and peanuts, biscuits, aperitifs, sweets bars of cooking chocolate, bars of dessert chocolate, honey, jam tinned milk, powdered milk, powdered eggs, yeast, pre-cooked puddings, tea, coffee, cocoa, herb tea, stock cubes, tomato concentrate, nutmeg, bird pepper, vanilla pods, spices and flavourings breadcrumbs, crispbread, sultanas, candied fruits, angelica; the[n] come tinned foods: tinned fish, tuna chunks, sardines in oil, rolle[d] anchovies, mackerel in white-wine sauce, pilchards in tomato sauce hake Spanish style, smoked sprats, lumpfish roc, smoked cods' roe tinned vegetables: garden peas, asparagus tips, button mushrooms baby runner beans, spinach, artichoke hearts, mange-tout peas salsify, diced vegetable salad; as well as sachets of dried vegetables split peas, lentils, broad beans, green beans, bags of rice, of past[a] products, macaroni, vermicelli, pasta shells, spaghetti, crisps mashed-potato flakes, and packets of soup powders; tinned fruit: apricot halves, pears in syrup, cherries, peaches, plums, packs of figs, boxes of dates, dried bananas, prunes; preserved meats and pre-cooked meals: corned beef, ham, *terrine* and *rillette* pâtés, chopped liver, liver pâté, boned meat in aspic, ox muzzle, sauerkraut, *cassoulet*, sausage and lentil stew, ravioli, lamb with potatoes and turnips, *ratatouille niçoise*, couscous, chicken with boletus and Bayonne ham, paella, and traditional veal *blanquette*.

The rear end wall and the larger part of the right-hand wall are reserved for bottles, stacked on their sides in plastic-coated wire racks in an apparently canonical order: first come the so-called table wines, then the Beaujolais, Côtes-du-Rhône, and that year's white wine from the Loire, the wines to be drunk young, Cahors, Bourgueil, Chinon, Bergerac; then the real wine cellar, the grand *cave* controlled by a wine list in which every bottle is entered by geographical origin, name of grower, name of supplier, vintage, date of entry, optimal maturity date, and, where relevant, date of leaving:

Alsace wines: Riesling, Traminer, Pinot noir, Tokay; red Bordeaux: Médoc vineyards: Château-de-l'Abbaye-Skinner, Château-Lynch-Bages, Château-Palmer, Château-Brane-Cantenac, Château-Gruau-Larose; Graves vineyards: Château-Lagarde-Martillac, Château-Larrivet-Haut-Brion; Saint-Emilion vineyards: Château-La-Tour-Beau-Site, Château-Canon, Château-La-Gaffelière, Château-Trotteveille; Pomerol vineyards: Château-Taillefer; white Bordeaux: Sauternes vineyards: Château-Sigalas-Rabaud, Château-Caillou, Château-Nairac; Graves vineyards: Château-Chevalier, Château-Malartic-Lagravière; red Burgundy wines: Côtes de Nuits vineyards: Chambolle-Musigny, Charmes-Chambertin, Bonnes-Mares, Romanée-Saint-Vivant, La Tâche, Richebourg; Côtes de Beaune vineyards: Pernand-Vergelesse, Aloxe-Corton, Santenay Gravières, Beaune Grèves "Vignes-de-l'enfant-Jésus", Volnay Caillerets; white Burgundy wines: Beaune Clos-des-Mouches, Corton Charlemagne; Côtes-du-Rhône wines: Côte-Rôtie, Crozes-Hermitage, Cornas, Tavel, Châteauneuf-du-Pape; Côtes-de-Provence wines: Bandol, Cassis; wines from the Mâcon and Dijon areas, ordinary wines from the Champagne vineyards – Vertus Bouzy, Crémant – and various Languedoc wines, wines from Béarn, from the region of Saumur, from Touraine, and wines from abroad: Fechy, Pully, Sidi-Brahim, Château-Maffe-Hughes, Dorset wine, Rhine and Mosel wines, Asti, Koudiat, Hochmornag, Egri Bikavér, etc.; and last of all come a few cases of champagnes, aperitifs, and various spirits – whisky, gin, kirsch, calvados, cognac, Grand-Marnier, Bénédictine, and, up on the shelving again, various cartons containing miscellaneous non-alcoholic beverages, effervescent and still, mineral waters, beer, fruit juices.

To the far right, finally, between the wall and the door – a thick wooden palisade with iron braces, and two large padlocks for closing it – comes the maintenance, cleansing, and miscellaneous supplies section: stacks of floorcloths, cartons of washing powder, detergents, descaling liquid, bleach products for unblocking wastepipes, supplies of ammonia bleach, sponges, products for polishing floors, cleaning windows, shining brass, untarnishing silver, for brightening glassware, floortiles, and linoleum, broomheads, Hoover bags, candles, spare matches, piles of electric batteries, coffee filters, soluble aspirin with added vitamin C, candle bulbs for chandeliers, razor blades, cheap Eau de Cologne in litre bottles, soap, shampoo, cottonwool, cottonbuds, emery nailfiles, ink cartridges, beeswax, paint pots, dressings for minor cuts, insecticides, firelighters, dustbin liners, flints for cigarette lighters, and kitchen paper towel rolls.

Abb. 5
Georges Perec, *Das Leben. Gebrauchsanweisung.*
Beschreibung des Kellers der Altamonts.

Fig. 5
Georges Perec, *Life: A User's Manual.*
Description of the Altamonts' cellar.

with an emphasis on familial traits (species) and the ethos of elementarism coursing through it. However, there are a number of places in the text in which Perec signals a shift of priorities, transitioning to the logic of the archive in which ad hoc adjacencies, exhaustive enumeration, and a multiplicity of relations are privileged. This tendency is most clearly evident in the section describing the species of "town." Perec's first observation about the town concerns how difficult it is to define it as a category of operation. He writes: "Don't be too hasty in trying to find a definition of the town; it's far too big and there's every chance of getting it wrong. First make an inventory of what you can see. List what you're sure of. Draw elementary distinctions: for example, between what is the town, and what isn't the town. Concern yourself with what divides the town from what isn't the town."[12] Though Perec's commentary appears to advocate for the categorization of a town, the text ultimately speaks to the impossibility of arriving at such a definition. Thus, rather than start from a category and populate it, Perec admonishes the reader to simply observe what is there, and to allow the figure to emerge from these observations. In this sense, taxonomic logic is supplanted by the logic of the archive as familial traits give way to the possibility of emerging figures and themes with imaginative and inventive potential.

In *Life: A User's Manual*, the transition from taxonomy to archive is complete, such that it is no longer appropriate to discuss the logic of the list in this context, but rather, the logics of the lists. In this transition the familial relations of the taxonomy that genealogically subsumes objects yields to the exhaustive nature of the archive that continually serializes its innumerable contents. Foucault describes the logics of the archive as follows:

The archive is the first law of what can be said.... But the archive is also that which determines that all these things said do not accumulate endlessly in an amorphous mass, nor are they inscribed in an unbroken linearity, nor do they

12 Perec 1997 [1974]: 76. In such statements by Perec, we witness the elision of his "day job" as a scientific archivist and his work as a writer. Though the practice of archiving may have trained Perec to be inherently suspicious of overdetermined definitions, the practice of empirical observation serves him well in both realms. And though, at first glance, invention that allows the figure to emerge ostensibly belongs to the habits of imaginative writing, numerous scientists allude to the importance of such moments of creativity in the process of scientific discovery.
13 Foucault 1972 [1966]: 126–131, in: Merewether 2006, 28f. Here, Foucault articulates the proactive manifestation of the archive, not as an institution whose sole function is to preserve, but rather as a sense of agency that, because it preserves, conditions all future articulations. This systemic framing of the archive is predicated upon the assumption that we say as much about our culture by what we chose to preserve and reify, which in turn determines, in some measure, how we act.

disappear at the mercy of chance external accident; but they are grouped together in distinct figures, composed together in accordance with multiple relations, maintained or blurred in accordance with specific regularities.... The archive is not that which, despite its immediate escape, safeguards the event of the statement, and preserves, for future memories, its status as an escape; it is that which, at the very root of the statement-event, and in which embodies it, defines at the outset *the system of its enunciability*....[13]

For Foucault, the archive does not impose a predetermined familial relation, but rather groups found things together until a theme or figure emerges. The archive is composed with respect to multiple relations, and thus its endgame is to differentiate discourses. Foucault's contention that the archive houses "statement-events" preserves the situation of the names and is consistent with Derrida's claims about the housing of the archive. With respect to Perec, what is so fascinating about his novel are the multiple logics of its construction. Examining the structure of the novel, the role of lists as organizational devices is impressive. The lists that structure the novel include the table of contents based upon various locales in the apartment building (four pages long), the index (sixty pages long), an alphabetical checklist of some of the stories narrated in the manual (four pages long), and a postscript listing

und dem Ethos des Elementarismus, der sie durchströmt. Es gibt jedoch eine Reihe von Stellen in dem Text, in denen Perec einen Prioritätenwechsel signalisiert und zur Logik der Archive wechselt, in der spontanes Angrenzen ausgiebige Aufzählungen und eine Vielzahl von Bezügen den Vorrang erhalten. Diese Tendenz wird sehr deutlich in dem Abschnitt, in dem die Gattung „Stadt" beschrieben wird. Perecs erste Beobachtung zur Stadt dreht sich um die Frage, wie schwer es ist, sie als eine funktionale Kategorie zu definieren. Er schreibt: „Nicht versuchen, allzu schnell eine Definition der Stadt zu finden: das ist viel zu groß, man hat alle Aussichten, sich zu irren. Zunächst einmal eine Bestandsaufnahme dessen machen, was man sieht. Das überprüfen, dessen man sich sicher ist. Unterschiede feststellen: zum Beispiel zwischen dem, was die Stadt ist, und dem, was die Stadt nicht ist. Sich für das interessieren, was die Stadt von dem trennt, was nicht Stadt ist."[12] Obwohl Perecs Kommentar für eine mögliche Kategorisierung einer Stadt zu sprechen scheint, ist im Text letztlich die Rede davon, dass es unmöglich ist, zu einer solchen Definition zu gelangen. Statt mit einer Kategorie zu beginnen und diese zu füllen, ermahnt Perec damit den Leser, lediglich zu beobachten, was da ist, und der Figur zu erlauben, sich aus diesen Beobachtungen heraus zu entwickeln. In diesem Sinne wird taxonomische Logik durch die Logik des Archivs ersetzt, da verwandtschaftliche Eigenschaften der Möglichkeit sich entwickelnder Figuren und Themen mit imaginativem und erfinderischem Potenzial weichen.

In *Das Leben. Gebrauchsanweisung* ist der Übergang von der Taxonomie zum Archiv vollzogen, so dass es nicht mehr angemessen ist, die Logik der Liste in diesem Kontext zu diskutieren, sondern eher die Logik der Listen. In diesem Übergang bringen die verwandtschaftlichen Beziehungen der Taxonomie, die Objekte genealogisch subsumieren, den umfassenden Charakter des Archivs hervor, das beständig seine unzähligen Inhalte in serielle Reihungen bringt. Michel Foucault beschreibt die Logiken des Archivs wie folgt:

„Das Archiv ist zunächst das Gesetz dessen, was gesagt werden kann... Aber das Archiv ist auch das, was bewirkt, daß all diese gesagten Dinge sich nicht bis ins Unendliche in einer amorphen Vielfalt anhäufen, sich auch nicht in eine bruchlose Linearität einschreiben und nicht allein schon bei zufälligen äußeren Umständen verschwinden; sondern daß sie sich in distinkten Figuren anordnen, sich aufgrund vielfältiger Beziehungen miteinander verbinden, gemäß spezifischen Regelmäßigkeiten sich behaupten oder verfließen... Das Archiv ist nicht das, was trotz seines unmittelbaren Entrinnens das Ereignis der Aussage bewahrt und ihren Personenstand als den einer Ausbrecherin für die zukünftigen Gedächtnisse aufbewahrt; es ist das, was an der Wurzel der Aussage selbst als Ereignis und in dem Körper, in dem sie sich gibt, von Anfang an *das System ihrer Aussagbarkeit* definiert."[13]

Für Foucault erlegt das Archiv keine vorbestimmte verwandtschaftliche Beziehung auf, sondern fügt eher gefundene Dinge zusammen, bis sich ein Thema oder eine Figur abzeichnet. Das Archiv setzt sich zusammen auf der Basis vielfältiger Beziehungen und

12 Perec 1994 [1974]: 76. In solchen Äußerungen Perecs zeigt sich das Zusammenziehen seiner Arbeit zum Lebensunterhalt als wissenschaftlicher Archivar und seiner Arbeit als Schriftsteller. Auch wenn die tägliche Praxis des Archivierens Perec darauf sensibilisiert hat, grundsätzlich misstrauisch gegenüber vorbestimmten Definitionen zu sein, ist ihm die Praxis der empirischen Beobachtung in beiden Bereichen sehr nützlich. Und obwohl eine Erfindung, die es der Figur erlaubt, sich angeblich zu entwickeln, auf den ersten Blick zu den Gewohnheiten des imaginativen Schreibens gehört, deuten zahlreiche Wissenschaftler die Bedeutung solcher Momente von Kreativität im Prozess der wissenschaftlichen Entdeckung an.

13 Foucault 1973 [1969]: 187f., in Merewether 2006: 28f. Hier bringt Foucault die proaktive Manifestation des Archivs zum Ausdruck, nicht als Institution, deren alleinige Funktion es ist zu erhalten, sondern eher als eine Art Agentur, die, weil sie erhält, alle zukünftigen Äußerungen bedingt. Diese systemische Einordnung des Archivs gründet sich auf der Annahme, dass viel über unsere Kultur ausgesagt wird durch das, was für die Erhaltung und Verdinglichung ausgewählt wird, was wiederum in gewissem Maße bestimmt, wie gehandelt wird.

all of the people Perec has quoted in the text (one-half page long). Following a single theme of the manual—the puzzle-maker—reveals how the multiple logics of the lists operate within the novel.

The theme of the puzzle-maker is certainly, for Perec, an autobiographical detail in his work. Perec was a lover of puzzles, particularly word puzzles, and went so far as to publish a lipogram entitled "La Disparition" in 1969, a three-hundred-page text that examines how much can be done with the French language, absent its most often-used letter "e."[14] In his essay "Think/Classify," Perec includes a section entitled "U: The World as Puzzle," that essentially critiques the futility of the project of classification. Here, Perec opines: "So very tempting to want to distribute the entire world in terms of a single code....Unfortunately this doesn't work, has never even begun to work, will never work."[15] This essay first appeared in 1978, the same year as his magnum opus, *Life: A User's Manual*, in which he includes a preface describing the respective agency of the puzzle-maker and the puzzler [→ figs. 6 and 7]: "From this, one can make a deduction which is quite certainly the ultimate truth of jigsaw puzzles: despite appearance, puzzling is not a solitary game: every move the puzzler makes, the puzzle-maker has made before; every piece the puzzler picks up, and picks up again, and studies and strokes, every combination he tries, and tries a second time, every blunder and every insight, each hope and each discouragement have all been designed, calculated and decided by the other."[16] With this description of the puzzle-maker as the novel's preface, Perec weaves a tacit analogy between the puzzle-maker and the author, the puzzler and the reader, simultaneously choreographing how the reader should encounter his text. As puzzlers, readers are empowered to craft their own narratives, but are reminded that meaning and understanding will always emerge from the dialogical relationship with the author.[17]

Through his cognizance of the cultural expectations of the list, the taxonomy, or the archive, Perec is able to actively undermine

14 Perec 1997 [1974]: xvi.
15 Perec 1997 [1974]: 190.
16 Perec 1988 [1978]: preface.
17 Here, Perec's views on textual interpretation align quite closely with those expressed by Roland Barthes in his seminal 1967 essay "The Death of the Author." In architectural discourse, the reciprocity between the conceptualization of the inhabitant and the design of the space parallels these questions of literary interpretation and the agency of the reader. See Adrian Forty's discussion of the modernist "user." Forty 2000: 312–315. See also Hill 2003.
18 Semper 2004 [1878]: 71.

certain assumptions about the list, while operating inventively on it. In the examples cited here, lists were assumed to privilege the epistemological over the ontological, lists were thought to prioritize similitude over difference, lists acted as *a priori* conditions of engagement, and lists were intended to be definitive and totalizing. When lists appear within the discipline of architecture, for example, a list of programmatic requirements, they too come with certain assumptions attached to them. Primary among these assumptions are the belief that program is fundamentally about locating people, objects and events, and that program constitutes a sort of hegemonic logic about how the building will eventually be inhabited and used. In Perec's able hands, the situation of the list is not simply about locating people, objects, and events, but extends to include the situation of discourses and meanings. The recurring figure of the puzzle-maker in Perec's writing potentially admonishes architects to eschew the hegemonic logic of program and acknowledge the role of the spatial inhabitants as co-creators, co-inventors, and co-conspirators.

In the first sentence of the prolegomena of *Style in the Technical and Tectonic Arts; or, Practical Aesthetics* (1861–63), Gottfried Semper wrote: "The nocturnal sky shows glimmering nebulae among the splendid miracle of stars—either old extinct systems scattered throughout the universe, cosmic dust taking shape around a nucleus, or a condition in between destruction and regeneration."[18] In a sentence that Werner Oechslin deems a *Jahrhundertsatz* (a "sentence of the century"), Semper instantiates his reflections on architectural style with an attempt at classifying the night sky through a parallel

ermöglicht damit am Ende die Unterscheidung von Diskursen. Foucaults Behauptung, dass das Archiv „Aussage-Ereignisse" enthält, bewahrt die Situation der Benennungen und stimmt mit Derridas Aussagen zur Unterbringung des Archivs überein. Das Faszinierende des Romans von Perec sind die multiplen Logiken seiner Konstruktion. Analysiert man die Struktur des Romans, ist die Rolle von Listen als Mittel zur Organisation beeindruckend. Zu den Listen, die dem Roman Struktur geben, gehören das Inhaltsverzeichnis, das auf den verschiedenen Schauplätzen im Mietshaus basiert (vier Seiten lang), der Index (sechzig Seiten lang), eine alphabetische Checkliste von einigen der Geschichten, die in der Gebrauchsanweisung erzählt werden (vier Seiten lang), und ein Nachwort, in dem alle Personen aufgelistet sind, die Perec in dem Text nennt (eine halbe Seite lang). Verfolgt man ein Einzelthema aus der Gebrauchsanweisung – den Puzzlehersteller – so wird deutlich, wie die multiplen Logiken der Listen innerhalb des Romas funktionieren.

Das Thema des Puzzleherstellers ist für Perec sicherlich ein autobiografisches Element in seiner Arbeit. Perec liebte Puzzles, insbesondere Wort-Puzzles, und veröffentlichte 1969 sogar ein Lipogramm mit dem Titel „La Disparition" [Das Verschwinden], ein Text mit dreihundert Seiten darüber, was alles mit der französischen Sprache ohne den am häufigsten verwendeten Buchstaben „e" möglich ist.[14] In seinem Aufsatz „Penser/ Classer" [Denken/Einordnen] überschrieb Perec einen Absatz mit „U. Le Monde du Puzzle" [U. Die Welt des Puzzles], das im Wesentlichen die Vergeblichkeit des Projektes der Klassifikation kritisch beleuchtet. Hier schreibt Perec: „Es ist so verführerisch, die ganze Welt nach einem einzigen Code aufteilen zu wollen ... leider funktioniert das nicht, es hat nicht einmal zu funktionieren angefangen, es wird nie funktionieren."[15] Dieser Aufsatz erschien 1978 zum ersten Mal, im selben Jahr wie sein großes Werk, *Das Leben. Gebrauchsanweisung*, in dem er ein Vorwort einfügt, das die jeweilige Institution des Puzzleherstellers und des Puzzlespielers beschreibt [→ Abb. 6 und 7]: „Man wird

daraus etwas ableiten, das sicherlich die höchste Wahrheit des Puzzles ist: allem Anschein zum Trotz ist es kein solitäres Spiel: jede Gebärde, die der Puzzlespieler macht, hat der Puzzlehersteller vor ihm bereits gemacht; jeder Baustein, den er immer wieder zur Hand nimmt, den er betrachtet, den er liebkost, jede Kombination, die er versucht und wieder versucht, jedes Tasten, jede Intuition, jede Hoffnung, jede Entmutigung, sind von dem andern ergründet, auskalkuliert, beschlossen worden."[16] Mit dieser Beschreibung des Puzzleherstellers als Vorwort des Romans webt Perec eine stillschweigende Analogie zwischen dem Puzzlehersteller und dem Autor sowie dem Puzzlespieler und dem Leser und choreografiert zugleich, wie der Leser seinem Text begegnen soll. Als Puzzlespieler werden die Leser dazu ermächtigt, ihre eigenen Erzählstränge zu spinnen, aber sie werden daran erinnert, dass Bedeutung und Verstehen immer aus der dialogischen Beziehung mit dem Autor entstehen.[17]

Aufgrund seiner Kenntnisse der kulturellen Erwartungen an die Liste, die Taxonomie und das Archiv war Perec in der Lage, aktiv bestimmte Annahmen im Zusammenhang mit der Liste zu unterminieren und gleichzeitig erfindungsreich damit umzugehen. In den hier zitierten Beispielen sollten die Listen das Epistemologische gegenüber dem Ontologischen bevorzugen, Listen sollten Ähnlichkeit gegenüber Unterschied eine höhere Priorität einräumen, Listen fungierten als apriorische Bedingungen der Verpflichtung, und Listen sollten endgültig und summierend sein. Wenn es Listen in der Architektur gibt, etwa eine Liste der bauprogrammatischen Anforderungen,

---

14 Perec 1994 [1974]: xvi.
15 Perec 1996 [1978]: 120.
16 Perec 1991 [1978]: 14.
17 Hier stimmen Perecs Ansichten über die Interpretation von Texten sehr stark mit denen von Roland Barthes in dessen wegweisendem Aufsatz „Der Tod des Autors" von 1968 [1967] überein. Im Architekturdiskurs gibt es in der Wechselbeziehung zwischen der Konzeptualisierung des Bewohners und der Gestaltung des Raums Parallelen zu diesen Fragen der Interpretation in der Literatur und der Institution des Lesers. Siehe Adrian Fortys Diskussion über den modernen „Nutzer", Forty 2000: 312–315. Siehe auch Hill 2003.

Pieces in puzzles of this kind come in classes of which the best-known are

the little chaps

the double crosses

and the crossbars

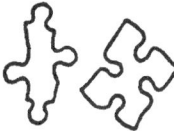

Abb. 6
Taxonomie der Bausteine des Puzzles aus der Präambel zu
Das Leben. Gebrauchsanweisung.

Fig. 6
Taxonomy of Puzzle Pieces, from the Preamble to
Life: A User's Manual.

Abb. 7
Puzzle pour un portrait de Georges Perec. Aus: La Poésie
dans un jardin – Festival d'Avignon, 1988.

Fig. 7
Puzzle pour un portrait de Georges Perec. From: La Poésie
dans un jardin – Festival d'Avignon, 1988.

hängen an ihnen ebenfalls bestimmte Annahmen. Vorrangig bei diesen Annahmen ist der Glaube daran, dass es beim Programm im Grunde um die Verortung von Menschen, Objekten und Ereignissen geht und dass das Programm eine Art hegemoniale Logik darstellt, wie das Gebäude schließlich bewohnt und genutzt werden wird. Durch Perecs literarisches Geschick geht es in der Liste nicht einfach nur um die Verortung von Menschen, Objekten und Ereignissen, sondern sie geht darüber hinaus und schließt das Platzieren von Diskursen und Bedeutungen mit ein. Die wiederkehrende Figur des Puzzleherstellers in Perecs Schriften mahnt möglicherweise Architekten dazu, die hegemoniale Logik des Bauprogramms zu meiden und den Bewohnern Rollen als Mitgestalter, Miterfinder und Mitverschworene einzuräumen.

Im ersten Satz der Prolegomena zu *Der Stil in den technischen und tektonischen Künsten oder praktische Ästhetik: ein Handbuch für Techniker, Künstler und Kunstfreunde* (1861–63) schrieb Gottfried Semper: „Der nächtliche Himmel zeigt neben den glanzvollen Wundern der Gestirne mattschimmernde Nebelstellen, – entweder alte, erstorbene, im All zerstobene Systeme, oder erst um einen Kern sich gestaltender Weltdunst, oder ein Zustand zwischen Zerstörung und Neugestaltung."[18] In einem Satz, den Werner Oechslin einen „Jahrhundertsatz" nennt, verdichtet und verbindet Semper seine Überlegungen über Baustil mit einem Versuch, den Nachthimmel durch eine entsprechende Identifikation von Invarianten zu klassifizieren.[19] Wie Cuvier Anlass zu einer Neupositionierung der klassifikatorischen Impulse für die Naturkunde gab, vermied Sempers Schema der Kategorisierung kunsthistorische Periodisierung zugunsten der Materie und der Fabrikation. Vielleicht deutet die Verwendung von Archiven, Listen und Taxonomien in Perecs literarischem Werk auf einen weiteren Wandel in der Klassifikation von Architektur hin. In Perecs Schriften ist eine Begegnung mit der Liste eine Begegnung mit der literarischen Erfindung. Durch die einfache Strategie der Inversion nimmt Perec ein typischerweise dekontextualisiertes Archiv und stellt

es in einen kreativen Dialog mit dessen räumlicher Umgebung; er spricht sich gegen die Überspezifizierung der Benennung aus, indem er sie mit einem offen-unfertigen kreativen Potenzial erfüllt; er lässt die restriktiven Lehrmeinungen der empirischen Beobachtungen als Selbstzweck hinter sich, indem er sie als Konstellationen positioniert, aus denen heraus sich schöpferische Figuren entwickeln können. In *Träume von Räumen* ermutigt Perec die Leser in geradezu hinterhältiger Weise, ihre Teelöffel zu hinterfragen – was kann die Architektur aus solchen Aphorismen lernen? Als Disziplin müssen wir fragen, welche Kategorien unserer Handlungen so banal, welche Listen so allgegenwärtig und welche Taxonomien so konventionell sind, dass sie unterhalb des Radars unserer kollektiven Aufmerksamkeit fliegen? Perec lehrt uns, dass diese verdinglichten Schemata uns ihr erfinderisches und schöpferisches Potenzial geradezu auf einem Silbertablett servieren.

18 Semper 1878: vii.
19 Klar 2005. Die Frage, warum dies ein Jahrhundertsatz für Oechslin darstellt, ist interessant. Mit dem Versuch, den Nachthimmel zu kategorisieren, gerät Semper mit seinen Bemühungen sofort zwischen die wissenschaftliche Quantifizierung und die Welt ästhetischer Eigenschaften. Und trotzdem scheinen sowohl die ästhetische Charakterisierung der Wahrnehmung des Nachthimmels als „mattschimmernde Nebelstellen … neben den glanzvollen Wundern der Gestirne" als auch die wissenschaftlichen Erklärungen „zerstobene Systeme" und „Weltdunst" fehlzuschlagen. „Ein Zustand zwischen Zerstörung und Neugestaltung" ist vielleicht die geeignetste Beschreibung für diese Wahrnehmung, insbesondere weil sich in ihr sowohl die wissenschaftliche Erklärung als auch die ästhetische Beschreibung wiederfinden, aber zugleich auch der historische Ansatz seinen Platz erhält.

identification of invariants.[19] Just as Cuvier occasioned a repositioning of the classificatory impulse of natural history, Semper's categorical schema eschewed art historical periodization in favor of matter and fabrication. Perhaps the use of archives, lists, and taxonomies in Perec's literary oeuvre portends another shift in architectural classification. In Perec's writing, an encounter with the list is an encounter with literary invention. Through the simple strategy of inversion, Perec takes a typically decontextualized archive and puts it into creative dialogue with its spatial setting; he mitigates against the overspecification of naming by imbuing it with open-ended creative potential, and he transcends the restrictive tenets of empirical observations as ends in themselves by positing them as a constellations from which generative figures can emerge. In *Species of Spaces*, Perec infamously encouraged readers to question their tea spoons—what can architecture learn from such aphorisms? As a discipline we must ask which categories of our operations are so mundane, which lists so ubiquitous, and which taxonomies so conventional, that they fly beneath the radar of our collective attention? Perec teaches us that these reified schemas are redolent with inventive potential.

19 Klar 2005. The question of why this is a sentence of the century for Oechslin is an interesting one. The attempt to categorize the nocturnal sky immediately positions Semper's classificatory efforts between scientific quantification and the realm of aesthetic qualities. And yet, both the aesthetic characterization of the experience of the night sky as "glimmering nebulae among the splendid miracle of stars" and the scientific explanations of extinct systems and cosmic dust seem to fall short. "A condition between destruction and regeneration" is perhaps the most apt characterization of the experience, largely because it accommodates both scientific explanation and aesthetic description, while simultaneously positioning the historical effort.

161

Fig. 8
Philippe Rahm architectes, Domestic Astronomy, Louisiana
Museum, Denmark, 2009.

Abb. 8
Philippe Rahm architectes, Domestic Astronomy, Louisiana
Museum, Denmark, 2009.

Fig. 9
Office of Metropolitan Architecture (OMA), Seattle Public
Library, Living Room, 2004.

Abb. 9
Office of Metropolitan Architecture (OMA), Seattle Public
Library, Living Room, 2004.

Archival Appendix

Housing the Archive: Philippe Rahm's Domestic Astronomy

If program is one of the taxonomic preoccupations for the discipline of architecture, then Rahm's 2009 project, Domestic Astronomy, takes the domestic program to task by imagining the climate as the determining factor in its distribution. In designing this apartment prototype, Rahm considered the temperature differential in the vertical axis of any spatial enclosure, governed by the climatic principle that heat rises. Rahm's invention was to render climate the locus of the project, and allow the various bits of domestic program to migrate vertically to their optimal temperature zones. Thus, the domestic topography is subject to new forms of organization according to climatic categories and atmospheric species. The bath hovers near the ceiling, the bed levitates just above the floor, and the conventional programmatic adjacencies for domestic architecture are all but forgotten. Perec's legacy, when viewed through the lens of Rahm's architecture, is to allow the paradigmatic situation of dwelling and its dialogue with the list of site attributes, or the taxonomy of conventional program, to leverage disparate forms of invention [→ fig. 8].

Naming the Species: Office of Metropolitan Architecture's Seattle Public Library

When Rem Koolhaas was commissioned to design the Seattle public library in 1999, there were certain conventions and expectations conjured by the library typology: stacks, reading rooms, a circulation desk. In lieu of these typological defaults, Koolhaas and OMA (Office of Metropolitan Architecture) proposed a mixing chamber, a living room, a Dewey ramp, and a meeting platform. Through a rigorous exploration of both the typology and contemporary practices of a library, the designers were able to occasion spatial invention through the very act of naming the program. The living room, for example, imbues a collective space of the library with a domestic horizon, while operating at a scale and level of transparency that facilitates another reading of the space as a public urban living room. Koolhaas deploys strategies of doubling and hybridization that allow this space to operate in the interstices between a private dwelling space for families, an institutional reading room, and a public space for collective activity. Here, naming is not an act of definition, but rather, of invention [→ fig. 9].

Letting the Figure Emerge: UNStudio's La Défense Offices and Shigeru Ban's Nomadic Museum

Letting the figure emerge from a multitude of empirical observations is often the result of relaxing classifications or reorienting categories. This de-specification yields invention by seeking unconventional correspondences between categories and the objects that populate them. Contemporary architectural discourse has facilitated such moments of invention through the de-classification of materials according to their use. This shift in priority expands the imaginative spectrum of the potential of materials within and outside of the discipline. Two examples of projects that locate invention in the de-classification of materials might serve to illustrate Perec's entreaty to allow a figure to emerge from the inventory. First, UNStudio's La Défense Offices in the Netherlands (1999–2004) alters the logic of the list by de-classifying a material's use. The material in question is a multicolored foil, originally manufactured for use in perfume bottles, but in this project it clads the glass panels of the interior courtyard to spectacular visual effect [→ fig. 10]. Similarly, Shigeru Ban's Nomadic Museum (2005) de-classifies and repurposes materials. Here, cardboard tubes are used structurally, shipping containers are deployed spatially, and teabags (with the tea removed) are pressed together and implemented aesthetically as a large billowing curtain against which the exhibition is featured. Thinking outside of the rigid logics of material classification allowed van Berkel, Bos and Ban to orchestrate a moment of unprecedented invention [→ fig. 11].

Heimstatt für das Archiv: Philippe Rahm, Domestic Astronomy

Wenn das Bauprogramm eines der taxonomischen Themenfelder der Architekturdisziplin ist, dann wird in Rahms Projekt Domestic Astronomy aus dem Jahr 2009 das Wohnprogramm einer kritischen Betrachtung unterzogen, da er das Klima als den bestimmenden Faktor für die Raumverteilung heranzieht. Beim Entwurf dieses Wohnungsprototyps stand für Rahm der Temperaturunterschied in der Vertikalen einer Raumhülle im Vordergrund: Dieser wird bestimmt von dem physikalischen Prinzip, dass Wärme aufsteigt. Rahms Erfindung war es, das Klima zum zentralen Element des Projektes zu machen und die unterschiedlichen Wohnbereiche aus dem Bauprogramm vertikal zu den für sie optimalen Temperaturzonen wandern zu lassen. Damit ist die häusliche Topografie neuen Organisationsformen entsprechend den klimatischen Kategorien und atmosphärischen Gattungen unterworfen. Das Bad schwebt nahe der Decke, das Bett erhebt sich leicht über dem Boden, und die Nachbarschaftsbeziehungen des konventionellen Wohnprogramms sind so gut wie vergessen. Wenn man Perecs Vermächtnis durch die Brille von Rahms Architektur betrachtet, besteht es darin, der paradigmatischen Situation des Wohnens und deren Dialog mit der Liste von Standortattributen beziehungsweise der Taxonomie des konventionellen Bauprogramms zu erlauben, das Beste aus disparaten Formen der Erfindung herauszuholen [→ Abb. 8].

Benennung der Gattungen: Office of Metropolitan Architecture, Seattle Public Library

Als Rem Koolhaas 1999 den Auftrag erhielt, die öffentliche Bibliothek in Seattle zu entwerfen, gab es gewisse Konventionen und Erwartungen, die von der Gebäudetypologie Bibliothek vorgegeben wurden: Regale, Magazine, Leseräume, Ausgabeschalter. Statt dieser für ein solches Gebäude typischen Standardeinrichtungen schlugen Koolhaas und das Office of Metropolitan Architecture (OMA) ein *mixing chamber* mit den modernsten Informationssystemen, ein Wohnzimmer, eine Dewey-Rampe und eine Begegnungsplattform vor. Durch ein rigoroses Durchforsten sowohl der Typologie als auch der aktuellen Funktionsweisen und Nutzungen einer Bibliothek konnten die Architekten allein durch den Akt der Benennung im Bauprogramm räumliche Erfindung ermöglichen. Das Wohnzimmer beispielsweise gibt einem Gemeinschaftsraum der Bibliothek einen Hauch von Häuslichkeit, während er in einem Maße und Umfang transparent ist, dass eine andere Lesart des Raumes nahegelegt wird als die eines öffentlichen urbanen Wohnzimmers. Koolhaas wendet Strategien der Verdoppelung und Hybridisierung an, wodurch dieser Raum etwas zwischen einem privaten Wohnraum für Familien, einem institutionellen Lesesaal und einem öffentlichen Raum für gemeinsame Aktivitäten werden kann. Hier ist Benennung nicht ein Akt der Definition, sondern eher der Erfindung [→ Abb. 9].

Die Figur entstehen lassen: UNStudio, La Défense Offices und Shigeru Ban, Nomadic Museum

Es ist häufig das Ergebnis einer Lockerung von Klassifikationen oder einer Neuordnung von Kategorien, wenn sich die Figur aus einer Vielfalt empirischer Beobachtungen entwickeln darf. Diese De-Spezifikation bringt Erfindung hervor, indem nach unkonventionellen Übereinstimmungen zwischen Kategorien und den Objekten, von denen sie bevölkert sind, gesucht wird. Der zeitgenössische Diskurs in der Architektur hat solche Momente der Erfindung durch die De-Klassifikation von Materialien entsprechend ihrer Verwendung erleichtert. Dieser Prioritätenwechsel erweitert das denkbare Spektrum des Potenzials von Materialien innerhalb und außerhalb der Disziplin. Zwei Beispiele von Projekten, bei denen die Erfindung in der De-Klassifikation von Materialien liegt, könnten dazu dienen, Perecs eindringliche Bitte zu erläutern, es einer Figur zu erlauben, aus der Inventarisierung zu entstehen. Das erste Projekt, La Défense Offices in den Niederlanden (1999–2004) von

Fig. 10
UN Studio, La Défense Offices, Netherlands, 1999–2004.

Abb. 10
UN Studio, La Défense Offices, Netherlands, 1999–2004.

Fig. 11
Shigeru Ban, Nomadic Museum, 2005.

Abb. 11
Shigeru Ban, Nomadic Museum, 2005.

UNStudio, ändert die Logik der Liste durch die De-Klassifizierung des Gebrauchs eines Materials. Es handelt sich um eine mehrfarbige Folie, die ursprünglich für die Verwendung in Parfümflaschen hergestellt wurde; aber bei diesem Projekt ist sie auf die zum Innenhof ausgerichteten Fassadenelemente aus Glas aufgebracht und lässt spektakuläre optische Effekte entstehen [→ Abb. 10]. In ähnlicher Form de-klassifiziert Shigeru Ban beim Nomadic Museum (2005) die Materialien und führt sie neuen Nutzungen zu. Hier werden Kartonröhren für konstruktive Zwecke eingesetzt, aus Frachtcontainern entstehen effektvoll Räume, und Teebeutel (aus denen der Tee entfernt wurde) werden zusammengepresst und ästhetisch ansprechend als luftige Projektionsflächen für die Ausstellung genutzt. Indem sie außerhalb der ausgetretenen Pfade der strengen Logik der Klassifikation von Materialien denken, können van UNStudios Berkel und Bos und Ban einen Moment noch nie da gewesener Erfindung inszenieren [→ Abb. 11].

Danksagung

Die Autorin dankt Susanne Schindler und Axel Sowa für deren unermüdliche redaktionelle Bemühungen und das aufschlussreiche Feedback. Ein Dank geht auch an Jane Rendell, die aufmerksam die Veranstaltung moderierte, auf der dieses Thema zum ersten Mal präsentiert wurde; von ihr habe ich viel über die Überkreuzung von Erzählung und Raumpraxis gelernt. Danken möchte ich auch Claire Sheridan und Alexander Brown für ihre Findigkeit und freundliche Unterstützung.

Acknowledgements

The author would like to thank Susanne Schindler and Axel Sowa for their tireless editorial efforts and insightful feedback. Thanks to Jane Rendell, who thoughtfully moderated the conference session in which this paper first appeared, and from whom I have learned much about the intersection of narrative and spatial practices. I would also like to thank Claire Sheridan and Alexander Brown for their resourcefulness and good-natured assistance.

Amy Catania Kulper ist Architektin und Architekturhistorikerin und -theoretikerin. Derzeit ist sie Assistant Professor of Architecture am Taubman College of Architecture and Urban Planning der University of Michigan. In ihren aktuellen Forschungsarbeiten bearbeitet sie die Frage der Konzeptualisierung der natürlichen Welt in einer Disziplin, deren zweigeteiltes institutionelles Erbe das Natürliche entweder als angewandte Wissenschaft oder als reine Kunst fasst. Ihre Fragen ergeben sich aus dieser künstlichen Unterscheidung und entstehen aus dem Wunsch, alternative Erzählstrukturen für die Einflüsse der Wissenschaft und des Szientismus auf den Architekturdiskurs herauszuarbeiten. Ihr geplantes neues Buch trägt den Arbeitstitel *Immanent Natures: The Laboratory as a Metaphor for Architectural Production*. Weitere Publikationen sind Beiträge in den in Kürze erscheinenden Büchern *Experiments: Architecture Between Sciences and the Arts* (Ákos Morávanszky und Albert Kirchengast, Hg.), *Intimate Metropolis: Urban Subjects in the Modern City* (Diana Periton und Vittoria di Palma, Hg.) sowie *Visions of the Industrial Age: Modernity and the Anxiety of Representation in European Culture, 1830–1914* (Amy Woodson-Boulton und Minsoo Kang, Hg.) und außerdem Artikel in *Journal of Architecture* und *Field: A Free Journal for Architecture* (in Kürze). Kulper schloss ihre Studien mit einem Master of Architecture an der University of Pennsylvania und einem Master of Philosophy und PhD an der Cambridge University ab.

Deutsche Übersetzung:
SAW Communications: Norma Keßler.

Amy Catania Kulper is an architect and architectural historian and theorist. She is currently Assistant Professor of Architecture at the University of Michigan's Taubman College of Architecture and Urban Planning. Her current research explores the conceptualization of the natural world in the context of a discipline whose divided institutional legacy frames the natural either as an applied science or a fine art. Her questions are lodged in this artificial distinction, and emanate from a desire to craft alternative narratives for the influences of science and scientism on architectural discourse. Her forthcoming book has the working title *Immanent Natures: The Laboratory as a Metaphor for Architectural Production*. Other publications include chapters in the forthcoming *Experiments: Architecture between Sciences and the Arts* (Ákos Morávanszky and Albert Kirchengast, eds.); *Intimate Metropolis: Urban Subjects in the Modern City* (Diana Periton and Vittoria di Palma, eds.); and *Visions of the Industrial Age: Modernity and the Anxiety of Representation in European Culture, 1830–1914* (Amy Woodson-Boulton and Minsoo Kang, eds.) as well as articles in *Journal of Architecture* and *Field: A Free Journal for Architecture* (forthcoming). Kulper received her PhD and MPhil from Cambridge University, and her MArch from the University of Pennsylvania.